# The Truths and Lies of Nationalism

*as Narrated by Charvak*

# The Truths and Lies of Nationalism
*as Narrated by Charvak*

Edited and with Annotations by
PARTHA CHATTERJEE

Cover image: *Still Life with a Skull and a Writing Quill*, oil on wood, 1628, by Pieter Claesz. Courtesy of the Rogers Fund, 1949, and the Metropolitan Museum, New York.

*The Truths and Lies of Nationalism as Narrated by Charvak* by Partha Chatterjee was first published by Permanent Black D-28 Oxford Apts, 11 IP Extension, Delhi 110092 INDIA, for the territory of SOUTH ASIA. First SUNY Press edition 2022.

Not for sale in South Asia

Cover design by Anuradha Roy

Published by State University of New York Press, Albany

© 2022 Partha Chatterjee

All rights reserved

Printed in the United States of America

No part of this book may be used or reproduced in any manner whatsoever without written permission. No part of this book may be stored in a retrieval system or transmitted in any form or by any means including electronic, electrostatic, magnetic tape, mechanical, photocopying, recording, or otherwise without the prior permission in writing of the publisher.

For information, contact State University of New York Press, Albany, NY www.sunypress.edu

Library of Congress Cataloging-in-Publication Data

Names: Chatterjee, Partha, author
Title: The truths and lies of nationalism as narrated by Charvak
Description: Albany : State University of New York Press, [2022] |
   Includes bibliographical references and index.
Identifiers: ISBN 9781438487779 (hardcover : alk. paper) |
   ISBN 9781438487786 (e-book) | ISBN 9781438487762
   (paperback : alk. paper)
Further information is available at the Library of Congress.

10  9  8  7  6  5  4  3  2  1

# Contents

|   | | |
|---|---|---|
| *Editor's Preface* | | vii |
| Introduction: Charvak Speaks | | 1 |
| 1 | All Nations are Modern | 5 |
| 2 | All National Borders are Accidental | 26 |
| 3 | Princes Have No Place in a Republic | 67 |
| 4 | India is Not a Hindu Rashtra | 101 |
| 5 | India is Not a Pluralist Secular Democracy | 132 |
| 6 | India is a People's Federation | 179 |
| 7 | People's Alliances Strengthen the Nation | 231 |
| 8 | The Nation Belongs to the Entire People | 274 |
| | *Index* | 321 |

# Editor's Preface

IN THE OLD DAYS, authors used to be commanded by the gods to write a poetical composition or a treatise on theology. Such things don't happen any more. That is the reason I find it awkward to explain the somewhat mysterious circumstances in which I came to produce this book.

While the Covid-19 pandemic was still raging in the autumn of 2020, I found, one evening, placed outside the door of my home in Kolkata, a sealed packet. Apparently, it had been left there sometime during the day. It did not come by post or any of the courier services that usually deliver mail because, if it had, someone would have rung the bell and I was home all day. In fact, the parcel did not bear any seal or inscription except my name and address written in English script in a confident cursive style rarely seen these days. My curiosity was aroused because the package did not look like a piece of junk mail. The thought that it might contain something more sinister did strike my mind – after all, the times were not exactly normal. But something in the look of the packet persuaded me that it should be examined.

After dutifully spraying the packet with a disinfectant, I unwrapped it and found, within cardboard covers and neatly tied in red string, what looked like a manuscript. On a closer look, that indeed turned out to be the case. The text was written by hand in prose in a widely spoken North Indian language that I had no difficulty reading. The first page began with a heading in two words: *Cārvāka uvāca*. It recalled a standard Sanskrit form in which a narrated story is reported, as, for instance, innumerable times in the Mahabharata, with the words "so-and-so said". In this case, the reader was meant to infer that the text had been spoken by a certain Charvak. But who put it down in writing? Was the original language the same as the language of the text? Was it a verbatim transcript or an edited reconstruction? There was no way of knowing. Indeed, there was a mystery of origins not only in the manner in which the text was delivered into my hands but in the attribution of authorship within the text itself. The speaker, Charvak, appears to be a person of an impossibly indeterminate age, since he claims to have been present in places and events separated by centuries. Perhaps the composer of the manuscript (assuming it is a single person, which may not be the case) intended to create a mythical persona from whose lips might emerge the principles of a new concept of Indian nationalism. The mode of address used in the text also suggests that it is spoken to a young North Indian woman, possibly a student, who is generally well informed but conventional in her views. But I prefer not to speculate too much.

On reading the manuscript in its entirety, I became convinced that, though it deals with highly controversial topics, it has enough serious and closely argued material to be both topical and thought-provoking for a wide readership today in India, and perhaps even elsewhere. For this reason, I decided not to publish the text in its original language but translate it into English. Admittedly, this adds a further layer of separation from the original text, whatever that might be. But I hope the reader will, on finishing the book, agree with me that ensuring the widest possible accessibility, including the possibility of convenient translation into various Indian languages, was more important in this case than fidelity to scholarly conventions. The only editorial supplement I have added is a minimal set of footnotes to clarify, expand, and where necessary correct factual information contained in the text.

I still have no idea how I happened to be chosen as a reader of the manuscript. Was I meant to be the medium for the circulation of this book in the public domain? Why was it not printed and published in the way hundreds of political tracts are put out every year, or circulated online? It is possible that whoever was responsible for choosing me thought I might be sympathetic to the views expressed in this text and thus might serve as a more accredited messenger than some nameless link on the web. To an extent, this is true. In particular, some of the arguments made in the chapter on Indian federalism echo what I have recently written, even though I would definitely not endorse all of the statements made in the manuscript. On the whole, even as I do not accept the reasoning on every contention made by the enigmatic Charvak, and indeed seriously disagree with some of them, I do feel that, despite its polemical style, the book deserves a patient reading. Of course, as is well known, most conversation these days is peppered with conspiracy theories. Much as I would like to believe that I have not been unwittingly drawn into some nefarious plot, I cannot entirely suppress the suspicion. Who knows?

As I worked during the winter of 2020–1 on translating and annotating the manuscript, protests built up against the new farm laws. Farmers from Punjab, Haryana, and Uttar Pradesh began to gather in massive protest sites around the national capital. I wondered what Charvak, wherever he is, was saying to his interlocutor on how the central government had made laws on a state subject without regard for the very different conditions of agricultural production and marketing in the different parts of the country – and merely to achieve an ideological vision of a nationally unified agricultural economy fully integrated with the big corporate business houses. Perhaps we will, in the near future, see a sequel to this manuscript, even if I am not chosen to be its messenger.

I had to make a few somewhat arbitrary decisions on the

styles of translation and transliteration. Much of the discussion in English on this subject in India, even in newspapers and the public media, is strewn with academic jargon, often referring to concepts and arguments offered by distinguished thinkers. The manuscript here uses a relatively simple conversational Hindustani style entirely devoid of such jargon. Indeed, I got the impression that whoever spoke or wrote this text was not familiar with most of the terms that are commonly used in our English debates. I have, therefore, tried as far as possible to consciously avoid slipping in those terms in which I would ordinarily converse if I were to speak in English. I say "as far as possible" because ingrained linguistic habits are not easy to consciously discard. I have also made an attempt not to erase the characteristic trace of an original Hindustani idiom by putting in its place a smart English phrase: what I have lost by way of elegance is hopefully made up by the necessary retention of authenticity.

The manuscript uses several Sanskrit words, phrases, and quotations. I have employed the standard convention of Romanisation with diacritical marks, except for words such as varna, rashtra, or jati that are now commonly used in Indian English. When translating into English, I have occasionally retained within parentheses some of the Hindi/Urdu words or phrases used in the original that I thought readers might be curious to know. In these cases, I have sometimes used diacritical marks to avoid confusion; at other times, if the words are in common use, I have dispensed with the diacritics. There are also some quotations in the manuscript from other Indian languages. Since I am not familiar with all of these languages, my transliterations may not always be accurate: for this, I beg the knowledgeable reader's pardon.

For place names, I have used spellings that were prevalent in British India when the reference is to that period, but current spellings when the context is recent: thus, Calcutta or Simla or Poona in the first case and Kolkata, Shimla, and Pune in the second. The original manuscript uses common Hindustani names in all contexts: thus, Kalkattā, Śimlā, Puṇe.

I am immensely grateful to Rukun Advani for the enthusiasm with which he has undertaken the publication of this book. In my long association with him going back nearly forty years, he has been unfailingly generous with his advice and help in publishing matters. I am also grateful to friends who have offered to help with translations of this book into several Indian languages.

1 March 2021                                                              P.C.

# Introduction
## Charvak Speaks

YOU KNOW SOMETHING about me, but not a lot. Let me tell you a little bit about myself.

They call me the great denier (*caram nāstik*) – one who questions the veracity of most things ordinary people hold to be true. They say I am a *nāstik* who denies the existence of the most sacred entities that people revere. The Brahmans nurse a special hatred for me. They say that while Buddhists and Jains may be nastik because they do not acknowledge the sanctity of the Vedas, they at least do not deny the existence of the next world (*parălok*). Charvak denies both! Charvak, the Brahmans say, is the *nāstik śiromaṇi*, the jewel in the crown of unbelief. They allege that I am a crude materialist (*jaḍavādī*) who preaches that no valid knowledge can be acquired by inference from facts obtained by direct perception, that there is no such thing as morality, and that the enjoyment of pleasure is the only object of human life.

And then there are the modern scholars armed with their tools of philological and historical analysis. Most of them claim there was no such person as Charvak, only an ancient school of materialist thought that went by that name. According to them, the Charvaka school was probably founded by someone called Bṛhaspati, although who that person was remains a mystery. There was Bṛhaspati the scholar of music, Bṛhaspati the writer of an *arthaśāstra*, and Bṛhaspati the compiler of a *dharmaśāstra*. Who was the Bṛhaspati who founded the Charvaka school of philosophy? Little do these learned men and women know of my complicated relation to the sage Bṛhaspati. The excuse these modern scholars give for their lack of clarity is that there are no texts in existence that were composed by the Charvaka philosophers themselves. Every scrap of information about them comes from others who have written on the views of the Charvakas, usually from a position of great hostility. Well, one feels a little sorry for these well-meaning modern scholars sitting in their book-lined studies, sending out platoons of eager research assistants to search for musty texts and commentaries in old libraries and archives. Let us leave them to their barren pursuits; they have worked hard and are entitled to their flights of speculative fancy.

In actual fact, I am neither a crude materialist nor a hedonist (*kāmuk*). But I am, if you wish to call me that, a sceptic (*saṃśayvādī*). I do not take common-sense truths at face value. Contrary to what the Brahmans say about me, I do not hold that no valid knowledge is possible through inference from facts. All I say is that such knowledge is conditional upon the observations on which the truth is claimed. Thus, if you tell me that we know the truth that the sun comes up in the east, I will not be so foolish as to deny that knowledge. But I will qualify it by saying that your truth is conditional upon the observations you have made so far of the sun's rising in the east, even though there may have been a million such observations. If you then insist that we are justified in inferring from those million observations the unconditioned and universal truth (*sāmānya jñān*) that the sun comes up in the east, I will object. What if the natural movement of the heavenly bodies is such that after moving in one direction for several thousand years, it reverses, entirely by natural causes, and begins to move in the opposite direction? What if that is the natural law? In that case, is it not possible that you might get up tomorrow morning and discover to your horror that the sun has risen in the west? Accuse me of splitting hairs, if you like, but I don't like muddled thinking. Knowledge by *anumān* or inference is, for me, conditional knowledge (*viśeṣ jñān*).

It is because of the same distaste for muddled thinking that I do not believe in reincarnation, or an extracorporeal soul that flies out of the human body after death and roams around as ghosts or spirits, residing in trees and ruined buildings, perhaps to re-enter some other human body. I do not believe in the efficacy of religious rites to bring about material or spiritual results. I do not believe in the next world, or fate, or the results of our karma in this life determining our next life. I do not believe in any of these things because there is simply no tangible evidence that anyone has ever been able to produce about their validity. For the same reason, I do not believe that there are supernatural causes of natural phenomena. In short, I am a realist (*vāstavāvādī*) who does not engage in fantastic imaginings and respects the limits of human knowledge. I speak the truth to the powerful few who spread dreams and lies to confuse and mislead the people in order to perpetuate their tyranny. No wonder the Brahmans hate me so much.

But it is not philosophy that I wish to talk about today. My subject today will be *rājănīti*, the principles of statecraft. You and your friends are obsessed with what you call *politics*.[1] You think you know its principles – all the things that are right and wrong in politics. Armed with that knowledge, you debate endlessly in your coffee shops and internet blogs and tweets, cutting off the king's head and carrying out daily revolutions. But do you know the truths and lies of politics? Unless you know what is true and what is false, how can you make judgements about what is right or wrong? So let me take up a subject over

---

[1] The word *politics* appears in the text as an English word.

which your friends have been greatly agitated recently. Who is a patriot and who is anti-national? Isn't that what you have been shouting about? Come, let me show you all the lies that have been told about nationalism. Along the way, I will also tell you about some of its truths.

# 1

## All Nations are Modern

THERE ARE NO ancient nations anywhere in the world. All nations (*rāṣtra*) are modern. Ancient Greece, ancient Egypt, ancient China, ancient India – all of them may have had great civilisations whose architecture, art, and literature are objects of admiration. But they were not nations. To realise this truth, you will have to forget for the time being the history you were taught at school. Because it is that history, drilled into your heads from the time you were children, and constantly renewed by national festivals and ceremonies, the speeches of your leaders, and novels, films, and television serials, that make it seem obvious to you that your nation is ancient. But I will show you that this is merely a conventional idea, a *saṃskār*. You take it for granted because everyone says it is so. In actual fact, it is not true. Your nation is not – indeed no nation on earth is – ancient. Only modern people can imagine it that way.

The modern Hindi word for nation – rashtra – makes this clear. The word rashtra merges the idea of the nation with that of the state (*rājya*). The nation is, as it were, represented by the state, just as the state stands for the nation. In effect, the Hindi word rashtra is today equivalent to the English term "nation-state".[1] If we take this meaning of the nation, then it is

---

[1] "Nation-state" appears in the text as an English word.

obvious that the Indian rashtra as a nation-state has only been in existence since the middle of the twentieth century. If you want to push that history a little further back by claiming that the Indian National Congress as an organised political body was the Indian rashtra in waiting, even that would not take you beyond the last decades of the nineteenth century. The Indian nation would still be a very modern entity.

But, you may ask, what about the great kingdoms and empires of the past? The empires of the Mauryas, the Guptas, the Delhi Sultanate, Vijayanagara, the Mughals, the Marathas – were they not great states? They certainly were. But they were empires, not nations. The various parts of those states were held together by military force and tribute-paying arrangements. That is not how the parts of a nation-state are supposed to be bound together. Even the Marathas held territories outside the Maharashtra region by the regular use of armed force and extraction of tribute from local rulers and populations who were looked upon as subjected peoples. The Marathas too had an empire, not a nation.

If you think about it carefully, the connection between nation and state, indicated by the word rashtra, is established by a third term. That term is "the people" (*lok*). When you talk about the nation, you do not immediately think of natural resources or ancient ruins or the Himalayas or the Vedas; you think of the people of India. Therein lies the crucial difference between the ancient kingdoms and the modern nation-state. Asoka or Akbar may have been great rulers; their subjects may even have been relatively happy and prosperous (let us grant that, for argument's sake). But the empire of Asoka or Akbar was not based on the sovereignty of the people. No one in those times could even think of such a concept. The people were subjects of the emperor whom they regarded as the sovereign. I am sure you know that popular sovereignty is a very modern idea which emerged in Western Europe and North America in the late-eighteenth century, spread to South America and other parts of Europe in the nineteenth, and then came to the countries of Asia and Africa in the twentieth. The revolutionaries in France, claiming to speak on behalf of the nation, demanded in 1789 that the people and not the king and his nobles must rule. They cut off the king's head. In North, and later South, America, the European settlers of the British and Spanish colonies declared themselves as nations, rebelled against the British and Spanish empires and proclaimed republics of the people. In Central and Eastern Europe, all through the nineteenth century, various peoples declared themselves as nations and demanded their own states. Without the claim to popular sovereignty, there can be no nation-state or rashtra. Therefore, all nations are modern.

At this point, if your mind is agile and you are following the discussion carefully, you may come back with a counterargument. Fair enough, you might say: let us grant that the nation as state is a modern phenomenon. The awareness of popular sovereignty and self-determination may also be something that has spread across the world only in recent times. But what about the people themselves? Can the people not be ancient? Could they not have memories and traditions that are thousands of years old? Could not the ancientness of culture give a people its identity?

I have to concede that this is a serious argument that demands a careful response. So you will have to be patient with me.

## An Ancient People?

Imagine yourself at Sarnath: you have probably visited the place before. What will you see there? You will see an impressive structure which you may recognise as a Buddhist stupa. You will see a sandstone pillar which, you will be told, was ordered to be built by the Emperor Asoka in the third century before the Common Era. There are inscriptions on the pillar which you will not be able to read, unless you happen to be a specialist: the language is an eastern Prakrit which, if read out to you, may sound vaguely familiar, but the script is Brahmi which is no longer in use anywhere. In the museum, you will immediately recognise the lion capital of Asoka, made thoroughly familiar by its reproduction on banknotes and government stationery. You will see the ruins of a Buddhist vihara which, the tourist guide may tell you, was where more than a thousand monks and scholars lived when the Chinese traveller Xuanzang visited the place in the seventh century. The entire place is now an archaeological monument: no one lives there and the only people you will see are tourists and pilgrims. The guidebook will tell you that the place became famous because that is where Gautama Buddha first preached his dhamma. Many of the things you see will seem quite familiar to you and, even if you were visiting the place for the first time, you will feel an exciting sensation of recognition.

But stop for a moment and ask yourself: who were the people who lived here when the place was inhabited and functional? What did they wear? What language did they speak? What did they eat? Since we know that this was a Buddhist monastery and place of pilgrimage, we could make the conditional inference (*viśeṣ anumān*) that the people who lived here were Buddhist monks and scholars. Therefore, they are likely to have read, written, and spoken Pali. Some of them may even have been fluent in Sanskrit. Since we know that monks and scholars came to Sarnath from many places in India and elsewhere, they must have also brought with them their native languages which not everyone would have understood. What about the people who lived in the neighbouring villages – the farmers and artisans and traders? What language did they speak? Well, they certainly did not speak Hindi as everyone in the area does now, because the Hindi language did not exist then. They probably spoke some variety of what the Brahmans call Prakrit (assigning it the lowly status of a coarse dialect carrying the pungent smell of virgin soil and wild forests, as distinct from their own supremely refined *devăbhāṣā*, the language presumably spoken by the gods). Anyway, whatever variety of Prakrit these people may have spoken, I can assure you that you would not have understood any of it. What did they wear? What did they eat? Modern historians have scoured through religious and literary texts and examined inscriptions and archaeological artefacts to come up with some answers. These are conditional inferences that you will find in history books. They are all valuable information – I am by no means denying that. But what makes you believe that those people living in and around Sarnath fifteen hundred years ago were your people? What is it that ties you and others of your kind – let us call them modern Indians – to those people in the ancient past?

Let me give you another set of examples. Make one more imaginative journey and take yourself to the pyramids of Egypt or, if you prefer, the Parthenon in Greece. I have never been to those places but have seen pictures. Once again, you will be faced with impressive structures that come from ancient times. Of course, you know they are ancient only because archaeologists and historians have told you so; how else could a non-expert tell simply by looking at the stones how old they are? But you know the pyramids (including the gigantic Sphinx) at the edge of the desert in Giza and the Parthenon on top of the hill in Athens are ancient monuments that have become famous icons of ancient Egyptian and Greek civilisations. They will be both familiar and unfamiliar to you, in the same way that Sarnath was, because you will know something about the people who lived there in ancient times, and may find out more about them by going to the library or searching the internet. There will also be much that you will not know. But would you ever feel that the people of ancient Egypt or Greece were your people? Never. So here is my question to you: what is it that makes you imagine the people of ancient Sarnath as your people but not those of ancient Egypt or Athens?

The answer is obvious, you will tell me. The remains of Sarnath are in the territorial region we call India; those of ancient Egypt or Greece are somewhere else, far away. It is geography that binds together the people of India today with those of ancient India.

To clarify your answer, let me ask you to do one more imaginative experiment: I promise this will be the last time I will ask you to do this. Imagine yourself walking through the ruins of Mohenjo-daro, the famous ancient city of the Indus Valley (or Harappan) civilisation. I did visit the place once some years ago. With its brick houses arranged in straight lines and rectangular blocks, a central marketplace, public buildings, baths, and covered drains, the planned city seems to have been built by a people with a sophisticated culture. There are debates among scholars about who those people were: we will come to that subject presently. But everyone is agreed that these ruins representing the urban phase of the Indus civilisation are from a period between 2600 BCE and 1900 BCE. They are also the earliest examples that have been found so far of an ancient high culture in the Indian subcontinent.

But remember, Mohenjo-daro is now located in Sindh province in Pakistan. If you are an Indian citizen, you will probably have some difficulty getting there. Does that pose a problem for modern Indians to claim its history as their own? Could you say, in the same way that you did in the case of Sarnath, that the people who lived in Mohenjo-daro four or five thousand years ago were your people? I know that is an easy question to answer. You will smile and say, "We have already decided that the nation-state is a modern creation but a people may be ancient. So why should the present boundaries of the nation-states of Pakistan and India prevent Indians from claiming the Indus civilisation as their own?" It is a good answer. But just to be aware of the implications, let me point out that history textbooks in Pakistan also begin with the story of the Harappan civilisation and claim the ancient people of the Indus valley as their people. They continue the story into the Vedic period and the rise of Buddhism in which Punjab and the north-western region of Pakistan played a very important part, the ancient city of Taxila being the major centre from where the Buddhist faith travelled to Central Asia and China.[2] That history is not inconsistent with your answer. The people of the modern nation-state of Pakistan claim as their own, for reasons of geography, the ancient tradition associated with the lower and upper Indus valley civilisations as well as Taxila, even though they date the beginning of the Pakistani nation from the Arab conquest of parts of Sindh in the year 711. But it means that the same ancient history and tradition may be claimed by different peoples; it may not be the exclusive property of one nation. Ancient history is like an inheritance shared by many. But your nationalist leaders will not be satisfied with that answer.

## An Ancient Hindu Nation?

Let us now come to the big debate over the people of the Indus Valley civilisation. Who were they? This much is known with

---

[2] I cannot tell if the manuscript here is referring to any specific textbook of Pakistan's history. But if I look at a book called *A History of Pakistan: Pakistan through Ages* (Lahore: Sang-e-meel Publications, 2007) by the famous archaeologist Ahmad Hasan Dani, I see the chapters proceed as follows: 1. Pakistan: The Indus Land, fed by the rivers coming down from the Himalayas; 2. The Dawn of Civilisation, describing the pre-Aryan and pre-Dravidian people, the urbanisation of the Indus valley and the mythologies of the Indus Civilisation; 3. Historical Kingdoms, from the invasion of Alexander, the Mauryan transformation, the Scythian-Parthians, Kushanas, Gandhara and the feudal rule of the Huns; 4. Rise of Muslim States, from Arab rule in Sindh and Multan to the Ghaznavids; and then chapters on Sultanate, Mughal, and British rule in the region.

a high level of certainty – at least that is what I have gathered from scholars. The existence of a civilisation of such antiquity was unknown to the modern world until the "mound of the dead" in Sindh was excavated by Rakhaldas Banerji in the early 1920s. Connecting Banerji's discovery of a set of seals in Mohenjo-daro with similar seals found a few years before by Daya Ram Sahni in Harappa in Punjab, John Marshall of the Archaeological Survey of India announced to the world in 1924 that a hitherto unknown ancient civilisation had been discovered in the Indus valley.

Since then, a large number of such Indus or Harappan sites have been found in a region straddling Balochistan, Sindh, Gujarat, Rajasthan, Punjab, and Haryana, indicating a Bronze Age people who practised agriculture, made pottery and metal objects, had urban settlements and seaports, and engaged in long-distance trade over land and sea. No one can tell what their language was, since the inscriptions on the Harappa seals have not been deciphered. There is also clear evidence that the various Harappa urban settlements were abandoned from around 2000 BCE. Why? The answers have become controversial.

British archaeologists who worked at the sites argued that since linguistic evidence from the Rig Veda and the ancient Persian Avesta indicated that the Vedic civilisation of the Sanskrit-speaking Indo-Aryans could not have been earlier than 1200–1500 BCE, the Indus Valley people were a distinct pre-Aryan "race" (*jāti*), very likely Dravidians.[3] In 1946, Mortimer Wheeler, looking at the positions where certain skeletons had been found on the Mohenjo-daro site, made the dramatic announcement that the ancient Indus cities had been subjected to a sudden and massive invasion by hordes of Aryan soldiers on horseback. Wheeler's theory is not taken seriously by scholars any more. The more common explanation for the emptying of

---

[3] The manuscript has *jāti* with *race* in English in parentheses.

the towns is some environmental calamity such as huge and repeated floods or, more likely, a prolonged drought, or an economic collapse such as the decline of trade. Most scholars today believe that the Harappan civilisation was in sharp decline well before the emergence of the Vedic people whose territories, though overlapping to some extent with the Harappan, were situated more to the north – in Haryana-Punjab, the North West Frontier Province (now Khyber-Pakhtunkhwa) and eastern Afghanistan. In this view, the Indo-Aryans, whose language, Sanskrit, is part of the Indo-European family of languages, migrated from Central Asia to the north-western parts of the Indian subcontinent over a spell of time after 1500 BCE.

Given the theories of race that were still strong in European anthropology and historical linguistics in the early-twentieth century, the question of the relation between the Indus and the Vedic peoples became entangled with racial distinctions. Thus, the people calling themselves *ārya* were described as fair-skinned outsiders who subjugated the dark-skinned Dravidians whom they called *anārya*. The Vedic varna classification came into use here because it could be interpreted to suggest that the four-caste hierarchy of Brahman, Kshatriya, Vaisya, and Sudra reflected variations in skin colour – the darker indigenous people being partially absorbed into the varna order at its lowest rungs. This overlooks the fact that the caste (*jāti*) order was extremely rudimentary in the early Rig Veda period and did not acquire any of the characteristics of the jati formations we know today. The explanations offered by these early British archaeologists were in fact based on extremely crude theories of race that have been discredited. But the Aryan–Dravidian racial distinction still casts its shadow on popular debates today.

Scholars holding the view that the Vedic peoples were immigrants who came after the decline of the Harappa cities point to the following pieces of evidence. Linguistic analysis suggests that the Rig Veda hymns were not much older than the *gāthā* of the ancient Persian Avesta which are dated at around 700 BCE. Hence, the Vedic peoples were certainly later than the peoples of the Indus-Harappa civilisation. Further, Vedic Sanskrit adopted many loanwords from Dravidian languages to refer to various material objects of common use. It also adopted the retroflex or *mūrdhanya* consonants, namely, the hard ṭ, ṭh, ḍ, ḍh, ṇ, common to most Indian languages but absent in other Indo-European languages. The retroflex appears to have entered Sanskrit from the Dravidian or Mundari languages spoken in India. Then there is the continued existence of stray Dravidian language speakers in northern India, such as the Brahui speakers of Balochistan, the Kurukh of Nepal, and the Oraon and Gond of central India. Finally, textual evidence suggests beyond any doubt that the Vedic peoples were adept in the use of horses and chariots with spoked wheels. To this day, there is no clear evidence that the Indus-Harappa people used horses. Recent scholars have been led by this evidence to conclude that, contrary to the old Aryan invasion story, the Aryan peoples migrated from Central Asia to northern India and, rather than driving the Dravidians to the south, largely mingled with the indigenous population, gradually absorbing them into a new social order marked by hierarchies and discrimination, assimilation as well as exclusion, cohesion as well as conflict.

But the idea of the Vedic Aryans as immigrants unsettles the deep nationalist desire to claim an ancient past for the Indian people. The heritage of an ancient civilisation whose record is preserved in the large Sanskrit literary canon and whose achievements rival those of classical Greece, as certified by leading European Orientalists, is held with enormous pride by modern Indians. That pride is severely dented if it has to be admitted that the Vedic Aryans were not the original inhabitants of this country and instead came from somewhere in Central Asia. Not only that, it is another blow to nationalist pride if it is claimed that there was in fact an earlier great civilisation in the

Indus valley bearing no relation to the Vedic people – one whose language and culture are unknown and whose subsequent fate remains to be investigated. Nationalist ideology is impatient with such cautious judgments.

So the rival claim has been made that the inhabitants of the ancient Harappan and Vedic civilisations were in fact the same people, indigenous to India. While the former lived mainly in the valleys of the River Indus, the latter were settled along the lost river Saraswati, part of whose course has been identified as the Ghaggar in eastern Punjab. The language of the Indus people was proto-Indo-European, that is to say, an earlier form of Sanskrit. Besides, even though there is very little material evidence of horses in the Indus civilisation, that absence does not by itself rule out the possibility that horses were in use. The proponents of the rival view therefore insist that instead of the Vedic Aryans having come to India from Central Asia, the migration had occurred in the other direction: Aryans first developed an indigenous civilisation in India – the Indus–Saraswati civilisation – which then spread through the migration of the Aryan peoples to Iran, Central Asia, and Europe.

In fulfilling its desire to establish the thoroughly native provenance of the ancient high civilisations of India, the rival theory runs into several difficulties. First, if the Indo-Aryans were the progenitors of the later peoples of Iran and Europe, then Sanskrit would have to be the mother of the Indo-European languages, which is definitely not the case. Second, how does one account for the presence of Dravidian languages in north India, or the fact that Sanskrit has retroflex consonants which are completely absent in other Indo-European languages? Surely, if Sanskrit was their mother, the languages of ancient Iran or Europe should have had Dravidian elements. Third, the argument stemming from the absence of evidence of horses in the Indus sites, while it could inject a useful dose of scepticism into overly confident assertions that the Harappan civilisation was radically different from the Indo-Aryan, does not constitute a positive claim about the presence of horses. But then, this is a classic case where the conclusion to be proved has been decided before the study is conducted or the evidence gathered. As a result, the evidence is made to suit the conclusion. The *a priori* object (*pūrvānumān*) here was to prove that the Vedic Aryans, the acknowledged progenitors of the Hindus, were native to India and were the same people who created the ancient Indus civilisation. The evidence had to be picked to prove this case: discovering the historical truth was not the main object of this exercise.

I should also point out the assumptions you are making when your heart swells with pride at the thought that your ancient ancestors had composed the great verses in praise of the Vedic gods (even though I suspect Vedic Sanskrit will sound as strange to you as ancient Mongolian). The Vedic literature, whether in verse or, as in the case of the Yajurveda, prose, is essentially liturgical (*upāsanā mantra*) – that is to say, it deals with the performance of the sacrifice or *yajña*. The only people involved in the Vedic sacrifice were kings, warriors, and ritual specialists (*purohit brāhmaṇ*). In other words, the religious culture around the Vedic *yajña* was confined to the elites of society. The vast mass of the people who lived in the north-western regions of the Indian subcontinent three thousand years ago were excluded from that culture. Indeed, women, the lower orders, and *anārya* people were prohibited from even hearing the Vedas being recited or sung. Further, the Vedas are full of stories of the *dev*, i.e. gods, led by Indra, fighting the *asur*. The gods usually won but only by the skin of their teeth, because the *asur* were also powerful beings. Who were they? In the early Vedas, they are divine creatures who refuse to accept the Vedic gods. But in the later Brāhmaṇa and Saṃhitā literature, they become identified with local enemy chiefs who are referred to with contempt as *dasyu* and *dāsa*, i.e. bandits and slaves. It is interesting, however, that several later ruling dynasties all over

India have in their mythical genealogies an ancestor with the name Asur. This indicates that peoples who were earlier opposed to the Vedic Arya later became incorporated into the political and social order while retaining a memory of their antecedents in their mythical history. Besides, the term *asur* when applied to non-Arya people or their leaders seems to indicate an acknowledgement on the part of the Vedic elites that the enemy had special magical powers. It has been speculated that this had to do with the fact that many indigenous people had knowledge of material processes, such as the extraction and use of iron, or healing methods, that the Vedic people did not have. Did you know that there still exists a so-called tribe in the present Jharkhand region that is called Asur whose traditional livelihood over centuries was iron smelting?

If you care for facts, you would have to admit that *ārya* in ancient India came to mean not a race (*jāti*) but an elite group of high status who could perform the Vedic rituals by reciting the proper Sanskrit mantras. Indeed, even among those who called themselves *ārya*, there were few for whom Sanskrit was the mother tongue: they spoke some other language and learnt Sanskrit as a language of distinction. Others in northern India, who were described as *prākṛtǎjan*, spoke one or the other Prakrit language belonging to the Dravidian or Mundari family but accepted borrowed words from Sanskrit to produce, after centuries, the early forms of the modern Indian languages as we know them. I have heard some teachers in your universities claim that, because Sanskrit literature has many instances of scholars from across the length and breadth of Bharatavarsha recognising each other as part of the same learned community, the idea of India as a nation has existed for centuries. I used to know many of these old pundits of yesteryears. Let me assure you that even if they recognised themselves as belonging to a *samāj* spread across the land from the Himalayas to the seas, that community certainly did not include carpenters and cobblers and blacksmiths, nor could the pundits have even remotely imagined the Kol or Bhil or Munda as part of any idea of India. When I listen to these debates, I wonder how your professors can waste their valuable learning in such thoroughly meaningless debates.

The point is that when you identify the ancientness of the Indian people with the Arya of the Vedas (regardless of whether you want to push it further back to an Indus–Saraswati civilisation), you are in fact choosing the ancient tradition of only a very small section. There are many other groups of modern Indians with completely different traditions (*paramparā*). The Tamil literary tradition, for instance, is ancient, going back to at least 450 BCE, and to this day it remains the least influenced by Sanskrit loanwords. The Sangam literature was produced between 300 BCE and 300 CE and a first-century text such as the *Thirukkural* can be read by a Tamil schoolchild today without any difficulty. Can you imagine an average student in a Haryana school reading the Rig Veda? If the Tamil had to think of themselves as an ancient people, why would they look to the Indus–Saraswati civilisation?

Let me also remind you of another curious, but very important, fact. Several different terms are used in the many Indian languages to refer to the modern meanings of nation, state, and people. In Hindi, as you know, the standard terms are *rāṣṭra*, *rājya*, and *lok* or *janatā*. Each of these words have a history in Sanskrit which connected them to political and social units in the past of varying sizes from a group of villages or a town (*janapad*) to a kingdom (*rājya*) to an empire (*sāmrājya*). But they certainly did not mean what they mean today: the current meanings in Hindi came to be fixed in the twentieth century. There is nothing strange about this, because, if you look at Europe, even though the words state, nation, and people come from Latin, they did not earlier mean what they now mean in the European languages. Other Indian languages picked other words—some from Sanskrit, some from other languages. Thus, in Bengali, the standard word used to mean nation is *jāti*, which also means caste; the word for state is *rāṣṭra*, which is completely different from its use in Hindi; the word for people is *jana*, *gaṇa*, or *lok*. In Odiya and Assamese, the most common term for nation is *deś*. In Telugu, too, nation is *desam* (remember the Telugu Desam party?), while in Tamil it is the same word in its Tamil form: *tecam*. The state is *rājya* in Kannada and Malayalam, but *rāṣṭram* in Telugu. Tamil uses very different words to mean the state: *arasu* or *maanilam*. I could go on with other examples from other Indian languages. All that they would show is that words borrowed from Sanskrit acquired completely modern, and often different, meanings in the Indian languages in the twentieth century to express political ideas that did not exist in the past.

I have talked so far of the major modern Indian languages. The so-called tribal peoples of central India—the Santal, Kol, Bhil, Oraon, Munda, etc.—all have oral mythical traditions (*paramparā*) whose historical provenance is hard to determine but are doubtless ancient. They speak languages that do not belong to the Indo-Aryan family but to the Austroasiatic and Dravidian families. If you take the oral tradition of the Santals, for instance, it is a long story of migration from one place to another—the names are impossible to locate on the map—caused by repeated attacks by well-armed enemies, until they managed to settle for a long spell of time in a country called Champa where each lineage such as Hembrom, Kisku, Murmu, Tudu, etc. built their own forts to defend themselves. But once more they were pounced upon by the Diku—outsiders—who forced them to move to the forests of the Santal Parganas. The Santal lore suggests that every time they cleared forests and settled down to a sedentary life, the agricultural and commercial society of the Diku, i.e. the society organised within the Brahmanical caste order, set their sights on acquiring that land. It is true, of course, that in the course of centuries of economic and political interaction, the so-called tribal communities of central India have accepted – some more than others – many features of the Puranic traditions. But even as they adopted various Puranic gods, they continued to maintain in their oral traditions an antagonistic relation with the Brahmanical religious order. And they certainly have nothing to do with Vedic traditions. And before you dismiss these tribal origin myths as merely oral traditions, let me remind you that the Vedas too were originally an oral, not written, tradition.

I have to push the point even further. If you remember the present boundaries of the Indian nation-state, how would you expect the Sikkimese, Khasi, Mizo, Naga, or Meitei people to identify with the ancient achievements of the Vedic Arya? Their origin myths, linguistic traits, and cultural practices suggest migrations from Tibet, Southeast China, Burma, Thailand, Indonesia, and perhaps even Oceania. If you are to continue to insist on the ancientness of the Indian people going back to the Vedic civilisation, you will have to exclude all of these people from the hallowed ranks of Indians. And at this point, I am not even raising the question of the explicitly anti-Vedic religions such as Jainism and Buddhism and their social foundations in caste, economic, and cultural conflicts, nor indeed am I opening the contentious question of Islamic traditions in India.

## The Evidence from Genetic Science

On the question of the early inhabitants of India, there is a new body of evidence that is now emerging. I have no training in these sciences myself, but I try to keep myself informed through conversations with specialists. If you believe in science, you should take this evidence seriously. Genetic scientists have developed methods of analysing DNA samples extracted from human skeletons found within archaeological sites. The analysis of Y chromosomes, mitochondrial DNA, and whole genome sequences from a growing number of genetic samples collected from several sites in India and Pakistan are yielding dramatic accounts of the early demographic history of this country. Let me tell you some of these stories.

You have probably heard that genetic scientists are now confident that the lineages of all humans everywhere in the world can be traced back to a common set of ancestors in Africa. You must realise the significance of this scientific finding before jumping to conclusions about these first modern humans who were different from the archaic species of humans such as *Homo erectus*, Neanderthals, and Denisovans. We do not know how these earliest modern humans looked. But the fact that their descendants now include Scandinavians, Japanese, Bolivians, Nigerians, Arabs, and every other people on earth makes it certain that the way we look today is the result of centuries of genetic mutation caused by migration as well as regional and local patterns of intermingling among peoples. The fact of common origin does not mean that there are no genetic differences between different human groups. But it does demolish claims to racial purity or inhabiting a country from time immemorial. All humans are, at some point or other in their ancestry, the children of migrants.

The earliest modern humans migrated about 70,000 years ago from Africa to Asia, most likely from present-day Eritrea across the Red Sea into present-day Yemen. Some of these migrants then moved further into India and found the central and southern parts of the country inhabited by archaic humans such as Neanderthals. One wave of migrants from Africa took a route below the foothills of the Himalayas, and the other along the coastline, to ultimately cross into Southeast Asia, East Asia and Australia. These migrants from Africa were in fact the First Indians.

Sometime between 45,000 and 20,000 years ago, the First Indians discovered the use of Microlithic tools. This led to a rapid increase in their population and the extinction of other, more archaic, species of humans. We know very little of Stone Age human societies in India because so few prehistoric sites have been excavated. Our interest seems to have been fixated on proving the ancientness of historical civilisations. But I will soon tell you why the prehistoric First Indians are so important for India's demographic history. The first signs of agriculture in South Asia are to be found from around 7000 BCE at a site called Mehrgarh in Balochistan. From this time, for the next three or four thousand years, there is an influx into the region of Iranian agriculturists who mix with the First Indians. These are the people who, between 5500 and 1900 BCE, created the Harappan civilisation which archaeologists now divide into the Early and Mature periods. The cultivation of barley and wheat had by then spread all across north-western India and the beginnings of rice cultivation can also be observed. The Mature Harappa period shows, as I have told you earlier, evidence of a developed urban society. The Late Harappa period between 1900 and 1300 BCE saw the decline and disappearance of that civilisation.

The people we call Aryans were pastoralists, not agriculturists or urban, who migrated between 2000 and 1000 BCE from the Steppe region of Kazakhstan to present-day Turkmenistan, Uzbekistan, and Tajikistan and then southwards into Afghanistan, north-western Pakistan, and northern India. These migrations brought the Indo-European languages and sacrificial religious practices into South Asia. Around the same time, there was another wave of migration, originating in China and moving through Southeast Asia, into eastern India. This brought the Austroasiatic languages and new varieties of rice cultivation into India. That in a nutshell is the demographic history of this country as constructed from genetic evidence.

You may remember a news item about a young American missionary called John Allen Chau who, in November 2018, went to the North Sentinel Island in the Andamans to preach Christianity to the reclusive hunting-gathering people living there. Sadly, he was killed and his body left on the beach. The Sentinelese are supposed to be among the world's last peoples to resist contact with outsiders. This might lead you to think that they must be the oldest surviving human community in India. But that is not necessarily the case. We know nearly nothing about when and from where they came, or whether their isolation is from ancient times or recent. What we do know from genetic evidence is that another indigenous people of the Andaman and Nicobar Islands, the Onge, of whom there are only about a hundred alive today, and who lived for a long time in relative isolation, are descendants of the First Indians who migrated from Africa. But before you draw any conclusions about the primitiveness of the Onge, let me tell you the much more remarkable fact that emerges from the study of whole genome sequences: some 50 to 65 per cent of all Indians have an ancestry going back to the First Indians. So the Onge are not exceptional at all. If you like to think racially, they belong to the same race (*jāti*) as most Indians. If you look at ancestry by mitochondrial DNA lineage, i.e. through the maternal line, the evidence is even stronger: between 70 and 90 per cent of the people of this country are descended from the First Indians. However, if you take the Y chromosome lineage – descent through the male line only – then only 10 to 40 per cent come from First Indians, because the genetic record of our mixture with later migrants is to be found in the patrilineal descent. The reason should be obvious. Successive waves of male migrants coming from elsewhere united with indigenous females to produce the mixed progeny we now call Indians.

I am reminded of the sociologist Benoy Kumar Sarkar, a learned and much travelled man whom I used to know. He taught in the Economics Department of the University of Calcutta in the 1930s.[4] He would come into class and ask all

---

[4] Benoy Kumar Sarkar (1887–1949) was a sociologist trained in Germany who taught at the University of Calcutta. Among his many books are

the Brahman students to stand up. Needless to say, in those days that was a large part of the class. He would then hold up a book with the photograph of a Santal woman and ask: "Do you recognise her? That is your great-grandmother. Go home and tell your parents that I showed you a picture of your great-grandmother." Professor Sarkar was being provocative. But even though he did not know of genome sequences, he was right in his intuition that the female line of descent of most Indians today, regardless of caste, goes back to Adivasi women who carry the longest lineage (*kul*) that is most widely shared across the country.

The pastoralists from the Steppes of Central Asia moved westwards into Europe around 3000 BCE and southwards into India around 2000 BCE. These are the people familiarly known as the Aryans, though scientists prefer to call them Steppe pastoralists. The interesting difference in the two migrations is that the Steppe pastoralists almost completely replaced the earlier inhabitants of Europe, whereas in India the First Indians, in their mixed form of the Harappa people, survived the migration and settlement of the Steppe pastoralists. The genetic trace of earlier hunter-gatherer populations can be found today among less than 10 per cent of Europeans, whereas the majority of Indians have whole genome sequences that belonged to the First Indians. If you take the evidence of languages, 95 per cent of people in Western Europe speak an Indo-European language, whereas only 75 per cent of Indians do so; some 20 per cent speak a Dravidian language. So perhaps I might provoke you by suggesting that Europeans are much more Aryan than Indians.

The genetic evidence makes it clear that almost all Indians have a mixture of First Indian, Harappan, and Steppe pastoralist ancestries, but in different proportions. These differences

---

*The Positive Background of Hindu Sociology* (1914), *Aesthetics of Young India* (1927), and *The Sociology of Population* (1936).

actually suggest that after a period of considerable mixing, population groups in India begin to mix less and less from around 100 CE, indicating the emergence of the endogamous caste (*jāti*) structures we all know well. How tight these endogamous groups actually were, how rigidly the prohibition on marrying across castes was observed, and how these caste formations varied across regions are questions to which genetic research is sure to provide useful answers in the days to come. It may also tell us much more of the fragmentation of castes and the emergence of new caste groups of which historians and anthropologists have spoken at such length. What is certain is that you can no longer claim any scientific evidence for believing in the Aryans as the original inhabitants of India or the Vedic civilisation as the ultimate source of Indian culture.

All I have shown you so far is that the attempt to trace the ancient past of the people who constitute the modern Indian nation to the Arya people of the Vedas is based far more on imaginative fiction than historical or scientific fact. But, as I have told you before, your national leaders are not the only ones to perform this feat. They have learnt it from European nationalists. How is it that, from the eighteenth century, European scholars, who were mostly Christian, began to imagine the pagan people of ancient Greece and Rome as their cultural ancestors? Most of these scholars looked down upon their contemporary Greeks and Italians as dirty, idle, and vulgar, hardly deserving the status of Europeans. That is to say, while claiming the civilisational inheritance of classical Greece and Rome for themselves, the pundits of Western Europe denied that gift to modern Greeks and Italians. Now think about this: how could the modern Scot or Norwegian imagine the people of ancient Athens as their people? The desire to have an ancient nation can produce wonderful acts of imaginative fiction. I will tell you later how that work of imagination actually takes place: it is a fascinating story.

2

# All National Borders are Accidental

You have been told a million times that your national territory is sacred, that the nation's borders come down to you from time immemorial. India's territory stretches, you believe, from the mountains in the north to the seas in the south: *āsamudra himācala*, from Kashmir to Kanyakumari. You may have also heard that stirring speech by Duryodhan in the Udyogaparva of the Mahabharata where he vows not to cede without a fierce battle even a speck of land, not even one as tiny as the point of a needle:

*yāvaddhi sūcyāstīkṣṇāyā vidhyedagreṇa māriṣa!*
*tāvadapyaparityājyam bhūmena pāṇḍavān prati.*

Of course, to appreciate the sentiment, you have to ignore the fact that Duryodhan was on the wrong side in the Kurukshetra war. In any case, there are more modern versions that national leaders proclaim these days: "We will not surrender an inch of our land to the enemy." But the poetic invocation of natural boundaries only produces a literary effect, as does the dramatic assertion of rightful possession over territory. For carrying out the actual business of running nation-states, such vague definitions, emotionally evocative as they may be, are quite useless.

Let me show you how the actual borders of the Indian state came into being.

Start with the northern borders which have recently come into the news because of the armed clash between Indian and Chinese forces in June 2020. India has a 1750-kilometre-long border with Nepal and two stretches of borders with China on either side of Nepal – one, of some 900 kilometres in the east, and the other, about 4000 kilometres in the west. Besides, there is a short stretch of border between Bhutan and India. As you know, the borders with China have been a matter of much dispute. So let us start from there.

### The Chinese Border in the East

The border on the eastern side does not have a lyrical Sanskrit name at all. Instead, it is called by a very matter-of-fact Scottish name: the MacMahon line. The history of this border is intimately connected with British imperial designs on Tibet. This is not a history that is taught in your schools and so you probably don't know these details at all. In 1878, by which time the British had established their administration in the hill regions of north-east India, they drew a so-called Outer Line roughly along the foothills of the Himalayas, more or less coinciding with the southern boundaries of present-day Arunachal Pradesh. In 1903, Francis Younghusband invaded Tibet with British Indian troops and imposed a treaty on that country.[1] But for various reasons, the idea of expanding the British Indian Empire into Tibet was not pursued any more. In 1907, Britain and Russia acknowledged Chinese suzerainty over Tibet. You must remember that for Britain, the main concern over the northern frontiers of the Indian empire at this time was not Tibet or China but Russia: Britain was keen to ensure that

---

[1] Younghusband's invasion of Tibet was actually in 1904, not 1903.

Russian expansion into western China or Tibet was checked. In any case, the mountainous frontier regions were not economically or strategically valuable, except for the Tawang area with its famous monastery which was an important trading centre in which the British had some interest. As a result, no serious attempt was made to demarcate the borders on the ground or impose strict administrative controls on the region. People and goods continued to pass from Tibet to the foothills and valleys of British Assam as they had done for centuries past.

In 1910, the Qing imperial government of China sent military forces to Tibet. The British responded by creating the administrative region called the Himalayan Frontier Tracts (later called the North East Frontier Agency or NEFA), pushing the Outer Line northward. Soon, however, the Qing Empire collapsed and in 1913 Tibet declared itself independent.

It is at this point that Henry MacMahon, a British civil servant, convened a conference at the famous Viceregal Lodge in Simla with delegates from Tibet and the new Republican government of China. It was agreed there that Tibet would be administered by the Dalai Lama under the suzerainty of China. Suzerainty was a legal concept invented by the British to describe in the language of the European law of nations the hierarchical arrangement of sovereign relations produced in Asia after the European powers acquired territory and influence.[2] Suzerainty meant overall sovereign authority without the powers of internal administration, something like the relations of the British Indian paramount power with the princely states of India. That is what the British thought China's relation should be with Tibet. But from there on, the story gets murky. There were two small maps showing very little detail that were appended in July 1914 to the Simla Agreement that were probably shown to the Chinese officials, but the maps have no signatures or initials on them. A more detailed map that included the MacMahon line

---

[2] The word "suzerainty" is written in English in the manuscript.

was signed as a bilateral agreement between Britain and Tibet with the Chinese side left out. The line ran from Bhutan in the west to some 200 kilometres to the east of the great bend in the Brahmaputra river, passing not through the foothills of the Himalayas as with the older Outer Line but over hill crests further north. But the Simla Agreement was rejected by the Government of India as incompatible with the 1907 Anglo-Russian convention by which Chinese suzerainty over Tibet had been recognised: how could Tibet sign an agreement with Britain and China as a third party of equal standing? Aitchison's *Treaties*, the authoritative collection of British treaties in the Indian subcontinent, put it on record that no agreement was reached in 1914 in Simla.

That is how matters stood until 1935 when, in the context of the internal upheavals in China and Japanese military threats to that country, Olaf Caroe, a British Indian administrator who was considered an expert on the northern frontiers, revived interest in the MacMahon line. The Survey of India published in 1937 a new set of maps showing the MacMahon line as the boundary between India and Tibet. More interestingly (some might say scandalously), Aitchison's *Treaties* was republished in 1938 with the announcement that the Simla Agreement was a binding treaty between Britain and Tibet. Earlier volumes of the *Treaties* were recalled and a false publication date of 1928 inserted. Needless to say, all is fair in the great game of empire. In April 1938, a small British force under the command of Captain Lightfoot occupied Tawang although control was ceded to Tibet soon after. In 1950–1, the Indian government asserted control over Tawang, including it within the borders of NEFA.

Ever since Younghusband's expedition of 1904,[3] the British had asserted certain extra-territorial rights over Tibet. In 1954, the Indian government under Jawaharlal Nehru recognised Chinese sovereignty over Tibet and gave up those colonial

---

[3] Here, the correct year is mentioned in the manuscript.

rights. By this time, of course, the People's Republic was well established in China. In 1959, Chinese forces occupied Tibet and the Dalai Lama escaped to India. The dispute over the MacMahon line flared up with the Chinese claiming – citing the original British position on the matter – that Tibet was not an independent country and could not have made treaties. Further, the Chinese were never shown the MacMahon line and no Chinese official had ever agreed to it. Thus, as far as the Chinese were concerned, the so-called Simla Agreement was null and void. Chinese maps still show 65,000 square kilometres of territory south of the MacMahon line as part of the Chinese province of South Tibet. In 1962, Chinese armed forces attacked Indian troops on the border and, within ten days, came all the way down to the vicinity of Assam. Everyone expected Assam to be overrun. I remember Prime Minister Nehru on the radio, his voice choking, as he said: "My heart goes out to the people of Assam." But the Chinese suddenly stopped and retreated to their original positions along the MacMahon line. That continues to be roughly the line of actual control. But the Chinese still dispute India's claim, based on the Simla agreement, to territories south of the MacMahon line now included within the Indian state of Arunachal Pradesh.

It is salutary to remember that Indian soldiers were sent out in 1962 to defend an imaginary line drawn by a Scottish civil servant on a map that no one is allowed to see because it is classified top secret. Can you tell me how the deaths of our soldiers had anything to do with the sacred territory of the Indian nation?

## The Chinese Border in the West

The frontier region in the western sector is known as Aksai Chin which in Persian means "the furthest part of China". We don't need to speculate on whether this name has any significance for the historical association of the region with China or India. As we will see later on several occasions, these investigations into the historical associations of names more often than not end up in a wild goose chase. So let us just say "What's in a name?" and move on.[4]

The mountainous region of Ladakh measures about 14,000 square kilometres, most of it above 5000 metres and passable at certain points only in the summer. The passes were traditionally used for trade between Tibet and the Xinjiang region of China. In Mughal times, the Namgyal rulers of Ladakh had intermittent tributary relations with the Mughals but were also frequently attacked and subdued by the Manchu and Qing Chinese authorities who controlled Tibet. In 1834, Zorawar Singh, a Dogra general belonging to the Sikh kingdom of Punjab, annexed Ladakh and attached it to Ranjit Singh's territories. Chinese troops halted the Sikh advance into Tibet and signed in 1842 a treaty at Chushul by which both sides agreed to refrain from further transgressions. Following the Sikh defeat in the Second Anglo-Sikh war in 1849, the Dogra state of Jammu and Kashmir became a princely state ruled by Gulab Singh under British suzerainty. Ladakh was part of Gulab Singh's kingdom. Sovereignty over Ladakh was inherited by India with the much discussed accession in 1947 of the princely state of Jammu and Kashmir.

However, the actual border between Ladakh and Tibet was never demarcated, largely because the mountainous terrain was for the most part uninhabited. In 1865, a survey official named William Johnson proposed a line that was found to be highly inaccurate. In 1893, Hung Ta-chen, a senior Chinese official, and George Macartney, the British consul in Kashgar, agreed on a line along the Karakoram mountains. This line

---

[4] It may be pointed out, especially in the context of discussions later in the manuscript, that V.D. Savarkar's well-known book *Hindutva* opens with a chapter called "What is in a Name?"

was favoured by the Government of India and was forwarded by Charles McDonald to the Qing government in Beijing for approval, but no response was received. In 1897, John Ardagh modified the Johnson line and placed it further west along the crest of the Kun Lun mountains, claiming that it was more defensible against Russian threats. Both the Johnson-Ardagh and Macartney-McDonald lines were used in various British maps of India. But no demarcation on the ground was ever attempted.

After 1947, the Government of India adopted the Johnson line as its official western boundary with Tibet. In 1957, it was discovered that the Chinese had built a 1200-kilometre road connecting Tibet and Xinjiang that passed 179 kilometres south of that line. Nehru claimed that the area was historically a part of Ladakh and hence belonged to India. Zhou Enlai rebutted the claim, arguing that the border had never been demarcated, that the Macartney-McDonald line was the only one ever proposed to China, and that the Chinese were in actual occupation of the land. As the dispute continued, China came to a settlement in 1963 with Pakistan on the trans-Karakoram part of the border between Tibet and Pakistan-controlled Kashmir: this agreed border was largely the same as the Macartney-McDonald line. India, in the meantime, continues to claim that China is in illegal occupation of Aksai Chin even though in actual fact it is fully administered by China as a part of Western Tibet and no agreed border has been demarcated. There are confrontations at times between Indian and Chinese troops facing each other across the line of control. The most recent one was in June 2020 in which lives were lost on both sides.

No matter which way you look at it, the imaginative evocation of the Himalayas as the natural northern boundary of India, standing from time immemorial as an immense snow-capped wall, has nothing to do with the country's actual borders, which are not only recent but in fact the result of the often confused but always self-interested actions of British imperialists.

Remember that when you next talk about the sanctity of the nation's territory. India's northern borders were created not by the gods but by our British rulers. And they left them in a confused and undefined state.

I am sure you have noticed the frenzy kicked up recently on social media by loud-mouthed patriots who swore they would sacrifice their lives to recover every inch of national territory in Ladakh stealthily occupied by the diabolical Chinese. I wish someone would tell them what kind of territories they are dreaming of defending. I have been some way up those barren hills in Ladakh though not to the heights where Indian and Chinese troops face each other. But I have known many soldiers who have done their duty there. Believe me when I tell you that those cliffs are not even remotely like the charming scenes you see when you go trekking in the Kumaon or Shimla hills. Not only are there no people living there, there are not even wild animals, not even a blade of grass. It is sheer rock that is covered for most of the year in ice and snow and temperatures go down to -30 degrees. Soldiers there will tell you that when they climb those treacherous rocks while patrolling, their main worry is not the enemy across the line of control but the cliff edges, the slippery ice, and the freezing cold. If they speak to you candidly, they will tell you that they don't know why lives must be put at so much risk to defend such worthless disputed property.

I have heard that when they met in 1959, Zhou Enlai told Nehru: "We have no real borders between us, only British maps. Let us make a bargain. You keep NEFA, let us keep Aksai Chin. That way, nothing will change on the ground."[5] But such is the force of national myth-making that it was beyond the power of any Indian prime minister to make such an agreement. Soldiers pay the price for our national vanity.

---

[5] NEFA (North-East Frontier Agency) is now the state of Arunachal Pradesh.

## Nepal, Bhutan, and Sikkim

The boundaries with China as shown in maps may be disputed, but precisely because of that reason, the actual borders on the ground are quite impenetrable. There are Indian troops along the line of control, even in the heights of Ladakh, where they face Chinese troops on the other side. The situation in Nepal, Bhutan, and Sikkim is, however, quite different.

One of the landmarks in the city of Kolkata is a tall memorial tower at the north-east corner of the Maidan. Most people know it simply as the Monument. A few knowledgeable persons might supply a more specific name: the Ochterlony Monument. In recent times, it has been renamed Shahid Minar in memory of the martyrs of the freedom movement. But no one knows what the Monument originally signified. In actual fact, the tower was raised to celebrate the victory in 1816 of David Ochterlony's troops in a two-year war with Nepal. Following the war, the East India Company concluded the Treaty of Sugauli by which Nepal gave up its control over Sikkim (including Darjeeling), Kumaon, Garhwal, and the western Terai. The war in the inhospitable foothills of the Himalayas had proved costly for the Company. Besides the surprisingly bold resistance put up by the enemy, a large number of its own troops had died of malaria. The British were not interested in further pursuing any aggressive goals in Nepal. Instead, they established a residency in Kathmandu and were happy to regard Nepal as a subsidiary ally, supplying Gurkha soldiers to their army in India and acting as a buffer against the Qing Empire in the north. Part of Nepal's border in the south with the kingdom of Awadh was agreed on in 1830 and that with the Company's territories some years later.

The lands on both sides were settled agricultural regions with regular revenue and police administrations. The border was for the most part open, with free movement of people along regular trade routes. After Indian independence, the Indo-Nepal treaty of 1950 confirmed that nationals of the two countries could travel across the border without passports or visas and could work in either country. That is roughly the situation that prevailed until recently when a new political situation emerged.

The Maoist insurgents gave up arms and entered the government in Nepal in 2008. The monarchy was abolished and a secular republic proclaimed. After prolonged negotiations between many parties, a new constitution was agreed upon in 2015. The Indian government, acting as the big neighbour, has always tried to exert its influence over Nepal's politics. Unhappy with certain provisions of the new constitution, the Madhesia community, consisting of people of Indian origin residing in the terai region of Nepal, mounted a blockade of the vital roads linking Nepal with India. The Indian government supported the blockade, causing much resentment in political circles in Nepal. In 2020, the Nepal government claimed that India had built a road over Nepalese territory in Kalapani. In fact, Nepal redesigned its official map to reflect the claim. India maintains that the border was clearly demarcated and that Nepal was being used as a proxy by China. K.P. Sharma Oli, the prime minister of Nepal, even claimed somewhat bizarrely that the real Ayodhya where Lord Ramchandra was born was in Nepal, confirming once more that a mythical birthplace of a mythical hero could be imaginatively transported anywhere. Perhaps a new chapter has been opened in the history of a border which until now was undisputed.

The British first engaged with the Namgyals of Bhutan in 1772 when the Koch ruler of Cooch Behar appealed to the East India Company for assistance against Bhutanese aggression. Although the Company's troops repulsed the attack, skirmishes continued until the middle of the nineteenth century when war broke out leading to Bhutan's defeat. As a result, Bhutan ceded in 1865 the Duars region of present-day West Bengal to the British who soon threw the area open to tea plantations. When, after protracted civil wars, the Wangchuk dynasty was established as the ruling monarchy of Bhutan, the British signed the Treaty of Punakha in 1910 by which Bhutan became a subsidiary ally, similar to an Indian princely state, with control over internal administration but ceding its foreign relations to the British Indian authority. In actual practice, however, Bhutan continued to exercise a fair degree of autonomy in managing its relations with Tibet. In 1949, the new Indian government signed an agreement with Bhutan by which it asserted control over that country's foreign relations, leaving internal sovereignty to the Bhutanese monarch. This position changed in 2007 when India agreed to recognise Bhutan as fully sovereign with complete autonomy to determine its external policy. Like Nepal, Bhutan's border with India is open and citizens of each country are free to travel and work in the other without passport or visa requirements.

Thus, even though it was once again British imperial policy that allowed Nepal to remain an independent country and conferred on Bhutan the status of a subsidiary ally, the significance of their borders with India is quite different from those of India's borders with other countries. But the fragility and arbitrariness of these boundaries are best brought out by the history of India's relations with Sikkim.

Ruled by the hereditary Chogyal, Sikkim was periodically attacked and occupied in the eighteenth century by Bhutan, the Gorkha kingdom of Nepal and the Qing government of Tibet. Following the Anglo-Gorkha war, Nepal surrendered in 1817 its control over Sikkim. But relations between Sikkim and the British administration in Bengal were not entirely cordial. In 1849, two British doctors exploring the mountains were captured by the Sikkim authorities, leading to a punitive expedition by the East India Company which culminated in Sikkim having to surrender the Darjeeling hills in 1853. Darjeeling, of course, was then turned into a summer resort and producer of some of the world's finest teas. The British were actually quite bloody-minded and reduced the Chogyal to a mere titular head, requiring him to govern under the supervision of the British

Indian authorities. Only in 1890 was Sikkim recognised as a British protectorate, but that too in an agreement with China on which Sikkim was not even consulted. By the twentieth century, Sikkim was given the status of a princely state.

After Indian independence, Sikkim organised a referendum among its citizens in which the majority rejected a proposal to join the Indian Union. Here, let me point out to you, is an example of the people of a princely state within British India actually voting to refuse the offer to join independent India. A treaty was signed between India and Sikkim in 1950 by which Sikkim was given the status of a protectorate with sovereignty over internal affairs, but with India retaining control over Sikkim's foreign relations and defence. The major political problem, however, was the influx of migrants from Nepal who soon outnumbered the local population. The Chogyal became deeply unpopular and there prevailed a climate of sustained unrest. In 1975, two months before Indira Gandhi declared a state of emergency, Indian troops occupied Gangtok and took control of the state. By a constitutional amendment, Sikkim first became an "associate state", an unprecedented and unique category. By a new referendum, an overwhelming majority of people in Sikkim then voted to abolish the monarchy, confirming India's annexation. Make a note of this point, because it will come up in a big way when we later discuss the thorny subject of Kashmir: the plebiscite or referendum has been used not once but several times, and not only in the case of Sikkim but elsewhere too, to settle the question of whether and under what conditions a particular territorial region was to be included within India. After the referendum of 1975, Sikkim became a full state within the Indian Union.

## The Hill States of the Northeast

It was not only India's borders with Nepal and Tibet that were defined as a result of British imperial actions. The very inclusion of the north-eastern states within contemporary India was also the somewhat chaotic result of British imperial policy. This is a tangled history about which few people care. But a brief sketch will help you get a sense of why the idea of India's sacred and inviolable borders, when tallied against the actual history of how those borders came to be defined, is so dubious.

The first of the hill peoples to come under British authority were the Garo. In 1816, East India Company officials pushed beyond the borders of the Bengal districts of Rangpur and Mymensingh to bring villages in the Garo hills under their revenue jurisdiction. Assam, of course, had long been under the rule of the Ahom kings, a dynasty of Tai ethnicity which had come from Yunnan in China in the thirteenth century. But the valley was invaded by the Burmese army in the early-nineteenth century. With the British victory in the first Anglo-Burmese war, the Burmese king renounced his claim to Assam which then came into British possession in 1826. British administration was then extended to the Khasi-Jaintia and Cachar hills in 1835. In 1866, the Naga Hills also came under British control. Not only that, you should remember that India's borders with Burma were also settled by British conquest: the Burmese defeat in the third Anglo-Burmese war resulted in the annexation of that country to British India in 1886. India's current borders with Burma date from that event.

Contrary to the widespread prejudices held about them in other parts of India, the hill peoples of the north-east were quite proficient in several branches of agriculture and manufacturing. They were excellent weavers of cotton fabric (today Naga or Khasi or Manipuri shawls have become items of fashion). Iron smelting was widely practised (as was the case with several Adivasi communities elsewhere in India). The Angami Nagas were able to get remarkably good yields of rice using terrace farming. There was also the prospect of wild rubber and wild tea, besides minerals including petroleum whose deposits were discovered in Assam from the 1860s. Hence, the British could have found the region economically useful. But they soon realised that because of its very different history and social conditions, the north-eastern region could not be administered in the same way as the rest of India. Assam was thus constituted into a Chief Commissioner's Province with much greater arbitrary powers given to the bureaucracy than elsewhere in India. The situation was complicated by the fact that besides thousands of relatively independent villages peopled by so-called tribal communities which did not have anything like a state formation, there were also six major states in the north-east whose rulers had acquired the status of Kshatriya kings and established certain Brahmanical practices in their courts. Among them, the British came to recognise the Koch, the Tripuri, and the Meitei states as the princely states of Cooch Behar, Hill Tipperah, and Manipur. The other three – the Ahom, the Jaintia, and the Kachari – were annexed. Yet another such state – that of the Buddhist Chakma people – was incorporated into Bengal as the district of the Chittagong Hill Tracts.

Several of the hill communities had a long history of resisting and staying away from the control of agrarian states in the plains. Their social organisation reflected this character of peoples without states. After several steps of trial and error, the British decided on a policy of segregating the hills from the plains. In the 1870s, an Inner Line was drawn, separating an area ultimately covering all the hill tracts of the north-east except the Khasi and Garo hills, which prohibited any person from outside from moving into or living in the area. Laws and regulations that applied to the rest of British India were not necessarily applicable here. A distinction emerged between a zone of administrative control in and around a British outpost and areas outside that zone where there was only "political control". In the former zone, the British initially interfered in the affairs of the hill peoples only when there were threats to the safety of British subjects, violations of the Inner Line, and intimidation of coolies and employees of tea gardens and neighbouring cultivators. Over time, and especially in the twentieth century, these administrative regimes would, of course, become more detailed and intensive. In the zones of so-called political control, especially in the Naga Hills, the British merely claimed a superior authority but left the local communities pretty much to themselves. There was no taxation, and even when there was headhunting or war between the tribes, the British seldom intervened. In the twentieth century, administrative control was gradually extended over larger areas of the hills. Even then, it was never quite clear if the region was part of British India or a "foreign jurisdiction" similar to the princely states. The constitutional reforms of 1935 created the category of "tribal areas" – areas "along the frontiers of India which are not part of British India or of Burma or of any Indian State or of any foreign State" – a sort of frontier region in limbo. Reforms such as elected ministries that were inaugurated in the provinces of British India in 1935 were not extended to these tribal areas. Such was the ambiguous status of the north-eastern hills at the time of Indian independence. I will explain to you later how, even after they became states of the Indian Union, these anomalies were not fully resolved.

Perhaps I should also ask you here if you know the reason why Burma is not a part of India. You probably think that is how it has been from time immemorial. But recent history which, as I have been showing you, has in most cases determined the actual borders of the country tells us something quite different. Burma became a province of the British Indian Empire in 1886. It was governed like any other province by members of the Indian Civil Service under laws made by the Government of India. When constitutional reforms were introduced in 1919, they were initially held back from Burma, but after protests they too were put in place. In fact, there were five seats in the central legislature in New Delhi for members from Burma. In 1937, when elected provincial ministries took office in the Indian provinces, the British took the political decision to take Burma out of the jurisdiction of the Government of India and create a separate crown colony directly under the British parliament. The British, of course, lost Burma during World War II when it was occupied by the Japanese. Burma eventually won its independence from the British in 1948. These accidental twists and turns are completely glossed over in your national histories. So the next time you are told about the timeless unity of the Indian nation, ask yourself why Nagaland is a part of India but not Myanmar, why Sikkim is a part of India but not Nepal or Bhutan, and you will begin to distinguish between the truths and lies of nationalism.

### The Punjab Border

Millions of words have been spent discussing the roots of the conflict that led to the partition of India in 1947. Some identify the Direct Action Day, declared by the Muslim League on 16 August 1946, as the momentous event that made partition inevitable. Others blame Gandhi's espousal of the cause of the Khilafat movement in 1919–20. Still others talk of the British imperial policy of "divide and rule" which set up separate electorates and reserved seats for Muslims in legislative bodies. Needless to say, there are also people who claim deeper historical knowledge and announce that it all began with Aurangzeb's bigotry or the pillage of India in the eleventh century by Mahmud of Ghazni or, even further back, the conquest of Sindh in the eighth century by Muhammad bin Qasim. But the historical truth is that the borders between India and Pakistan were drawn by about half a dozen men in the space of less than six weeks in July and August of 1947. That is how actual national borders are often drawn. It is time you stop romanticising national borders because they can be made and unmade with nothing more than paper, pencil, and the force of law.

It all began with Mountbatten's decision in April 1947 to advance the date of the transfer of power to 15 August of that year. This meant that all political negotiations and administrative arrangements had to be completed at great speed. When it was decided in the same month that Punjab and Bengal would be divided in order to respect the Sikh and Hindu demands in the two provinces not to go with Pakistan, it became clear that the delimitation of boundaries would become a contentious issue. Mountbatten initially toyed with the idea of involving the United Nations in settling the boundaries in Punjab and Bengal, but Nehru rejected the idea because it would take too much time. In any case, the authorities in London would have none of it because the transfer of power in India had to appear to the rest of the world as one involving only the British and the Indians: no one else could be allowed to have a say. In the end, it was decided to appoint a boundary commission for each of the two provinces, with four high court judges – two each nominated by the Congress and the Muslim League – and both commissions to be chaired by Cyril Radcliffe, a London barrister who had never been to India. It was anticipated that the Indian judges on the commission would uphold the views of their parties: the inevitable deadlocks that would follow, therefore, had to be broken by an impartial British chairman. Radcliffe's unfamiliarity with India's politics was considered a good qualification in projecting his lack of bias.

As it happened, the commissions functioned very differently in the two provinces. In Punjab, neither the Congress nor the Muslim League was organised enough to make the legal or technical arguments in claiming territory for the two new states. The Sikhs, mobilised under Tara Singh, were the most vociferous in publicly demanding that their interests be protected. But because they were mostly concentrated in the central districts of the province, they were also geographically the most vulnerable. In the end, with the Congress and Muslim League nominees unwilling to concede ground, Radcliffe drew the borders of the two new Punjab provinces virtually singlehanded.

Since there was no time for a fresh survey and demarcation on the ground, Radcliffe decided to adopt the existing district and tehsil boundaries. This meant that as far as the borders between India and Pakistan are concerned, natural boundaries had no role to play; only the existing administrative boundaries drawn by the colonial state for its revenue and policing purposes mattered. In fact, since Indian rivers are notorious for changing course, Radcliffe clearly stated in his award that even when the boundary ran close to a river, it was the administrative line and not the physical course of the river that would define the international border. Radcliffe's basic task was to determine the relative proportions of Muslims, Hindus, and Sikhs and define two blocks of contiguous areas, one with a Muslim majority and the other a Hindu-Sikh majority. The two criteria – religious majority and contiguous area – could not be strictly followed simultaneously, even after dividing up districts, as a result of which the majority criterion had to be sacrificed in certain instances in order not to end up with scattered pieces of Indian and Pakistani territory. In addition, Radcliffe decided that, given the importance of the irrigation system in Punjab, the canals that watered the different districts should not be separated from their headwaters. This too meant that the religious majority principle had to be overruled in certain cases.

In the end, Radcliffe's line separated the two largest urban concentrations in Punjab – Lahore and Amritsar – which were only twenty-five miles apart, but awarded the Muslim-majority districts of Gurdaspur and Ferozepur to India to preserve the integrity of their irrigation systems. Since the line necessarily passed through the central part of Punjab, it meant that some of the major Sikh shrines went to Pakistan, even though a part of Lahore district with a large Sikh concentration was separated out and added to the Indian territory.

It is sometimes alleged that Radcliffe was forced by Mountbatten, who in turn was being prodded by Nehru, to make the Gurdaspur award in order to give India a land route into Kashmir which, of course, had not yet chosen to join either India or Pakistan. Since Radcliffe destroyed every single piece of paper in his possession, it has been difficult for historians to verify the truth of this allegation. But it is worth remembering that in 1947, all road and rail communication into Jammu and Kashmir went through Lahore and Sialkot and there was only one road through Gurdaspur which, however, could not be used throughout the year. In fact, when India agreed in October 1947 to the Maharaja's request to send troops to Kashmir, they had to be airlifted because there were no roads that could be used. It seems more reasonable to accept the argument that in this case Radcliffe was more concerned about irrigation than any future Indian strategic interest in Kashmir. It is, however, true that Gurdaspur provided a physical connection between the territories of Jammu and Kashmir and the Indian dominion without which its accession might have been far more contentious, perhaps impossible. On the other hand, there is evidence that on Ferozepur, Mountbatten did urge Radcliffe to award the Muslim-majority district to India because the princely state of Bikaner whose parched lands were fed by canals originating in that Punjab district was threatening to join Pakistan unless Ferozepur was given to India.

The announcement of the Radcliffe award was delayed until 17 August 1947, well after power had been transferred to the two new dominion governments. Perhaps the idea was to absolve the British of any responsibility of dealing with its consequences. What ensued was a horror story matched by few other episodes in modern world history. The careful balancing of religious majorities with contiguous territory turned out to be an academic exercise of no import. The only thing that was true was the administrative line that defined the new border. As for the rest, killing, looting, arson, rape, and the terror-stricken flight of millions ensured that overwhelming religious majorities would be established on either side of the international boundary cutting through the heart of Punjab. On hindsight, it seems clear that it would not have mattered at all if Radcliffe had drawn his line a little this way or that: the same distribution of population would have emerged on the two sides. Do you need any more proof in support of my claim that national borders are the results of historical accident? If you have not read it, do read Saadat Hasan Manto's story "Toba Tek Singh" which describes far better than I can ever hope to do the absurd reality of how the Punjab border was actually drawn.

### The Bengal Border

The Bengal border was decided somewhat differently, mainly because the parties concerned were far better organised and prepared to make an effective representation of their demands before the Radcliffe commission. The Muslim League, of course, had argued for the inclusion of an undivided Bengal in Pakistan and most Muslim members of the Bengal Assembly had voted that way during the crucial session on 20 June 1947. The Hindu members of the Assembly, on the other hand, including those from the Congress, the Hindu Mahasabha, and most members belonging to the Scheduled Castes, had voted in favour of the partition of Bengal. Once the boundary commission was announced, it became clear that political and intellectual circles in Hindu Bengal were devoting a great deal of thought and research to devise strategies for best representing their case for territory.

The Congress, for instance, whose case was put forward by the lawyer Atul Gupta, decided to adopt a complicated, and somewhat devious, strategy of presenting the commission with two separate proposals – one called the Plan and the other the Scheme. The Congress Plan made no ambitious claims. Taking the police station or thana as the basic territorial unit, it claimed areas where Hindus numbered at least 55 per cent of the population. In addition, invoking the principle of contiguous territory, the Plan asked for no more than six thanas with Muslim majorities in Rangpur, Rajshahi, and Malda, besides the district of Murshidabad where Muslims were 56 per cent of the population. Kaliachak thana in Malda was claimed because that is where the headwaters of the Bhagirathi river which flowed past Calcutta was located: this is where the Farakka barrage would be built in the 1960s. Murshidabad was claimed because it would, first, physically join the northern and southern districts of the new province, and second, retain the integrity of the river system around the crucially important region around Calcutta. Khulna, on the other hand, although it had a small majority of Hindus, was considered economically unimportant and could, at a pinch, be given up in exchange for Murshidabad. The new province of West Bengal envisioned by the Plan would have a Hindu majority of 70 per cent. Clearly, the strategic objective behind the Congress Plan was to achieve a territorial unit that was politically and administratively the most governable: the Muslim population would be a small minority and the Congress would be overwhelmingly the dominant political force.

But the Congress provincial leaders were aware of the fact that this rather minimalist Plan would be difficult to sell to a public that was being treated every day to the most fantastic territorial claims flaunted by the Hindu Mahasabha and other Hindu outfits. So Atul Gupta also put before the Radcliffe commission a second proposal called the Congress Scheme. It was this Scheme rather than the more limited Plan that was publicised in the press along with a map showing the division of the two Bengals that the Congress was apparently endorsing. The Scheme demanded Jessore, Khulna, the Chittagong Hill

Tracts and parts of Dacca, Bakarganj, and Faridpur districts as territories of India. With this public posture, the Congress leaders were hoping to cope with the inevitable disappointment of a much reduced final award by putting the blame on the intrinsic unfairness of the departing imperial power.

Interestingly, the Congress Plan was not the most minimalist Hindu plan on offer. A ginger group within the Bengal provincial Congress, consisting of district leaders from Burdwan, Hooghly, and Midnapore, and led by Jadabendra Panja and Atulya Ghosh, put forward a plan for an even smaller and tightly bound West Bengal. This would consist only of the Hindu-majority and Congress-controlled districts of southwestern Bengal, Calcutta, 24-Parganas, and Khulna. It was willing to give away even Hindu-majority districts of the north such as Darjeeling and Jalpaiguri, as well as Dinajpur, Malda, Murshidabad, Nadia, and Jessore. Clearly, when staking their claims to territory, the politics of post-partition government was already being anticipated by the realist politicians of the Bengal Congress: they wanted a territory firmly under their control.

It is also worth noting that the all-India leadership of the Congress did not intervene at all in these provincial negotiations in Punjab and Bengal. In fact, when Congress leaders from those provinces approached their national leaders for advice or help, they were told that it was Congress policy to let the boundary commission deal with the matter; Congress leaders would not interfere with what was essentially a legal-administrative process. Perhaps there was politics at play here too. Given the highly communal rhetoric and passions blowing across Punjab and Bengal at the time, it was inevitable that the drawing of boundaries dividing the two provinces would be looked at almost exclusively along the lines of religious division. Local leaders too, including those from the Congress, would perforce have to take up the Hindu cause, because the Muslims and Sikhs were being represented by the Muslim League and the Akalis;

otherwise, the Congress would have to cede the position to the Hindu Mahasabha. In such a situation, it was prudent for the all-India Congress leadership, once again with a view to its post-independence tasks of government, to stay away from these contentious communal debates raging in the two provinces.

One should also mention that even though the official Muslim League position was to claim the entire Muslim-majority province of Bengal for Pakistan, there was a more realist view that acknowledged that the overwhelmingly Hindu-majority districts of south-western Bengal could not be easily claimed. As early as 1943, the East Pakistan Renaissance Society, a group of leading young Muslim intellectuals of Bengal, produced a map of East Pakistan that excluded those districts. As far as Bengal is concerned, the idea of drawing borders so as to produce culturally homogeneous national units had become well established.

In the end, Radcliffe's award largely followed the Congress Plan. Murshidabad and Nadia (minus the Kushtia subdivision) were given to West Bengal to preserve the integrity of the Bhagirathi river system so crucial to the port of Calcutta. In exchange, Khulna went to Pakistan. East Bengal now had a population that was 71 per cent Muslim, while West Bengal had a Hindu majority of 70.8 per cent. The two northern districts of Jalpaiguri and Darjeeling, however, were left unconnected with the rest of West Bengal, even after Dinajpur district was bifurcated and each half awarded to the two new states. It was only with the reorganisation of the Indian states in 1956 that a sliver of land was transferred from Bihar to West Bengal in order to provide the latter with the territory for road and railway connections between Malda and Darjeeling districts.

Curiously, the Radcliffe commission awarded the eastern district of the Chittagong Hill Tracts, where 90 per cent of the people were Buddhist, to Pakistan. The reason was that there could be no possible contiguity with West Bengal, even though the district had common borders with Assam and the princely state of Tripura. Interestingly, the Bengal Congress did not claim the district in its Plan.

## Plebiscites

While we are on the subject of the borders of East Bengal, we should remember that the Assam district of Sylhet, populated largely by Bengali-speaking Muslims, was claimed by Pakistan. The issue was settled by a referendum in June 1947 with about 60 per cent voters wanting to join the new Pakistani province of East Bengal. Sylhet, minus the Hindu-dominated subdivision of Karimganj, was taken out of Assam and joined with East Bengal. That is one of two instances within British India where the people, rather than politicians and bureaucrats, were asked to decide whether they would like to live in India or Pakistan.

The other instance was the North West Frontier Province (NWFP). In 1946, the NWFP legislative assembly had a Congress majority and was governed by a Congress ministry headed by Khan Sahib, brother of Khan Abdul Ghaffar Khan (locally known as Bacha Khan), the famous Gandhian leader of the Khudai Khidmatgar. But the governor of the province was Olaf Caroe, the same wily civil servant I mentioned when talking about the disputed border between Ladakh and Tibet. If the decision to join India or Pakistan was left to the members of the assembly, as happened in the cases of Punjab and Bengal, then, given the Congress majority, NWFP would become an island province of India surrounded by Pakistani territory on one side and Afghanistan on the other. Caroe did not think that was a good idea at all, because with the Soviet threat from the north and the ongoing civil war in China, he was worried that British strategic interests would be jeopardised by a strong Congress presence in the region. Shrewdly noticing that the Muslim League had in fact got more popular votes in the 1946 elections, even though the Congress won more seats because of its sway over the less densely populated rural constituencies, he persuaded Mountbatten that a popular referendum would produce a more legitimate path for the future of the province. Ghaffar Khan realised that a close election, even if it produced a narrow verdict in favour of India, would lead to violent disturbances. He appealed to Gandhi and the Congress. But Gandhi was not taking part in the final act of cutting up the country, and the Congress, already forced into accepting the partition of Punjab and Bengal, was not keen to throw another spanner into the process of transfer of power. So Ghaffar Khan and the Khudai Khidmatgar decided not to participate in the plebiscite: 99 per cent of those voting chose to join Pakistan. NWFP is now known as the Pakistani province of Khyber-Pakhtunkhwa.

Perhaps I should also mention in passing why Afghanistan was never a part of British India. It was not for want of trying on the part of the British. The Afghan region has a history of political and cultural links with northern India going back to ancient times. The Vedic peoples were settled in the region, as were the so-called Indo-Greek rulers. Gāndhārī, the spirited mother of the Kauravas in the Mahabharata, came, as her name indicates, from the place now known as Qandahar, as did her brother, the wily Śakuni. Gandhara was the main route through which Buddhism travelled from India to Central Asia and China. The British were particularly interested in conquering the region because of its geopolitical importance, being at the confluence of Russia, China, and Iran. In the first Anglo-Afghan war, troops of the East India Company occupied Kabul in 1839 but were decimated in an uprising of Afghan tribesmen in 1842. The British installed Dost Muhammad as Amir and concluded an agreement with him. But the Russian Empire continued to threaten British interests in the region. In 1878, the second Anglo-Afghan war was launched which again proved very costly. The British were forced to withdraw in 1880 after coming to another settlement with an Amir of their choice.

Conquest having failed, they had to be satisfied with accepting Afghanistan as a buffer against Russia.

Finally, in 1919, soon after the Jallianwala Bagh massacre in Amritsar, Amir Amanullah ordered Afghan troops to march across the Khyber Pass into Indian territory. At the time, British Indian troops had just returned from long spells of combat abroad in the First World War and were being demobilised. Their morale was quite low. But the Afghan attack was repulsed with British, Dogra and Gurkha troops under the command of Brigadier General Dyer, infamous for his role in the Amritsar killings, along with bombing from the air. The war concluded with the British recognising Afghanistan under King Amanullah as an independent country, while the latter accepted the Durand line as the international border. That still continues to be the border between Afghanistan and Pakistan.

## Enclaves

The most outlandish story about the accidental character of national borders concerns the so-called Chhit Mahals on the India–Bangladesh border. A chhit mahal (which literally means a scattered village) is an enclave, usually of one or two villages, belonging, say, to India, but surrounded by Bangladeshi territory, or belonging to Bangladesh and surrounded by Indian territory. After partition in 1947, there were some hundred or so Indian enclaves in East Pakistan, mostly in the district of Rangpur, and a similar number of Pakistani enclaves in the princely state of Cooch Behar. But that is not all. Some Indian enclaves contained Pakistani counter-enclaves within them, as did some Pakistani enclaves which had Indian counter-enclaves. There was even one Indian enclave in East Pakistan which had a Pakistani counter-enclave which in turn contained an Indian counter-counter-enclave.

How did this ridiculous state of affairs come into being?

Since rational explanations are hard to find, people have come up with fantastic stories. It is said that the Maharaja of Cooch Behar used to play the dice game of *pasha* with the Maharaja of Rangpur in which they would stake their mahals or revenue villages. Depending on who won on which day, the villages along the border between Cooch Behar and Rangpur became scattered possessions of the two rulers. That is why a chhit mahal is sometimes called *pasha mahal*. Whoever invented the story was probably thinking of the infamous dice game in the Mahabharata in which Yudhiṣṭhir staked and lost his kingdom. Winning and losing mahals at *pasha* were, after all, part of a hallowed royal tradition in this country.

The more reasonable explanation is probably that revenue administration in the state of Cooch Behar was not as thorough and systematic as in the Mughal province of Bengal. When the British established their administration in Rangpur district, they discovered they had revenue-paying villages within Cooch Behar territory, just as Cooch Behar had revenue villages in Rangpur. With due regard to their relations with the princely state, the British decided to leave things that way. Had Cooch Behar been a British Indian district, I am quite sure the enclaves would have been merged within one or the other district a long time ago.

The existence of the enclaves meant that there were Bangladeshi citizens living in a Bangladeshi enclave inside India. The enclave would be fenced. The gates would open in the morning. People who needed to go to a government office or children going to school would have to walk through Indian territory to go to the office or school in Bangladesh. Indian citizens living in an Indian enclave within Bangladesh faced a similar situation. It was an absurd state of affairs.

But even though the insanity of the situation was obvious to everyone, it took almost seventy years to resolve it. The reason for the delay is nothing more than the petty sentiment of national pride that made people in both countries throw a tantrum about how many square kilometres of land each side would gain or lose by an exchange of enclaves. In the end, an agreement was reached between India and Bangladesh in 2015 to merge the enclaves into the surrounding administrative unit. Residents of each enclave were given the option of continuing to stay where they were or moving to the country of their choice. That is one accidental gift of history – an absurdly confused border – that seems to have been finally straightened out.

## Islands in the Sea

Most people do not always remember that the territories of India stretch beyond its shores and include several islands in the sea. How did that happen? The answer is the same as the one we discovered for the land borders: the accidents of British imperial policy.

The Lakshadweep islands, with a total land area of only 32 square kilometres, lie between 200 and 400 kilometres from the coast of Kerala. The islands were part of Tipu Sultan's territories and passed into the control of the East India Company after Tipu's defeat and death in 1799. Peopled mostly by Malayali Muslims, the islands were administered by the British as part of Malabar district of the Madras Presidency. After independence, when state boundaries were reorganised in 1956, the Laccadive, Amindivi, and Minicoy Islands were separated from Kerala and made into a Union Territory. The name was changed to Lakshadweep in 1973. The British did not attach much strategic or economic importance to the islands. They have been developed into a tourist destination only in the last two or three decades.

That is a fairly straightforward story. The curiosity lies in why some of the other islands in the same region did not become part of India. The Maldives, for instance, are a thousand kilometres from the western coast of India. In the eighteenth century, the islands were ruled by their sultan under the hegemony of the

Dutch. When the Dutch were ousted from Ceylon by the British in 1796, the Maldive Islands became a British protectorate, administered from Colombo. The population of the islands is predominantly Muslim and speak a language similar to Sinhalese. During the Second World War, the Maldives acquired a significant strategic interest for the British as a convenient base in the Arabian Sea for the Royal Air Force. As a result, they did not figure in the negotiations over the independence of India or Ceylon, since the British were keen to retain control over the islands. The Maldives became an independent country in 1965 and the British closed their military base there in 1976.

The question never asked is why Ceylon, now Sri Lanka, was not administered by the British as part of their Indian empire. The island is separated from the southern tip of India only by a narrow strait and there have been countless political, economic, and cultural interactions across those waters for centuries. The coastal areas of the island were occupied first by the Portuguese and then by the Dutch. The British ousted the Dutch in the early-nineteenth century and, after waging war on the independent kingdom of Kandy in 1815, established their rule over Ceylon. This was the period when a group of liberal reformers in Britain, influenced by utilitarian philosophy, began to look to the eastern colonies as a laboratory for putting into practice their progressive schemes for a more representative form of government. They found the established conventions of East India Company administration in India too conservative and too entrenched. With the exception of figures like Macaulay and Bentinck in Bengal, the liberal utilitarians did not make much impression in India. But Ceylon proved a much more favourable and fertile ground. The Colebrook–Cameron reforms of 1833 established executive and legislative councils, which later became an elected representative government in which elite sections of the different communities in Ceylon could take part. Thereafter Ceylon was treated by British officials as a colonial entity entirely different from India, with its own civil service. In fact, at a time when, despite the Motilal Nehru report and the urging of the Congress, the British refused to expand the suffrage in India, the constitutional reforms of 1931 introduced universal adult suffrage in Ceylon. That is why Ceylon was never part of the historical process that produced nationalist politics in India.

To turn further west across the Arabian Sea, did you know that Aden, the port city on the southern coast of Yemen, now bombed into rubble in course of the civil war there, was administered as part of the Bombay Presidency from the beginning of the nineteenth century to as recently as the 1930s? The British acquired the port during the Napoleonic wars and turned it into a crucial commercial and naval hub in the Indian Ocean region. Through the nineteenth century, business in Aden came to be dominated by a group of Parsi and Jewish merchants with close ties to the city of Bombay. In 1932, when arrangements were under way for constitutional reforms and elected provincial ministries in India, the British decided to shift the administrative control of Aden from the Government of Bombay (which would soon have a Congress ministry) to the central government in New Delhi. The Parsi businessmen of Aden fought very hard to keep the port city under the charge of Bombay, but failed. In 1937, the British decided that Aden was too strategically important to be left at the mercy of the uncertain political future of India and turned it into a crown colony administered directly from London. Aden became the capital of the independent republic of South Yemen in 1970.

## The Andaman and Nicobar Islands

Once again, nothing except British colonial conquests and policies explain why these islands across the Bay of Bengal are a part of India. They are less than 300 kilometres from Myanmar and only 150 kilometres from Indonesia, whereas the nearest shores of the Indian mainland are more than a thousand kilometres away. The British established a naval base and penal settlement in Chatham Island in 1789; this later became the town of Port Blair. The penal settlement was a curious European institution where convicts were sent in the belief that they would reproduce their species in isolation, without fear of contaminating the higher breed of humanity living in civilised society. The largest and most famous such penal colony was in Australia. The penal settlement in the Andamans became active after the Anglo-Burmese war of 1852 and the suppression of the revolt of 1857 in India. Several hundred Burmese prisoners of war and mutineers from northern India were brought to the islands and settled in fenced villages.

The Andaman Islands were inhabited at this time by several thousand indigenous peoples belonging to a dozen tribes. They were hunters and gatherers who had lived in isolation and resented the intrusion of foreigners who were cutting down their forests and desecrating their sacred spaces. Between 1859 and 1863, bands consisting of several hundred men of the Jarawa tribe, armed with axes, knives, and bows and arrows, carried out successive attacks on convict villages, killing a few convicts and capturing several others. In most cases, the unarmed convicts were unable to resist and, in trying to escape, usually jumped into the sea. Interestingly, the Andamanese attackers were particularly hostile towards the gangmen who led the convicts in clearing forests and were apparently quite friendly towards ordinary convicts who were in chains. On a few occasions, British naval guards opened fire on the attackers. In one incident, a British doctor of Port Blair was attacked by a group of aborigines, while in another, a British sailor who apparently molested an Andamanese woman was killed.

Imagine the situation. Indians who had rebelled against the British had been captured and sent off to a distant island where they were supposed to clear forests and settle down in a penal colony. The indigenous peoples of those islands resisted this encroachment on their lands; the Indian convicts bore the brunt of their attacks. The rebels of 1857 are celebrated in your national history as heroes and martyrs. Have you ever heard of the indigenous people of the Andamans being described as Indians who also fought against British rule? You think of the Andaman Islands as an inseparable part of India. But do you think of the Andamanese people as Indians too? Then why are they missing from the history of resistance to British rule?

Actually, the subsequent story of the encounter of the Andamanese people with modern civilisation is even more shocking. Once the initial hostilities subsided, British officials tried to initiate a more friendly approach towards the indigenous people of the islands. What resulted was the spread of two deadly diseases – syphilis and measles – brought into the islands by settlers and sailors. In 1858, the Andamanese population was estimated at around five thousand, divided into twelve tribes. By 1921, only five hundred or so, belonging to the Onge and Jarawa tribes, survived. In 1951, there were only 150 Onge and 50 Jarawa left; all the other tribes had become extinct. This is a story of colonisation you thought could only come from the Americas, where European conquerors wiped out native populations. Yet it happened on what you claim is Indian territory. In today's language, you should call it a genocide of indigenous people.

Let me now propose a little mind game. Suppose there is today, somewhere in the Andaman Islands, a young Onge woman who has, through extraordinarily fortunate circumstances and hard work, gone to school and college. She has found out all there is to know about the history of her people. Now, suppose you are that young woman. What would you think of the Indian nation and your place in it? As an Onge woman, would you still be able to shout slogans about the greatness of Indian civilisation? That is the test you must pass before you can make tall claims about the proud identity of the Indian people.

By the early-twentieth century, there were some 15,000 convicts in the Andaman Islands, mostly Hindus and Muslims from northern India, and about 2000 Burmese. Apart from the first lot of war prisoners and rebels, most of the others had been convicted of violent crimes such as murder and armed robbery. After an initial period of hard labour, these men were allowed to send for their wives and settle down in a penal village with a plot of land which they could cultivate. The few women convicts were also allowed to find male partners. In this way, there emerged a culturally hybrid population of ex-convicts and their children.

Nothing much happened in the Andamans in the nineteenth century to bring the islands into public attention in India, except for the murder of Lord Mayo, the viceroy, in 1872. He was on a visit to Port Blair when he was stabbed to death by Sher Ali Afridi, a convict. This is the only successful assassination of a viceroy in the history of British India. But the killing was not politically inspired. I know some writers have tried to explain this as an act of jihad, inspired by Wahabi ideology. Don't believe that story. Sher Ali was a god-fearing man with a fiery temper. He had killed a cousin in a family feud and confessed to his crime. When he was captured after he had stabbed the viceroy, he said he wanted to take revenge on the superintendent of police and the viceroy who, he thought, were responsible for the harsh sentence he had been given. He said that God had instructed him to kill the *lat sahib*.

From the beginning of the twentieth century, however, the Andamans became entangled with the political history of Indian nationalism. A new jail had just been built at Port Blair, with a central tower and seven three-storeyed wings, each with rows of cells. There were nearly 700 cells in all. This was also the time when a new wave of armed resistance developed against British rule. Now it was a new generation of middle-class Indians from Bengal, Punjab, and Maharashtra who took the lead.

The Cellular Jail has become famous, or infamous, in Indian history because that is where hundreds of nationalist revolutionaries were imprisoned from the early years of the twentieth century. Political prisoners were sent to the Andamans in two spells, corresponding to two waves of armed resistance to British rule – the first between 1910 and 1920 and the second in the 1930s. A large section of the 133 prisoners in the first group were from Punjab and included prominent leaders of the Ghadar movement, such as Prithvi Singh Azad, Bhai Parmanand, Sohan Singh Bhakna, and Kartar Singh. The prisoners from Bengal in the first group included prominent revolutionaries such as Barin Ghosh, Upen Banerjee, Hem Kanungo, Indubhusan Roy, Sachin Sanyal, and Pulin Das. Also among them were two brothers from Maharashtra – Vinayak Damodar and Ganesh Damodar Savarkar. The 366 political prisoners sent to the Cellular Jail in the 1930s were principally from Bengal and included revolutionaries such as Trailokya Chakravarty, Gopimohan Saha, Ganesh Ghosh, Satish Pakrashi, Batukeswar Dutt, Harekrishna Konar, Niranjan Sen, Narayan Roy, Manoranjan Guha Thakurta, Mohit Moitra, Loknath Bal, Ananta Singh, Subodh Roy, and Khoka Roy. Many of the Bengal revolutionaries became communists during their time in the Cellular Jail.

There is every reason for Indians to feel a strong emotional attachment to this place where some of their bravest patriots were confined and subjected to harsh, often brutal, punishment. Separated from the mainland by hundreds of miles of water, denied contact with family or friends, the morale of the prisoners was put to the severest test. It is remarkable how many of them still managed to keep up their political resolve and wait for the day when they might be released and returned to the mainland. I know there are many stories of how some famous revolutionaries supposedly renounced their politics of resistance and appealed to the British to release them. Don't be too quick to make negative judgments. These were men of sharp intelligence and great tactical cunning. They had political projects which looked far into the future. Later on, I will have more to say on this matter.

But the fact remains that the Andamans became a part of Indian nationalism only because the British had conquered the islands and kept political prisoners there; there is no other historical or cultural connection. The islands were occupied by the Japanese during the Second World War, after the British had been thrown out of Malaya and Burma. It was the only piece of British Indian territory actually occupied by the Japanese. The Indian National Army led by Subhas Chandra Bose was given formal charge of the islands. Bose himself visited Port Blair, raised the national flag there and renamed the Andaman Islands as Shaheed Dweep and the Nicobar Islands as Swaraj Dweep. But, of course, the islands went back into British hands following the defeat and surrender of Japan.

After independence, two wings of the Cellular Jail were demolished and a part of it has been turned into a hospital. It has also become a memorial to the revolutionaries who were imprisoned there. As is to be expected, there is politics over which names are given prominence. Given the political preferences of the party in power in New Delhi recently, V.D. Savarkar has emerged as the most celebrated patriot connected to the Cellular Jail. I will have more to say about Savarkar later. Without diminishing in any way his patriotism and bravery, let me say that the two regions of India where historical memory is most intimately tied to the prison in the Andamans are Punjab and Bengal. They had by far the largest number of political prisoners there. Recently, Prime Minister Narendra Modi visited Port Blair and, as if emulating Subhas Bose, gave new names to three of the islands: Ross Island is now to be called Netaji Subhas Chandra Bose Dweep, Neil Island is now Shaheed Dweep, and

Havelock Island will be Swaraj Dweep. The islands, it seems, have still not been fully nationalised: it is work in progress.

The Nicobar Islands, located to the south of the Andamans, are inhabited by some 30,000 indigenous people who are ethnically similar to the people of Southeast Asia and speak languages belonging to the Austroasiatic group, similar to Khmer, Vietnamese, and Mundari. These islands were in the possession of the Danish East India Company from 1756, but several attempts to establish a settlement there failed, mainly because of the ravages of malaria. The British purchased the islands from the Danes in 1868 and made them a part of their Indian empire. The colonial presence on the Nicobar Islands was never very deep, except for the activities of a few Christian missionaries who converted most Nicobarese people to Christianity. In recent times, unlike the Andamans which have been settled by farmers from Bengal and labourers and traders from different parts of India, and developed as a tourist destination, the Nicobar Islands remain relatively isolated, owing to the setting up of a major base of the Indian Navy.

## French and Portuguese Territories

So far we have only talked about British territories that were transferred to India at the time of independence. But there were also territories in India that were held by two other European imperial powers for several years beyond 1947. The French were in occupation of Pondicherry, Mahé, Yanam, Karaikal, and Chandernagore. The Portuguese held Goa, Daman, and Diu. The reason why the British, even after they had established complete dominance over the Indian subcontinent, allowed these territories to remain with France and Portugal had to do with diplomatic alliances in Europe. The French Indian territories were twice seized by the British during their wars with France but were returned after peace was established. Portugal was a subordinate ally of Britain which promised to defend the former's colonial possessions everywhere in the world. Britain was not going to put pressure on Portugal to give up Goa.

The transfer of power negotiations between British officials and Indian political leaders did not include any reference to the French or Portuguese territories. For a few years after independence, the French enclaves continued to exist surrounded by Indian territories. Negotiations with France went smoothly. In 1954, the French possessions were handed over to India. Chandernagore is now the town of Chandannagar in the Hugli district of West Bengal. Pondicherry is now the Union Territory of Puducherry but its colonial antecedents are still retained in its peculiar territorial composition. Puducherry consists of four districts located in different parts of southern India: Puducherry and Karaikal districts are each surrounded by territories of Tamil Nadu, Yanam is located within the East Godavari district of Andhra Pradesh, and Mahé is on the coast of Kerala. You must admit that no matter what they declaim in public, Indians are strongly attached to their colonial histories – not just in connection with Britain but also France.

The story of the Portuguese possessions is quite different. Portugal had held colonial territories in India since the early sixteenth century, much before the British. After India became independent in 1947, Portugal, ruled by the dictator Antonio Salazar, claimed that its overseas territories were not colonies but integral parts of the country. Hence, it not only refused to negotiate with India but declared its opposition to all attempts at decolonisation of Portuguese territories in Africa and Asia. But popular opposition to Portuguese rule in Goa had grown from the 1920s. Led by Tristao de Braganza Cunha, an engineer educated in Pondicherry and Paris, the Goa Congress Committee carried out propaganda against Portuguese colonial rule and developed close ties with the freedom movement in India. Persecuted by the Portuguese authorities, T.B. Cunha shifted to

Bombay to continue his anti-colonial work from there. In June 1946, when talks were under way for the transfer of power in India, Congress Socialist leaders such as Ram Manohar Lohia, along with Cunha and Julião Menezes, launched a satyagraha movement in Goa. There was a crackdown and Cunha was arrested and sent to prison in Portugal for eight years. He returned to Bombay after his release in 1954 and died in 1958. Have you and your friends who are so proud of your national heroes ever heard of T.B. Cunha?

There were also groups like the Azad Gomantak Dal whose methods were not confined to peaceful protests. They secured arms from India, with the assistance of Indian authorities, and carried out a subversive guerrilla campaign in Portuguese Goa, attacking police stations, military installations, and banks. The Portuguese came down hard on the revolutionaries. Narayan Naik and Dattatreya Deshpande spent many years in prison in Portugal and Angola, while Vishwanath Lawande and Prabhakar Sinari escaped from prison and returned to India to raise a large force and carry out raids from across the border. Have you seen these names in your pantheon of national revolutionaries?

Indian diplomatic efforts to force Portugal to give up Goa were ineffective because, with the hardening of the Cold War, the United States and Britain were not well disposed towards non-aligned countries like India which, they thought, were for all practical purposes leaning towards the Soviet side. Debates in the United Nations Security Council became sharply polarised, with the Soviet Union supporting anti-colonial causes in Asia and Africa. Prominent among these were the armed liberation movements in the Portuguese colonies of Angola and Mozambique.

In July 1954, members of the Azad Gomantak Dal, led by Vishwanath Lawande, along with their allied groups in Gujarat, attacked police stations in Dadra and Nagar Haveli, two enclaves that were part of the Portuguese district of Daman. The Indian government fully supported this action by blockading the enclaves and preventing the Portuguese authorities from sending reinforcements. A few days later, the Portuguese administrator and his police forces surrendered. Dadra and Nagar Haveli were liberated from colonial rule, although they would be legally integrated into India only after 1961.

The Western powers did not react kindly to the forcible seizure of Dadra and Nagar Haveli and strongly criticised the role of the Indian government. With the Salazar regime adamant in its refusal to negotiate, the Indian government decided in 1961 to use force. In December of that year, Indian troops moved into Goa as well as Daman and Diu. There was a parallel assault from the sea by the Indian Navy. The Portuguese garrisons and the single naval vessel were utterly inadequate to resist the onslaught and, despite fiery messages from Salazar to fight to the last man, gave up their arms. Goa was annexed in less than twenty-four hours, practically without bloodshed.

The military action by India led to much controversy in diplomatic circles. A motion against India did not pass in the United Nations only because of the Soviet veto. Although countries like Nasser's Egypt (then the United Arab Republic) fully supported India and refused the use of the Suez Canal to Portugal to ship military reinforcements to Goa, the United States and Britain were very critical of the Indian action. They were particularly incensed by what they alleged was Indian hypocrisy: while India had always lectured the rest of world on non-violence and peaceful methods for resolving conflicts, here it was using military force to annex territory. To some extent, the fault did lie with the Indian political leaders of the time. They could not effectively make the case that Goa was not a dispute between two sovereign nations that had to be resolved through international law and diplomacy but rather a matter of the right to self-determination of the people of Goa and liberation from colonial rule. True, Nehru did accuse the

Salazar government of looking at the world through sixteenth-century concepts of conquest and colonisation, but still allowed India's case to become entangled in diplomatic niceties, mainly because of the moralising tone it had adopted. Its case would have been strengthened if a plebiscite had been held in Goa after the Portuguese colonial regime was overthrown. But India had tied itself in legal knots, on the one hand, by not carrying out the UN-mandated plebiscite in Kashmir and, on the other, relying on British imperial maps and treaties for its claims on the Chinese border. While it put up a weak defence in international courts, it proceeded slowly in the matter of integrating Goa, Daman, and Diu with the Indian constitutional system. They became a Union Territory in 1962 but only after 1974, when the authoritarian regime in Portugal collapsed and democracy was established there, was there a proper treaty normalising the inclusion of the Portuguese territories into the Indian republic. Only then did the people of Goa finally begin to fully participate in the democratic process in India.

I hope you will now admit that the boundaries of the Indian nation-state are neither natural gifts from the gods nor borders that Indians have themselves drawn. They are, for the most part, borders created by the British rulers of this country who were pursuing their own interests as a colonial power. The only significant political acts of the Indian state that changed the country's borders were the annexations of Goa and Sikkim. Whatever legal or diplomatic controversies there might be over those actions, subsequent events prove that the people of those regions were willing to join the political arena of India's federal democracy.

This only reminds us that territories are not like immovable property; they come with people who cannot be evicted by the force of law. The legitimacy of territorial boundaries in today's democratic age ultimately depends not on geography or law or military strength but on the will of the people. Remember that

India stretches not only from Kashmir to Kanyakumari but also from Lakshadweep to the Andaman Islands and from Goa to Nagaland. All of the places included within those borders are legitimately part of India not because there are treaties and laws but only if the people in all those places willingly agree to live together within the same constitutional system. That is the only true test of national belonging.

3

## Princes Have No Place in a Republic

THE INDIAN STATE (*rājya*) today does not consist only of territories that were once under the colonial rule of Britain, France, and Portugal. In 1947, nearly 40 per cent of the Indian subcontinent consisted of about 550 so-called native states ruled by princes who, by virtue of treaties with the British paramount power, had internal sovereignty to run the administration but not the right to establish diplomatic relations with foreign powers.[1] The British appointed a Resident in each state to advise and keep a watch over the princely administration and reserved the power to take it over if there was misgovernment or problems with succession. The history of how these states became parts of India and Pakistan after 1947 is largely forgotten. Probably all you have been told is that Sardar Patel, the iron man, who was Home Minister in Nehru's cabinet, used his masterly political skills to get all the princes to join India. Perhaps you also believe that if only he had been allowed a free hand, the Kashmir problem would not have arisen at all. Nothing can be further from the truth.

---

[1] There were 565 princely states in 1947.

## The Princely States on the Eve of Independence

As negotiations proceeded in 1946 between the British authorities, the Congress, and the Muslim League over the transfer of power, the princes were very much in the picture. They assembled in the Chamber of Princes, one of the houses of the central legislature where the major states (those entitled to gun salutes) had permanent seats and the others sent members from among themselves. Even though they were invited to join the newly elected Constituent Assembly, most princes were reluctant to do so. They were very concerned about their status after the British left and most wanted assurances that they would not come under the domination of a popularly elected Congress government. As a result, one of their persistent demands was that paramountcy should not pass to any successor government, whether India or Pakistan. Rather, with the end of British rule, paramountcy should lapse and the princely states regain full freedom to enter into whatever new treaty relations they wished. British negotiators accepted this argument. Congress leaders too realised that lapse of paramountcy would be an advantage because the new government would not have to deal with the varied and enormously complicated treaty obligations with the princely states; they could begin on a clean slate. But not everyone had the same idea of what should follow from the end of paramountcy.

Several of the larger states were inclined to first assert their independence before entering into negotiations with the new government. They were emboldened by the words of Wavell, the departing viceroy, in January 1947 that nothing would be imposed on the princes without their consent. In June 1947, Travancore and Hyderabad announced their decisions to form independent sovereign states and establish diplomatic relations with other countries. The hundreds of smaller principalities could not, of course, do the same because they did not have the resources to function as viable independent states. Nawab Hamidullah Khan of Bhopal, the chancellor of the Chamber of Princes, argued that all the princely states should join to form a third state alongside India and Pakistan. The All India Congress Committee (AICC) strongly disagreed with the theory that the lapse of paramountcy meant that the princes were no longer under any obligation to the Government of India. Independence of the princely states, the AICC said, could not be an option. Nehru went a step further and announced that any princely state which did not enter the Constituent Assembly would be declared a hostile state and treated accordingly. Jinnah, on the other hand, stood for the right of princes to declare independence. Even then, by early July 1947, with only six weeks to go for the transfer of power, very few princes had made up their minds.

Besides the top leaders, princes, and officials involved in these negotiations, there was another force at play: the people who lived in the princely states. Several states had organised movements, usually called Praja Mandal, which demanded representative government; some were in favour of integration with India. The strength of these movements varied from state to state. The States People movement, supported by the Congress, was quite strong in the Gujarat states as well as in some of the Orissa states. In Travancore and Cochin, the movement was led by local Congress leaders who wanted a merger of the two states into a United Kerala. In the Telangana region of Hyderabad, the movement was taken over by a communist leadership which launched a guerrilla armed struggle against the feudal landlords of the nizam's state. In Jammu and Kashmir, the people's movement under the leadership of Sheikh Abdullah's National Conference also organised peasants against landlords and demanded that the maharaja grant representative government. The princes too had varied attitudes towards the idea of giving their subjects a role in government. Some states such as

Mysore, Cochin, and Travancore had representative assemblies; other rulers, however, were determined to resist any attempt to allow popular representatives to curtail their autocratic powers.

Constantly advised by Mountbatten, the Congress leaders chose to move cautiously. Towards the end of July 1947, the viceroy announced in the Chamber of Princes that after the accession of a princely state to one of the two dominions, the dominion legislature would have the power to make laws on only three subjects in relation to the state – defence, external affairs, and communications including railways, shipping, and airlines. In all other matters, the state would continue to govern itself, unless it voluntarily chose to enter into additional agreements with the dominion government. In the interests of security, good government, and the welfare of their subjects, he strongly advised the princes to join one of the two dominions. By all accounts, this was a very effective speech by Mountbatten, with Patel by his side. It assured many, if not most, of the princes that the departing British power would ensure that the new Indian government give them a legitimate and secure place within the new constitutional order. Thus began the process by which the princes signed instruments of accession stating the three subjects on which they ceded their powers to the Government of India.

I must point out something important about the position taken by the Congress government under Nehru and Patel on the question of the princely states. By taking the cautious bureaucratic approach of negotiating the terms of accession with each prince, the government chose not to assert the political claim that hereditary princes could have no place in a republican nation-state and that the future of the princely states should be determined by their people and not their rulers. The left wing of the Congress, including Nehru, Subhas Bose, and the socialists had long demanded this, but the right wing, including Patel and Rajendra Prasad, with the blessing of Gandhi, believed that the princes should be won over to the national cause. As I will show you, even in cases where the States People movement was strong, Patel preferred to use it as a bargaining chip rather than a political demand. Even though he knew very well that most princes had been against the Congress-led national movement and some actively persecuted nationalist campaigners within their territories, he did not want to encourage a general popular mobilisation against the princes. The result of this conservative approach was that instead of involving the people of the princely states in a political process of coming together with the people of the rest of the country, the Indian government engaged in secret negotiations with the princes, often resorting to threats, false promises, betrayals, and, in a few cases, military force, to achieve the task.

Although Vallabhbhai Patel laid down the overall objectives and policy of the government in carrying out these negotiations, he did not get involved in the details. That job was performed by a bureaucrat by the name of V.P. Menon. Menon was not a member of the Indian Civil Service. In fact, he began his career in the early 1920s as a typist and clerk in the newly established Department of Constitutional Reforms in the Government of India and acquired such specialised expertise in constitutional matters that he not only took charge of that department but became a close adviser to three viceroys – Linlithgow, Wavell, and Mountbatten. After the interim government took office in 1946, he came close to Patel who created a new States Ministry and put Menon in charge.[2] Patel relied entirely on Menon to make sure that the princes joined the Indian dominion without too much fuss. Menon was the real architect of the bureaucratic achievement called the integration of the Indian princely states. By his own admission, he acted as Patel's hatchet man.

[2] V.P. Menon was Secretary, Ministry of States, in the Government of India during 1947–50. Vallabhbhai Patel was the Minister of States until his death in December 1950.

## Unions of States

Even though the princes had been assured that the Indian government would not interfere except in matters of defence, foreign affairs, and communications, Patel and Menon were clear that the object should be to ultimately integrate the princely states with the main body of the Indian state. It was the unity of the Indian state with which they were most concerned, not the political involvement of the people. The main instrument that Menon used was to pool together neighbouring states into a regional union with a single administrative structure. He tried to persuade the princes that if they were left to themselves, they would find it hard to cope with the demands that would come from their subjects. Thus, instead of threatening their rule, joining the Indian state and accepting the new constitution would actually make their position more secure. This was, of course, a patently false promise, not meant to be kept. But many of these states were at this time witnessing the rise of the Praja Mandal which demanded a share in government. Menon astutely used this as an argument in favour of accession. When the ruler of Bhavnagar, unnerved by the popular agitation, agreed to accept a form of elected government, Menon arranged for Patel to inaugurate the event, sending the message to the other rulers of Kathiawar that Menon had the full backing of the Indian government. In some states in Orissa, Adivasi people, taking the side of the local ruler, rose up against caste-Hindu farmers and the proposed construction of the Hirakud dam. The disturbances got so bad that Menon threatened to take over the administration, no matter what the rulers wanted. When C.P. Ramaswami Aiyar, the diwan of Travancore, insisted on remaining independent, Menon pointed out "the communist menace" that was threatening to spread across Kerala and even managed to get Mountbatten to reiterate the point. Did the state have enough administrative and military resources to fight a communist uprising?

Maharaja Hanwant Singh of Jodhpur tried to bargain for concessions by negotiating with both dominions. Apparently, Jinnah gave him a blank sheet of paper with Jinnah's signature as well as a fountain pen and asked the maharaja to write down whatever concessions he wanted. When Menon said these were impossible concessions, Hanwant Singh declared he would join Pakistan. Menon took the maharaja to meet Mountbatten who explained to him that, since he was a Hindu, as were most of his subjects, for him to join Pakistan would be a violation of the spirit of the partition. When Mountbatten left the room, Hanwant Singh pulled out a revolver, pointed it at Menon, and shouted that he was not going to sign anything dictated by a bureaucrat. Menon replied that killing him would not get the maharaja better terms. In the end, some of Hanwant Singh's demands were conceded and Jodhpur acceded to the Indian dominion.

To compensate for what would essentially be a surrender of sovereignty, the princes were offered generous annual pensions, called privy purses. These were negotiated separately in each case. For some reason, the Gujarat states, of which there were more than 300, some no larger than a few villages, got much bigger purses than states in other parts of the country. I don't know if this had something to do with the fact that Gandhi's father had been an official in a Kathiawar state or that Patel was a Gujarati. In any case, when several states were brought together into a union, its constitutional head was not a governor as in the provinces but a Rajpramukh, usually the ruler of the largest state in the union.[3] There were lots of princely egos that had to be placated. The Maharaja of Udaipur insisted that his position among the Rajput princes was such that a mere

---

[3] It should be remembered that before the promulgation of the Indian constitution in 1950, the units inherited from British India were called provinces (*pradesh*) while the former princely states were called states (*rajya*). The manuscript here follows this nomenclature. The Constitution of India of 1950 divided the two categories into Part A and Part B states.

title of Rajpramukh would not be appropriate; as a result, he was given the unique position of Maharajpramukh of the Rajasthan Union. The Maharaja of Travancore wanted to be called Perumal, the traditional title of a Kerala chief, but had to be satisfied with being Rajpramukh. In Mysore, the former ruler was allowed to use the title Maharaja instead of Rajpramukh.

There was a historic rivalry between Indore and Gwalior, the two major Maratha states which were once, before the British conquest, rulers of much of northern and western India, including all the Rajput states of Rajasthan. Breaking the promise that large and viable princely states would not be taken over, Menon, with the support of Patel, put pressure on Yeshwant Rao Holkar and Jivaji Rao Shinde (styled Scindia in British India) to merge into the Union of Madhya Bharat.[4] Holkar wanted to revive the idea of a third state of Princely India and complained that the Indian government was out to abolish the Maratha states while leaving the Rajput states alone. He suggested that the question of the merger of Indore with Gwalior should be put to a plebiscite of their people. Menon was aware of the deep feelings of rivalry between the subjects of the two rulers and did not want to test the popular will. Instead, he pointed to the spectre of a democratic revolution threatening all the princes. If Holkar and Shinde decided to continue on their own, the agitations for democratic government would definitely increase and the rulers might lose everything. It would be far better for them to accept their privy purses and an assured place as constitutional heads of the union. To balance their claims to superior status, it was decided that the new government of Madhya Bharat would have its summer capital in Indore and winter capital in Gwalior, even though there was no difference in the climate of the two places.

---

[4] The manuscript has Shinde with Scindia in parentheses.

The Nawab of Bhopal had taken the lead in arguing for a separate independent state of Princely India which, of course, did not materialise. Following independence, the Praja Mandal movement in Bhopal began to demand a popular government. Patel wanted Bhopal to merge with the Madhya Bharat Union while the local Congress leaders suggested a plebiscite. Menon reassured them that the future of the people of Bhopal was secure in the hands of Nehru and Patel and a plebiscite was unnecessary. In the end, in June 1949, Bhopal became a Chief Commissioner's province with an elected legislature and a ministry. Nawab Hamidullah Khan, who was an ambitious and capable figure in the Muslim League, expected to become Governor General of Pakistan after Jinnah's death but was blocked by Liaquat Ali Khan. Bitterly disappointed by the turn of events, he abdicated in favour of his daughter and retired from public life.

The integration of princely states also threw up new questions about the role of religion in the new republic. When the smaller states of East Punjab agreed to merge into a union, Patiala resisted, only to be threatened with the prospect of isolation. After the Patiala and East Punjab States Union (PEPSU) was formed, the Akali Dal insisted that the Union should have a Sikh premier. This was an early indication of a demand that would reach its peak in the 1960s in the movement for the separation of Punjab and Haryana. In Alwar and Bharatpur, the rulers and some top officials were alleged to have ties with Hindu communal organisations and encouraged violence against Muslims at the time of partition. The Maharaja of Alwar was even suspected of being involved in the assassination of Gandhi, although nothing was finally proved. Patel decided that, in the interest of maintaining communal peace, the administration of Alwar and Bharatpur should be taken over by the Indian government. In the case of Travancore-Cochin, the union came with the transfer of the Devaswom management of numerous Hindu temples, including their huge lands, funds, and treasure, from the two rulers to the new government. This opened up a new set of issues for the management of religious institutions by a secular republic. In the north-east of India, there were twenty-five Khasi hill states, whose people were mostly Christian, under elected chiefs called Siems who were internally self-governing but functioned under the governor of Assam. They could not be treated in the same way as the princely states. Ultimately, the internal autonomy of these tribal peoples of north-east India was sought to be secured through Autonomous Hill Councils listed in the sixth schedule of the Indian constitution.

We see, therefore, that although paramountcy was supposed to have ended with the withdrawal of British rule, the States Ministry of the Indian government under Patel did not shrink from using its administrative powers to bring the princes into line. An interesting example was the case of Maharaja Pratap Singh Gaekwad of Baroda who was alleged to have committed serious financial improprieties in his handling of public funds and was involved in a scandalous second marriage. After attempts failed to bring him to account, the Government of India decided in April 1951 to no longer recognise Pratap Singh as the ruler of Baroda and instead appointed his eldest son Fatehsingh to the position. In a sense, paramountcy never ended in India; it was still being ruled like an empire.

## States in the New Constitutional Order

As a result of the process of integration, alongside the provinces inherited from before independence, India came to be constituted by several unions of states such as Saurashtra, Madhya Bharat, Patiala and East Punjab, Travancore-Cochin, and Rajasthan. In some cases, such as the Eastern States Union of the Orissa states, the Chhattisgarh Union, and the Vindhya Pradesh Union, the unions were dissolved after some time on grounds of administrative convenience and the territories merged with Orissa and the Central Provinces. In the case of small states that did not share contiguous territories, the rulers were persuaded to accept a privy purse and merge their states with the neighbouring province.

You should remember that the accession, especially of the larger states, to India could not be achieved unilaterally; it required a political agreement. The initial promise to the princes was that, after accession, the Indian government would make laws applicable to the states only on three subjects – defence, foreign affairs, and communications. Legal intervention on any other subject would require the agreement of the state. Accordingly, each of the large states and each union of states was allowed to have its own constituent assembly, consisting of nominated as well as elected representatives, to define the exact relation of the state with the central government. Each union was governed by a ministry headed by a premier, responsible to a representative legislature. Of all the states, only Saurashtra, Jammu and Kashmir, Mysore, and Travancore-Cochin managed to set up constituent assemblies. The Government of India asked B.N. Rau, a senior civil servant and constitutional expert, to draft a model constitution for the states, but the draft was not acceptable to all of them. By the middle of 1949, after most of the states had been merged with neighbouring provinces and several unions seemed incapable of coming up with effective constituent assemblies, the Indian government came round to the view that a separate constitution for each state would not be desirable. The better option would be to incorporate whatever special provisions were necessary for the states in the body of the Indian constitution itself and have the states sign new instruments of accession recording their acceptance of the constitution.

This was the origin of Articles 370 and 371 of the constitution which allowed for temporary special provisions for what were then called the Part B states. Thus, a special provision was made in Article 370 on relations between Jammu and Kashmir and the Indian government until the state's constituent assembly finished its work, while Article 371 provided for parts of the constitution not to be applied to a Part B state by presidential order, this becoming necessary since Mysore and Travancore-Cochin were still negotiating the exact terms of acceptance of the constitution. The Saurashtra constituent assembly had by then resolved to accept the Indian constitution in full and had disbanded itself. Patel was completely clear that, even though uniformity was desirable, special conditions had to be accepted for some of the larger states because their integration could not be achieved only by legal or administrative force; it needed a political pact. I am reminding you of this history to point out that you are wrong when you believe that Jammu and Kashmir came to have its own constituent assembly and administrative autonomy because of Nehru's weakness or the Congress Party's appeasement of Muslims. Special provisions were not unique to Kashmir: those were the terms under which several other princely states agreed to accede to India and accept the Indian constitution. After the 1952 general elections, all of the Part A and B states of India came to have Congress governments, except Jammu and Kashmir where the National Conference was in power. Therefore, it became politically quite easy to get all the other states, including Mysore and Travancore-Cochin, to accept the Indian constitution in full. After 1952, therefore, while Article 370 continued to be in force in relation to Kashmir, Article 371 became merely an enabling article by which, in later years, several other states such as Nagaland, Mizoram, Manipur, Assam, Maharashtra, Gujarat, Andhra Pradesh, Sikkim, and Goa would be given special powers on various subjects. Most of these special provisions were the result of agreements reached at the end of prolonged political agitation. If you look at the various sections of Article 371 today, you will not realise that the reason it was originally framed was to give Mysore and Travancore-Cochin a special status until they could come to an agreement on their acceptance of the constitution. That is no reason for you to be misled by the false history you are taught.

Let me also tell you about the princely states that joined Pakistan, of which there were only a handful. The Nawab of the Punjab state of Bahawalpur joined Pakistan soon after independence. The Balochi states of Kalat, Makran, Las Bela, and Kharan were joined into a union within Pakistan. In 1955, Bahawalpur and the Balochi states were merged with the neighbouring provinces of Punjab and Balochistan. A few tribal states like Chitral and Swat in the north-west acceded to Pakistan in 1947 and remained autonomous until 1969. Similarly, the tribal state of Hunza in northern Kashmir was an autonomous region within Pakistan until 1974.

## A Little State Called Junagadh

Among the Kathiawar states was a small princely territory called Junagadh ruled by an eccentric nawab who cared more for his hundreds of dogs than his subjects. On 15 August 1947, Nawab Mahabat Khan exercised his option and announced his decision to join Pakistan. This caused a commotion among the people of Junagadh and put the Indian government in a fix. In strictly legal terms, the Junagadh ruler was entirely within his rights to accede to Pakistan. But the political problem was that most of Junagadh's population was Hindu. They did not want to live in Pakistan. Besides, if the accession went through, Junagadh would become a little pocket of Pakistani territory surrounded by hundreds of Kathiawar states, all of which were about to join India. The Government of India protested, and even Mountbatten tried to exert his influence to stop Pakistan from accepting the accession. More importantly, political organisations in Junagadh began to mobilise demonstrations demanding that the nawab change his decision, join India and carry out democratic reforms.

The diwan of the state, Shah Nawaz Bhutto, a senior politician of Bombay and Sind (and father of Zulfikar Ali Bhutto who would later become prime minister of Pakistan), stuck to the legal position that the ruler, in exercising his option to join Pakistan, was not obliged to consult his subjects. There was an angry exchange of letters between the Indian and Pakistani governments, and even some talk of referring the matter to the United Nations. Nehru and Patel did not think that was a good idea. But they did everything to encourage the Praja Mandal movement in the state to step up its agitation. On 25 September, the Kathiawar Congress leaders announced that the Junagadh nawab had lost the allegiance of his subjects and a provisional popular government had been formed with Samaldas Gandhi as its head. This government set itself up in Rajkot, outside Junagadh territory.

With agitations mounting, the situation in Junagadh deteriorated. Government officials in two enclaves administered by Junagadh clashed with the agitators. On 21 October, Indian troops moved in to take over these enclaves and surround Junagadh. The nawab realised that his time was up. He packed his favourite dogs and some of his family into a plane and left for Karachi, leaving many of his wives and children behind. The agitators ran amok, indulging in loot and arson. Unable to tackle the situation, Shah Nawaz Bhutto opened negotiations, offering to hand over the administration not to the provisional government but directly to the Indian authorities. Liaquat Ali Khan, prime minister of Pakistan, complained bitterly that India had used military force to drive away the nawab but, realising that the Indian government was in control of the situation on the ground, proposed that the future of Junagadh be decided by a plebiscite conducted jointly by India and Pakistan. Patel, who was deeply suspicious of popular initiatives that were not tightly controlled by an organised leadership, was against a plebiscite.

The facts that the nawab had abdicated and that the majority Hindu population was clearly in favour of joining India were, for him, sufficient. As soon as the new administration had taken charge, Patel visited Junagadh where he was given a massive reception. He went to the coastal village of Prabhas Patan where the historic Somnath temple, infamously destroyed a thousand years ago by Mahmud Ghaznavi, was located and promised that the Indian government would rebuild the temple.

In the end, it was decided that a popular referendum would put a stamp of legitimacy on a legally dubious annexation. In February 1948, a plebiscite was held in Junagadh by the Indian authorities. Not surprisingly, more than 99 per cent voted in favour of accession to India.

## Hyderabad

If Junagadh was a tiny kingdom whose ruler could be tackled without much difficulty, Hyderabad was not. It was the most populous and, in many ways, the most important princely state with territories spread over as many as four of the present states of India – Telangana, Andhra Pradesh, Karnataka, and Maharashtra; 85 per cent of its population was Hindu, but the ruling elite, concentrated in Hyderabad city, was predominantly Muslim and most positions in the bureaucracy, police, and army were occupied by them. Mir Osman Ali, the nizam, had ruled for more than thirty-five years, imagining himself to be a monarch of a stature equal to those of the major kingdoms of the world. I must also mention that he was a great patron of education and culture. He established Osmania University as a leading centre of learning in southern India and presided over a distinct and sophisticated Hyderabadi culture that was shared by both Muslim and Hindu upper classes.

But in 1947, he was put in a difficult situation. The ruling circle in Hyderabad, threatened by Congress agitators in the city and a communist guerrilla movement in the Telangana countryside, was firmly against coming under the domination of a Congress-led Indian government. Fanned by the propaganda of a Muslim political organisation, the Majlis-e-Ittehad-e-Muslimeen, and supported by a militia called the Razakars led by Kasem Razvi, a fanatical agitator from the small town of Latur, the pressure was mounting on the nizam to join Pakistan. Jinnah too sent emissaries to Hyderabad, promising support. But the nizam knew that going with Pakistan would provoke a serious reaction among the Hindu population of his state. Besides, Hyderabad would then become a part of Pakistan separated by the sea and hundreds of miles of Indian territory and could not depend on military help from Pakistan. He, therefore, insisted that he be allowed to form a sovereign independent dominion with membership of the British Commonwealth.

Until early 1947, British authorities appeared to support the view that with the lapse of paramountcy, the princely states would regain full sovereignty and the freedom to enter into new relations with other states. But as soon as Mountbatten arrived on the scene and declared his partition plan in June 1947, he made it clear that independence of the princely states was not an option the British government would recognize. Even as he accepted that the nizam had the full right to accede to either Pakistan or India, he strongly advised the latter option for the sake of geographical viability and domestic peace.

But Nizam Osman Ali was unwilling to take a decision in a hurry. He began a protracted and thoroughly deceitful series of talks with both India and Pakistan, seeking to put off for as long as possible the inevitable surrender of his sovereignty. He was aided and abetted in this disastrous effort by several advisers. Let me quickly take you through some of the terms of these negotiations to show you what kind of special status Mountbatten and Patel were prepared to give to Hyderabad to secure its accession. If the nizam had been a little more realistic and not squandered all his chances by holding out for too long,

Hyderabad would have had far more autonomy than Kashmir ever did.

The story begins with the nizam's decision to get rid of the services of the able civil servant Mirza Ismail as his prime minister in May 1947. Ismail had a realistic view of the political future confronting the princely states and knew that popular government could not be resisted for long. He advised the nizam that, given the geographical location of his state and the clear preference of the majority of his subjects, the best option for him was to accede to India after negotiating concessions that would secure his constitutional position. But the Majlis, and especially Razvi, launched a virulent propaganda against Ismail, alleging that years of service in the Hindu courts of Mysore and Jaipur had corrupted him and rendered him insensitive to the interests of the Muslim states. The nizam gave in, elevated the Nawab of Chhatari to the position of prime minister, and brought in Walter Monckton, a London barrister, to negotiate on his behalf.

From July to October 1947, talks were held between New Delhi and Hyderabad on what was called a "standstill agreement" that would spell out what each side could and could not do until a final constitutional arrangement was reached. While Mountbatten and Patel held meetings in New Delhi, V.P. Menon shuttled back and forth between the north and the south of the country. At the Hyderabad end, the nizam and Monckton kept open a parallel track of negotiation, often secretly, with Jinnah. But Patel had a mole by the name of Aravamudh Aiyangar in the nizam's executive council who kept the Indian home minister fully informed of every move that was being discussed among the nizam's advisers. After several inconclusive meetings and near misses, caused mainly by the nizam's indecisiveness, an agreement was finally reached in October 1947. The Hyderabad negotiators took the agreement back to the nizam's executive council which, after three days of debate, accepted it. But on the night before Chhatari and Monckton were supposed to fly back to New Delhi with the document signed by the nizam, a crowd of some 20,000 laid siege to their houses and prevented them from leaving. The next morning, Kasem Razvi harangued the nizam into scrapping the agreement and disbanding his negotiating team. Chhatari and Monckton both resigned.[5] I am quite certain that the nizam was fully in the know of Razvi's plans and allowed him to act in this outrageous way so that the signing of the agreement could be further delayed.

But it is instructive to note how much the Indian government was prepared to concede. The Hyderabad team began in July 1947 by ruling out accession to India but suggesting a treaty on defence, external affairs, and communications and exchanging ambassadors with both India and Pakistan. The nizam, it appears, was contemplating purchasing from Portugal a port in Goa and so demanded a corridor through Indian territory to the Goa coast. This is an indicator of the absurd lengths to which his dream of sovereignty was driving him. Needless to say, the Portuguese dictator Salazar promptly turned down the proposal when it was put to him. As talks proceeded in August 1947, the Hyderabad team began to explore the concessions that might be extracted from India in exchange for accession. A claim was made for the districts of Berar which had been ceded by treaty to the East India Company in 1853 and later merged with the Central Provinces. Some murmurs were also heard for adjustment of boundaries with the so-called Ceded Districts in the south and the Northern Circars in coastal Andhra which had been seized by the British in the eighteenth century. In response, Mountbatten dismissed the territorial claims but agreed to grant a railway line from Hyderabad to an Indian seaport. The condition was that the state must accede to India on the three subjects and that foreign relations had to

---

[5] Besides the Nawab of Chhatari and Walter Monckton, there was a third member of Hyderabad's negotiating committee – Sultan Ahmed.

be carried out exclusively through Indian diplomatic channels. If the nizam was still reluctant to accede to India, the governor general suggested that the matter be put to a plebiscite as had been done in the North West Frontier Province. The nizam's advisers did not want to touch the plebiscite proposal since, given the communal composition of the population, the result was a foregone conclusion. Ultimately, the nizam agreed to accede on these terms in October, only to have the deal scuttled by Kasem Razvi.

By then, the Hyderabad matter had become entangled with developments in Kashmir where an attack by Afridi tribesmen from the north had forced Maharaja Hari Singh to accede to India and seek military help. India airlifted troops to Kashmir to halt the attackers but, by November 1947, the matter had gone to the United Nations and there was an imminent possibility of war between Pakistan and India. At this time, Mountbatten flew to Lahore to persuade Jinnah to agree to plebiscites in both Kashmir and Hyderabad. Jinnah agreed to the Kashmir plebiscite but refused to include Hyderabad in the arrangement. The talks failed. It is important for you to know that as far as Patel was concerned, he was at this time completely prepared to let Kashmir go to Pakistan if Hyderabad would join India. I myself heard him say in a huge rally in Junagadh in November 1947 that whereas Pakistan was always comparing Kashmir to Junagadh, the real comparison should be between Kashmir and Hyderabad. He said he had repeatedly told Pakistan's leaders that India would agree to a plebiscite in Kashmir if Pakistan would accept one in Hyderabad.[6]

By November 1947, the nizam's government had been, for

---

[6] The reference is very likely to a meeting in Junagadh on 13 November 1947, where Patel said, "Pakistan attempted to set off Kashmir against Junagadh. When we raised the question of settling this problem in a democratic way, Pakistan at once told us they would consider this matter if we applied that policy to Kashmir State. Our reply was that we would agree to Kashmir

all practical purposes, captured by Kasem Razvi and the Majlis-e-Ittehad-e-Muslimeen. There was constant propaganda about the importance of preserving the identity of Hyderabad as a Muslim state. The nizam too openly declared his inclination by appointing, on Jinnah's recommendation, Laik Ali as his prime minister. Laik Ali had just served on Pakistan's delegation to the United Nations and accepted the nizam's offer on condition that he would not be expected to arrange for Hyderabad's accession to India. Patel responded by appointing K.M. Munshi, a veteran Gujarat Congress politician, as India's agent-general in Hyderabad.[7] The appointments showed clearly that positions had hardened on both sides. In January 1948, Hyderabad banned the circulation of Indian currency in the state and provided a loan of Rs 20 crores to Pakistan. By March, Munshi was reporting to Patel that Hyderabad had the strength to hold out against diplomatic and economic pressure and would not agree to either accession or a plebiscite. The only recourse left for India was the use of military force.[8]

What was called Operation Polo was planned by the Southern Command of the Indian army from March 1948, under the explicit orders of Nehru but without the knowledge of

---

if they agree to Hyderabad." Vallabhbhai Patel, *For a United India: Speeches of Sardar Patel* (New Delhi: Publications Division, 1967), p. 11.

[7] Kanhaiyalal Maneklal Munshi (1887–1971) was Home Minister in the Congress government of Bombay in 1937–40, Governor of Uttar Pradesh from 1952 to 1957 and, after leaving the Congress Party in 1959, was a co-founder of the right-wing Swatantra Party. He was also a distinguished Gujarati novelist and founder of the Bharatiya Vidya Bhavan, an influential literary and educational institution.

[8] The public records show no communication from Munshi in March 1948 with these words. But Munshi's letter to Patel of 21 May 1948 has the following: "This governmental machine has all the desire and potentiality to accede to Pakistan, if circumstances favour, and will not reconcile itself to a closer association with India. It will have to be displaced." Durga Das, ed., *Sardar Patel's Correspondence*, vol. 7 (Ahmedabad: Navajivan Publishing House, 1973), p. 150.

Mountbatten or General Bucher, the commander-in-chief. When the governor general got to know of it, he was particularly offended by the code name Polo which he thought was intended to personally mock him, since it was well known that he was a great polo enthusiast. The military plan was ostensibly meant for the Indian government to intervene if there was a massacre of Hindus in Hyderabad. But Mountbatten was due to leave India in June. Regardless of the slight, he decided to make one last attempt to find a solution short of armed invasion.

Talks were resumed. Monckton was once again assisting the nizam. Laik Ali expressed a willingness to consider an elected legislature and constituent assembly but, in order to preserve the character of Hyderabad as a Muslim state, insisted that half of their members should be Muslim. New Delhi's proposal, conveyed through Munshi, was that the Hindu majority must be recognised and the Muslim reservation should be kept to 40 per cent. After some haggling, there appeared to be a consensus on a Hindu–Muslim formula of 55:45. Although neither Nehru nor Patel liked the idea of communal representation being continued in independent India, both appreciated that the Hyderabad solution required special concessions.

With a week left before his departure from India, Mountbatten made a trip to Dehradun to meet Patel who was convalescing there after a heart attack and persuaded the home minister to drop the condition that the interim government in Hyderabad should be formed after consultations with the major political parties and with parity between Hindus and Muslims. This, Mountbatten believed, would finally produce an agreement in which the nizam would agree to a plebiscite by adult franchise, supervised by an independent authority, to decide on the question of accession, establish a constituent assembly to initiate responsible government, and form an interim government until the accession was formalised. Hyderabad would not be required to follow all the laws passed by the Indian dominion but could, at the request of the latter, pass similar laws. It would be allowed to maintain its own army of up to 20,000. As you can see, this was far more than was ever allowed to Jammu and Kashmir.

But when this plan was put to the Hyderabad delegation, Laik Ali came up with new demands. He also complained about an economic blockade that was throttling essential supplies to Hyderabad. No agreement was reached by the time Mountbatten left on 21 June. When Munshi asked Patel about the settlement, Patel replied: "What settlement? The settlement has left for London. By god's grace, we have had a narrow escape."[9]

What was Nizam Osman Ali thinking? Why did he allow himself to be virtually held prisoner by Kasem Razvi and his followers who, defying every realistic assessment of the options, wanted Hyderabad to join Pakistan? There was, of course, the constant encouragement he was getting from Jinnah who, even though Pakistan could hardly offer much assistance to Hyderabad to resist Indian pressure, wanted the nizam to delay acceding to India as long as possible, if only to keep the issue unsettled until the Kashmir matter was resolved. The nizam must also have been apprehensive of the power that Congress agitators and Hindu nationalists might wield if Hyderabad joined India, and K.M. Munshi's presence did nothing to assuage his worries. Besides, the communists were creating havoc in the Telangana countryside, attacking landlords and officials, and it was not clear if joining India would help the nizam's government on that front. But most of all, Osman Ali seems to have persuaded himself that with India militarily engaged in Kashmir, there was no real threat of armed intervention in Hyderabad. I don't know what private advice Monckton gave him, but certainly Laik Ali did nothing to break the nizam's illusion.

The Razakars, in the meantime, had spread a reign of terror on Hindus in Osmanabad and Nanded in Marathwada,

[9] Munshi does report an exchange with Patel more or less to this effect. K.M. Munshi, *The End of an Era* (Bombay: Bharatiya Vidya Bhavan, 1957), p. 177.

and Bidar and Gulbarga, now in Karnataka. These were areas in which democratic mobilisations such as the States People movement were poorly developed. The Razakars imposed levies on propertied Hindus who were usually unable to resist; those who did were subjected to violence, including murder and rape. Even officials of the nizam's government co-operated with the Razakars, believing it was the only organisation capable of defending the Muslims of Hyderabad against an Indian assault. Reports of atrocities committed by the Razakars on Hindus were prominently reported in the Indian press and were being compiled by the States Ministry for the attention of Vallabhbhai Patel. Once negotiations stalled after Mountbatten's departure, Kasem Razvi launched a tirade against India, threatening to unleash 500,000 Razakars if a single Indian soldier crossed into Hyderabad soil. He began to make fantastic claims of liberating the Muslims of north India and flying the Asafjahi flag on top of the Red Fort. Ironically, he provided the pretext for the Indian invasion.

Jinnah died in Karachi on 11 September 1948. On 12 September, C. Rajagopalachari, the governor general of India, sent a telegram to Hyderabad declaring that, since the nizam's government had failed to control the Razakars as well as the communists, the Indian government could no longer remain a silent spectator and leave its troops stationed at the border. The next day, in what was euphemistically called a "police action", an entire armoured division headed by a lieutenant-general, assisted by bombers of the air force, crossed into Hyderabad. Its declared job was to restore law and order.

After a few initial skirmishes, the Hyderabad State army retreated and surrendered in a matter of days. It was really in no position to fight a much superior force. The nizam declared a ceasefire on 17 September. K.M. Munshi immediately went on the air to broadcast the news of the liberation of Hyderabad. He had assumed that he would be appointed Governor of Hyderabad. He was sternly reprimanded by both Nehru and Patel and told he was not to get involved in any ceremonies or give instructions on administration. Major General J.N. Chaudhuri was appointed the military governor. Patel was absolutely clear that India had taken the state by military force, not political negotiation, and it was up to the military commander to restore order.

To the extent there was resistance to the Indian army, it was put up by the Razakars. More ominously, the news of the arrival of Indian soldiers led to the outbreak of communal violence on a massive scale in many parts of Hyderabad state. I am sure this is a story you have never heard before, because it is not talked about in India. Everyone has heard of the horrific killings in Punjab at the time of partition. But did you know that some 50,000 civilians were killed in Hyderabad following the invasion of the Indian army? Most of them were Muslims. If you don't believe me, look at the report sent to Nehru and Patel by a fact-finding committee, headed by Pandit Sunderlal, a highly respected Congress leader, which visited Hyderabad in December 1948. Patel dismissed the report, saying he gave more credence to the military officers who were keeping the peace on the ground and who had not reported any such violence. The report was never published and has only been recovered from the archives recently. You should ask your friends to read it.[10] It will give you a different picture of the price that was paid by ordinary people for a "police action" brought about by the grand ambitions of state building by viceroys, nizams, and ministers.

The report points to the sudden transformation in power equations caused by the Indian invasion when it says that the four districts worst affected by the communal violence were precisely the ones where Hindus had suffered the most from

[10] The Sunderlal Committee Report on its goodwill mission to Hyderabad in November-December 1948, addressed to the Prime Minister and the States Minister, was accessed from the Nehru Memorial Museum and Library, New Delhi, and published by A.G. Noorani in the magazine *Frontline* in March 2001. Since then, the report has been reprinted in several publications.

the oppression of the Razakars. But the retaliation took a terrible toll of lives. The committee estimated the number of people killed after the army action in those districts alone to be at least 18,000. In the town of Latur, the killings went on for twenty days and only 3000 of the 10,000 Muslims there were still around; 1000 had been killed and the others had fled. There were rapes, abduction of women, loot, arson, grabbing of property, and desecration of mosques – all of the characteristic features of major communal riots in independent India. There were even stories of forcible conversion into the Hindu religion – symbolic, of course, intended to humiliate the victims and announce to the world that with the arrival of the Indian army Muslims were no longer in power in Hyderabad.

Unlike Junagadh, there was no plebiscite in Hyderabad. The nizam signed the instruments of accession and became the Rajpramukh of the state. The communists accepted the integration of Hyderabad with India, withdrew their movement in Telangana, and surrendered arms in 1951. General elections were held in Hyderabad in 1952, along with the rest of the country, electing a Congress ministry. The forcible accession was finally legitimised by the democratic participation of the people. After the linguistic reorganisation of states in 1956, Hyderabad was divided into Telugu, Marathi, and Kannada regions and merged with the states of Andhra Pradesh, Bombay, and Mysore. But was the identity of the Hyderabadi people erased? Did they happily accept all that had happened to their land (*mulk*) and forget their history? If so, why did the Telangana movement rise up in the 1990s precisely in those districts that once belonged to Hyderabad state, demanding separation from Andhra Pradesh, and winning that demand in 2014? Think about that.

## The Kashmir Tangle

You have heard so much about the Kashmir problem all your life that you probably think you know everything about it. So

I will be brief. But I must tell you that I have a rather complicated relation, not all of which is happy, with that wonderful place and its people.

Kashmir is a land of great philosophers and poets. Many years ago, I had a very public quarrel with one of the greatest of them – the Brahman logician Bhatta Jayanta who was a favourite of King Shankaravarman and his queen, Sugandha. I must confess I have a prejudice against scholars who curry favour with powerful people. But Bhatta Jayanta was a scholar of true brilliance whose intellect I much respected. Now, it so happened that in one of his light-hearted moments, the Brahman wrote a play in which he tore into the doctrines of every single sect (*sampradāy*) – Vaidik, Shaiva, Vaishnav, Buddhist, Jain – and showed each one as full of fallacies and contradictions. But he ended by advising the king that although no religion was perfect in itself, they were all streams that flowed into the great river of universal truth. Hence, the best policy was to tolerate all of them. Even nastik religions like Buddhism and Jainism should be allowed. The only people who were to be forcibly banished from the kingdom were the Nilambaras who, Jayanta said, were a threat to the whole varnashram order because men and women of the sect defied the rules of family and marriage, performed indecent songs and dances, and had sex in public. I challenged Bhatta Jayanta and defended the Nilambaras who, it is true, did reject the whole Brahmanical varnashram system but did not behave in the outrageous way in which the Brahman had depicted them. For this, I was thrown out of the kingdom of Kashmir and was not able to go back for many years until the reign of the good king Zainul Abedin.[11]

But let us keep aside my story and talk about the much debated history of the accession to India of Jammu and Kashmir. The reason why it was a princely state and not a part of

---

[11] Bhatta Jayanta was a Kashmiri philosopher of Nyaya who lived in the ninth century. He was a contemporary of King Shankaravarman of Kashmir.

British India is also curious. You should know that history. At the time of the first British war against the Sikhs in 1846, the Dogra family of Gulab Singh led the most powerful faction within the Sikh court in Lahore. When the war ended, the minor king Duleep Singh was required to pay the British an indemnity of one and a half crore rupees. Unable to raise the money, the Sikh king ceded to the East India Company a large part of his territory in eastern Punjab as well as Jammu and Kashmir. But Hardinge, the governor general, thought the expense of protecting the mountainous northern borders would be prohibitive. At this point, Gulab Singh, the Dogra general in the Sikh army, offered to buy Jammu and Kashmir for a payment of seventy-five lakh rupees. In return, he was recognised by the Company in the Treaty of Amritsar of 1846 as an independent native prince. In accordance with the local style, Maharaja Gulab Singh announced his loyalty to the Company by making an annual present of a horse and twelve goats. This was later changed to a more decorous annual gift of two shawls and three rumals. People in Kashmir have not forgotten that they were bought by the Dogra kings for a mere seventy-five lakhs. In 1946, on the centenary of the Treaty of Amritsar, the poet Hafeez Jalandhari wrote:

*Mulk par qabzā hamārā hai pachattar lākh mem̐,*
*Māl ye sab hamne mārā hai pachattar lākh mem̐.*
*Ye maveśī ho ke adamzād, sab hai zarkharīd,*
*Inke bacche, bacchīyām̐, aulād, sab hai zarkharīd.*
*Ho nahīm̐ sakte kabhī āzād, sab hai zarkharīd,*
*Tā qayāmat khanmāl barbād, sab hai zarkharīd.*
*Lūṭ lī insān kī qismat pachattar lākh mem̐,*
*Bik gaī kaśmīr kī jannat pachattar lākh mem̐.*
*Mard kā sarmāye mehnat pachattar lākh mem̐,*

---

Jayanta is famous for his treatise *Nyāyamañjarī*, and a play called *Āgama ḍambara*. Sultan Zainul Abedin ruled Kashmir from 1420 to 1470.

*Auratoṁ kā jauhare ismat pachattar lākh meṁ.*
*Mulk, millat, qaum, māl-vo-jahāṁ pachattar lākh meṁ.*
*Hāṁ, pachattar lākh meṁ, hāṁ, hāṁ, pachattar lākh meṁ.*[12]

I should mention that Hafeez Jalandhari moved to Pakistan after independence and even joined the forces that tried to liberate Kashmir from Indian rule. I am told he was injured in action in 1948. He also wrote the Qaumi Taranah, Pakistan's national anthem, which is so full of Persian words that I cannot understand it. But let me get back to the main story.

At the time of independence and partition in 1947, Maharaja Hari Singh, like the rulers of Hyderabad or Bhopal or Travancore, was trying not to join either of the two dominions. He was in a particularly difficult position: 77 per cent of his subjects were Muslim but they were unevenly distributed. In the Jammu region, Muslims were 60 per cent and Hindus 40 per cent, whereas in Kashmir 92 per cent of the people were Muslim. There was also a part of his kingdom – Ladakh – where most of the people were Buddhist. What added to the complication was that there was an active and organised popular movement in the state which campaigned against the monarchy and demanded representative government. This movement began in the 1930s as the Muslim Conference, but changed its name in 1939 to the National Conference and admitted non-Muslim members. Under the leadership of Sheikh Muhammad Abdullah, it affiliated

---

[12] The poem is called "Pachattar lakh ka sauda" [The Seventy-five lakh deal]. A rough translation: We came to possess the country for seventy-five lakhs; we got the whole loot for seventy-five lakhs. Whether cattle or human, they are all our slaves; their sons, daughters, and their offspring, all are our slaves. They will never be free, they are all our slaves; they are ruined until doomsday, they are all our slaves. We have looted their destiny for seventy-five lakhs; Kashmir's paradise was bought for seventy-five lakhs. The fruits of men's labour bought for seventy-five lakhs, the jewel of women's virtue bought for seventy-five lakhs. Country, nation, community, all of life's possessions, bought for seventy-five lakhs. Yes, for seventy-five lakhs; yes, yes, for seventy-five lakhs.

itself to the States People movement closely associated with the Indian National Congress. In 1941, a section of the National Conference split and revived the Muslim Conference which, led by Ghulam Abbas, aligned itself with the All India Muslim League. Given this complicated situation, the maharaja knew that whether he joined India or Pakistan, his decision would anger one or the other section of the population. He preferred not to have to decide.

All of the rail and road connections between Kashmir and the rest of India passed through what became the Pakistan side of Punjab. In fact, until the military conflict at the end of October 1947, the postal services of Kashmir were operated by the Pakistan postal department. The single road through Gurdaspur which would later become the Pathankot–Jammu corridor was then not an all-weather road. In August 1947, Pakistan signed a standstill agreement with Jammu and Kashmir pending the latter's accession to one of the dominions. India, however, put forward various conditions including foreign relations and control over the J&K army. This suggests that while the Indian leaders recognised the difficulty faced by the maharaja, they were nevertheless trying to secure something like an accession in the guise of a standstill agreement. But the maharaja did not take the bait. You should also remember that at this time Sheikh Abdullah had been put in prison by the maharaja for his anti-monarchical and pro-democracy agitation.

Given the logic of the partition of the country, the general expectation was that Hyderabad should join India and Jammu and Kashmir join Pakistan. But in each of these cases, internal politics made the choice difficult for the ruler. As I have told you before, India put a lot of pressure on the nizam but an influential political organisation in the kingdom, encouraged by Pakistan, managed to block any agreement. In Kashmir, on the other hand, there was very little initiative on the Indian side. V.P. Menon, who was shuttling between different state capitals in the months before and after partition, paid no attention to Kashmir. It seems as though the leaders in New Delhi were satisfied to see that the inevitable decision was taking so long in coming. Jinnah, on the other hand, remarked several times that Kashmir was a ripe fruit waiting to fall into his lap.

But as in Hyderabad, there were some in Kashmir who were impatient and unwilling to wait. Supporters of the Muslim Conference in Mirpur, Poonch, and Muzaffarabad, and Muslim League activists in Gilgit-Baltistan in the north, launched a campaign in the Pakistani press, accusing the government of not doing enough to secure the accession of Kashmir to Pakistan. There are some reports that Jinnah himself authorised the campaign of armed tribesmen from the North West Frontier Province, Chitral, and Hunza to take Kashmir by force. If so, he made a bad miscalculation that gave the maharaja a good reason to seek Indian help and the Indian government the chance to ask for his accession to India. For the people of Kashmir, it was the beginning of the long road to endless tragedy.

On 22 October, tribal raiders crossed into Jammu and Kashmir from the NWFP. The Kashmir situation was in more ways than one a mirror image of that in Hyderabad, because most senior positions in government as well as the army were held by Hindus and Sikhs while Muslims were to be found only in the lower ranks. Faced with an enemy that had arrived to liberate Kashmir from the hands of an unpopular Hindu ruler, the Muslim soldiers in the J&K army deserted and joined the raiders who managed, in two days, to take Muzaffarabad and reach the outskirts of Baramulla. At that rate, they were likely to reach Srinagar in another two days. The Dogra chief of staff of the maharaja's army had to put up a resistance at Uri with barely a hundred men; everyone else had deserted.

Maharaja Hari Singh panicked and sent an urgent message to New Delhi on 24 October, seeking immediate military assistance. You should remember that at this time the British Indian armed forces were still being partitioned, with officers and men choosing one or the other dominion principally on the basis of religion. Field Marshall Claude Auchinleck was the supreme commander of the armed forces of both India and Pakistan. Further, all the commanders-in-chief of the army, navy, and air force of the two countries were British. Thus, even though there was much nationalist passion in both countries, especially in the context of the horrifying civil violence of partition, the two national armies were not yet fully formed.

The implications of the impending fall of Srinagar were stark. Not only would there be a communal massacre in Kashmir, but the inevitable retaliation that would follow in other parts of northern India, where the wounds of partition violence were still raw, could be catastrophic. The Indian leaders were unanimous that something had to be done. But Mountbatten argued that India would have a proper legal basis for sending troops to Kashmir only if the maharaja first signed the instruments of accession granting India the power to act in matters of defence, foreign affairs, and communication. He also insisted that, given the communal distribution of the population, the legitimacy of the accession would only be secured if, after the raiders had been expelled and normality restored, it was put to a popular vote. Nehru argued that, in accordance with the policy adopted for the other states, the maharaja would have to appoint a representative government and agree to convene a constituent assembly. V.P. Menon was sent to Srinagar with these instructions. He returned on 26 October with the maharaja's letter of accession in which he also announced his decision to appoint Sheikh Abdullah as the head of an interim government.

The airlifting of troops and equipment to Kashmir was quite an achievement. Besides the resources of the air force, a large number of commercial airplanes were mobilised. As soon as a few battalions were assembled in Srinagar, Indian troops began to push back the intruders. But in areas like Poonch, where retired Muslim soldiers of the British Indian army joined the raiders, and the northern region of Gilgit, where the J&K army as well as the local administration declared its loyalty to Pakistan, the population was clearly hostile to the maharaja's decision to join India. In the meantime, Pakistan furiously disputed Kashmir's accession to India, alleging that it had been procured by force and fraud. Once Indian soldiers began action in Kashmir, Jinnah ordered General Gracey, the head of the Pakistan army, to send troops. Gracey referred the matter to Auchinleck, the supreme commander, who immediately explained to Jinnah that since Kashmir had now become a part of India, the entry of Pakistani troops would amount to a foreign invasion, in which case all British officers in the Pakistan army would have to be withdrawn. Jinnah had to take back his order.

Given the way the situation was developing in Hyderabad and Kashmir, Mountbatten was extremely concerned at the possibility of war between the two dominions. In early November, he flew to Lahore to persuade Jinnah to accept plebiscites in the two states: that, he said, would resolve the matter in a democratic way. As I have told you before, Jinnah was keen on a plebiscite in Kashmir but not in Hyderabad. Soon, the matter became an international dispute, with debates in the United Nations where India continued to insist that the accession of Jammu and Kashmir to India would be ratified by a plebiscite.

The comparison between Hyderabad and Kashmir is important because, even though no one in India remembers that history, that is exactly how they were seen at the time – two equivalent cases where the ruling monarch was of a different religion from that of the majority of his subjects. India insisted that the nizam ascertain the popular will in Hyderabad because it knew which way most of the people would vote. The matter was more complicated in Kashmir. Sheikh Abdullah was clearly the leader of the most organised popular movement in the state and had a very strong following in the Kashmir valley. He was also ideologically close to the progressive sections of the Indian National Congress. But popular sentiments were quite different in the western parts of Jammu and in the northern regions of Gilgit-Baltistan. Would Sheikh Abdullah's influence have swung the result in favour of India had a plebiscite been held in 1950 or 1951? I am not sure. In fact, I believe that Abdullah was put in the same situation that Khan Abdul Ghaffar Khan faced in the NWFP when the plebiscite was held there in 1947. Even if he had won the vote by a small majority, Bacha Khan knew that he would have to face an open rebellion by his opponents. He chose to withdraw from the contest. Abdullah took the more difficult course of trying to create a space of autonomy for Kashmir which could only be viable if it was guaranteed by both India and Pakistan. Sadly, he only managed to create suspicion and distrust among the rulers in New Delhi. In 1953, Nehru removed him from power and put him in prison for ten years.

What followed in Jammu and Kashmir was the slow but effective administrative integration of the territories on either side of the line of control into the governing apparatus in Pakistan and India, respectively. In Azad Kashmir and Gilgit-Baltistan, this did not lead to much political conflict since the people were from the beginning inclined towards Pakistan rather than India. On the Indian side, a constitution was promulgated for the state of Jammu and Kashmir in 1956, while Article 370 of the Indian constitution allowed for the extension to the state of laws made by the Indian parliament. Politically, following the dismissal of Abdullah's government, Kashmir saw a succession of puppet governments created through party splits, defections, and rigged elections. There has been a sustained spirit of resistance among the people, especially of the Kashmir valley, to being ruled from Delhi. Calls for freedom (*āzādī*) have been met with increasing force so that Kashmir is today the most militarised region in the whole world. Many thousands of people have been killed there in recent years – by the security forces as well as by militants.

I know your friends are very exercised by the idea that, had it not been for Nehru's weakness, Indian troops, instead of stopping at the line of control, should have moved forward and brought the whole of the state under Indian jurisdiction. Then there would have been no Kashmir dispute at all. This is turning history into fantasy. The reason why military operations had to be suspended was not merely that the real possibility of open warfare between India and Pakistan led to international pressure through the United Nations, but the political reality that popular support for joining India was non-existent on the other side of the line of control. The only significant reason why one part of Jammu and Kashmir became a part of India was the support that Abdullah's National Conference enjoyed in the valley. This support did not extend to the other areas of the state. The ruler's choice in this case counted for nothing, as witnessed in Junagadh and Hyderabad. It was under Abdullah's leadership that Jammu and Kashmir joined India on the assurance that it would have its own constitution and the accession would be ratified by a plebiscite. This history is now not only forgotten; it is being actively falsified.

In August 2019, Article 370 was revoked and Ladakh was separated from the rest of Jammu and Kashmir. The two new units are no longer states but union territories, under far more direct control of New Delhi than before. You must have your own opinion about this event. All I will say is that it puts a real question mark on what kind of nation India wants to be. Let us now talk about that subject.

# 4

# India is Not a Hindu Rashtra

WHAT KIND OF nation did India want to be in 1947? Was there a vision of its national identity that was shared by the people and their leaders? These days, you hear learned people talk a lot about "the idea of India".[1] What they mean by that are the thoughts of great Indian writers and philosophers on the core principles of Indian history and culture. These thoughts are the product of deep erudition and reflection. But did they have any impact on the actual political events that turned India into what it is today? I have my doubts but agree that the question is worth looking into. So let me begin with the ideas on Indian nationalism that are most influential today and look back to where they came from, why they became influential and what effect they have had on the country.

## Hindutva and Hindu Rashtra

I am sure you hear these words very often and suspect you know what they mean. I have also mentioned the name Vinayak Damodar Savarkar before. It is time to talk about him at length.

Savarkar, as I have told you, was a revolutionary who was convicted by the British for organising what they described as terrorist acts and sent to prison in the Andaman Islands. His

---

[1] This phrase occurs in English in the original manuscript.

elder brother, Ganesh, better known as Babarao, was also a revolutionary who was sent to the Andamans. As a law student in London, Vinayak Savarkar was very active among Indians in Britain and France, carrying out propaganda against British rule in India, criticising the obsequious pleadings of Congress leaders and advocating armed resistance. The British police kept a close watch on him and regarded him as the most dangerous among Indian political activists in Britain. While in London, he wrote a book in Marathi on the revolt of 1857 which was soon translated into English. The book was banned in India. You should get a copy and read it.[2] You will see that even though he was not a trained historian and did not have access to any archives, Savarkar was still able to read the histories of the so-called Indian Mutiny written by British authors and turn them around into a truly inspiring nationalist history of what he called the first war of Indian independence. Most importantly, he saw the revolt as one in which the Muslims and Hindus of India were united in their struggles and sacrifices. He did believe that the Muslim conquerors of India were foreigners who had subjected the Hindus to violence and oppression. But by the middle of the eighteenth century, the Marathas had established *de facto* Hindu rule over Hindusthan. By the middle of the nineteenth century, after a hundred years of British domination, Hindus and Muslims had equally become the victims of colonial rule. Hence, when the rebels of 1857, having ousted the British from Delhi, offered the crown of Hindusthan to Bahadur Shah Zafar, it was an act of generosity on the part of the Hindus and a recognition that they accepted the Muslims of the country as fellow-sufferers and comrades-in-arms.

There are many critics of Savarkar who question his devotion to the nationalist cause even in his early years. I don't think that criticism is at all deserved. While in London, the British police

---

[2] The book is now available in English under the title *The Indian War of Independence, 1857*.

began to look for him for being involved in the assassination of a British official in Nasik. Savarkar managed to escape to Paris where the French police arrested him and handed him over to the British. He was put on a ship to India but when it docked in Marseilles, the wily Savarkar escaped through a porthole. Unfortunately, he was apprehended again, brought to India, tried and convicted.

During his imprisonment in the Cellular Jail in Port Blair, Savarkar did write several letters to the British authorities expressing regret for his actions and pleading for his release. These letters are cited by his critics to argue that Savarkar had become a turncoat and a toady of the British. My own view is very different. Savarkar was a political tactician to his very bone; all of life was for him a field of *kūṭanīti*. He felt deeply frustrated at having to spend all those years in a faraway prison, without any contact with his friends and political associates. More importantly, he was greatly disturbed by the turn in India's nationalist politics brought about by Gandhi. He believed Gandhi's brand of non-violent resistance would make India a weak nation. He was also alarmed by Gandhi's alliance with the Khilafat movement which brought masses of ordinary Muslims into the nationalist movement but under the belief that they were fighting for the survival of the Islamic caliphate represented by the Sultan of Turkey. Savarkar thought Indian Muslims were being encouraged to proclaim allegiance to a sacred authority located outside their own land. After his last mercy petition was turned down in 1920, he and his brother were transferred in 1921 from Port Blair to Ratnagiri jail and subsequently to Yerawada prison in Poona. He was released in 1924 but on condition that he would not leave Ratnagiri district for five years. Savarkar resumed active politics in the 1930s. But by then his political priorities had completely changed.

While in prison in Ratnagiri, Savarkar wrote a book in English called *Essentials of Hindutva*. The manuscript was smuggled out of prison and published in 1923. It did not carry his name;

instead, the author was described as "A Mahratta".[3] What is remarkable about the book is that while its subject is Indian politics, nowhere is there even a mention of British colonial rule in India and the struggle to put an end to it. In fact, Savarkar seems to be imagining a near future when the British are no longer in charge: Indians must decide who will be included within the nation as its true citizens. Hence, the question he asks is "Who is a Hindu?" because the nation, he claims, is "Hindusthan" – not the Hindustan of old which was a name coined by foreigners in a foreign language, but Hindusthan, a name of pure Sanskrit derivation.

## The Hindu in History

Savarkar spends many pages of his book arguing that the Aryans who settled on the banks of the Sindhu (Indus) river called themselves Sindhu and their land Sindhusthan. The name Sindhu was pronounced Hindu by the ancient Persians. The Greeks called the river Indus and the land India. What you must note in Savarkar's tortuous arguments on this point is that he accepts that the Aryans came to India from Central Asia to settle down on the lands along the Indus. He was too well read and rational to make silly claims about the Aryans being the original inhabitants of India. What he disputed was the assumption that the name Hindu was something given to Indians by foreigners. Rather, he says, in their relations with other peoples, the Aryan settlers of India described themselves as Sindhu. The name was

---

[3] Savarkar's book was first published in 1923 as *Essentials of Hindutva* by A Mahratta. A revised edition was published in 1928 under the title *Hindutva: Who is a Hindu?* It carried the full name of the author. The title page also carried two Sanskrit epigrams. The first summarised Savarkar's definition: "A HINDU means a person who regards this land of BHARATAVARSHA, from the Indus to the Seas as his Father-Land as well as his Holy-Land that is the cradle land of his religion." The other sets out the main political task: "Who delivers this our Nation of Sapta Sindhus who endows us with wealth, do thou O! Lord, hurl thy mighty thunder-bolt to destroy our enemies – the Dasas."

then transformed to Hindu when it was later adopted by the various Prakrit languages. I am not convinced by the evidence Savarkar provides from various Sanskrit sources to prove that the Aryans called themselves Sindhu and their land Sindhusthan. It is particularly disappointing that he draws extensively from the *Bhaviṣyapurāṇa*, a fake text that Savarkar knew to be a modern creation, probably written as recently as the nineteenth century. But I do not think the point about names is really crucial for his argument about the Hindu nation. Let scholars of ancient India fight over it; we need not be detained by their debates.

You must also remember that when Savarkar was writing his book, the existence of an earlier Harappan civilisation was still unknown. The mound at Mohenjo-daro had just been excavated but the historic significance of the discovery was only announced in 1924. Hence, he did not have to deal with the problem of a developed urban civilisation preceding the Aryans. He simply assumed that the people who lived in India when the Aryans arrived were primitive and uncivilised.

What is really interesting is the next step that Savarkar takes in creating a modern national myth. The Aryans, he says, spread out from their initial settlements on the Indus to other parts of the country. They sometimes came into conflict with the indigenous peoples, whom they called Anarya. But, Savarkar insists, the more powerful and persistent process was the mixing of peoples through the original Aryans intermarrying locals to produce a thoroughly mixed race – "a vast synthesis", as he describes it. A number of polities were created and destroyed until, with Ramchandra's conquest of Simhala, the whole country from the Himalayas to the seas was brought under the rule of a single sovereign. That is when Arya and Anarya were bound together as one people and the Hindu nation was born.[4]

---

[4] In Savarkar's words: "At last the great mission which the Sindhus had undertaken of founding a nation and a country, found and reached its geographical limit when the valorous Prince of Ayodhya made a triumphant entry into Ceylon and actually brought the whole land from the Himalayas to the

You should note two points here. First, Savarkar thinks of the Hindu race as one that was produced by the admixture of an Aryan people who came from elsewhere to settle in India with the local people.⁵ Second, the Hindu nation (*rāṣṭra*) was created when the entire country from north to south was politically united under a single sovereign power because the Anarya people of the south swore allegiance to Ram of Ayodhya. In other words, even though the Hindu people are racially a mix of Arya and Anarya, the political unity of the nation was the result of the Aryans proclaiming their sovereignty over the others. Despite the vast synthesis, the priority of the Aryans – the Sindhu people – as the civilising force that created the Hindu nation is clear. Keep that in mind as you follow Savarkar's argument.

If this was the golden age of the Hindu nation, it did not last. The rise of Buddhism as a universal religion preaching non-violence and spiritual harmony made the nation weak and incapable of defending itself.⁶ Asoka created a large empire and spread the spiritual message of the Buddha all over the world. But his successors could not defend the country against the barbarian invasions of the Shakas and the Hunas. Savarkar's judgment on the political role of Buddhism is merciless. The

---

Seas under one sovereign sway. The day when the Horse of Victory returned to Ayodhya unchallenged and unchallengeable, the great white Umbrella of Sovereignty was unfurled over that Imperial throne of Ramachandra the good, and a loving allegiance to him was sworn, not only by the Princes of Aryan blood but Hanuman, Sugriva, Bibhishana from the south – that day was the real birth-day of our Hindu people. It was truly our national day: for Aryans and Anaryans knitting themselves into a people were born as a nation." *Hindutva: Who is a Hindu?* (Bombay: Veer Savarkar Prakashan, 1969), pp. 11–12.

⁵ The word for "race" used in the manuscript is *jāti*.

⁶ In Savarkar's words, "mealy-mouthed formulas of Ahimsa and spiritual brotherhood." Savarkar seems to suggest that the Buddhist appeal to non-violence was not sincere. His intended target may have been the Gandhian creed.

world, he says, is full of brutal men who are driven by the lust for wealth and power; they are not swayed by messages of peace and goodwill. They could be stopped not by righteousness but only by the superior force of arms. The barbarian invasions produced a reaction. The Gupta Empire under Vikramaditya began to revive the Vedic religion as the binding force to unite the Hindu nation as a strong polity. It was necessary, says Savarkar, to build a common church to create religious support for the new national state.

It is important to understand the significance of Savarkar's criticism of Buddhism because it is actually an oblique criticism of Gandhi's politics. The message of non-violence and love may be spiritually uplifting but it is of no use – in fact, dangerous – in the real world filled with enmity and violence. More importantly, Buddhism was a universal religion, proclaiming brotherhood of all peoples. It did not protect and preserve a national centre that could be the exclusive sacred land of the Hindu nation. This is what the reaction to Buddhism achieved under the Gupta Empire. I should also mention something that few people know. Among Savarkar's voluminous literary writings in Marathi is a musical play written in 1931 called *Saṅgīt sannyāsta khaḍga* in which a Shaka king takes the vows of non-violence from the Buddha but, when his kingdom is attacked by an invading army, realises that compassion and non-violence cannot subdue cruelty and violence. The play ends with the words: "Doomed is the nation which believes that renunciation is the highest dharma." The reference to the Gandhian doctrine is unmistakable.[7]

Following the decline of Buddhism, the revival of the Vedic religion restored the symbolic importance of the Sindhu. Savarkar admits that the reaction was excessive, because it

---

[7] The play is included in V.D. Savarkar, *Samagra Sāvarkar Vāṅmaya*, vol. 7 (Pune: Maharashtra Prantik Hindusabha, 1965), pp. 539–640.

brought back and even exaggerated the cruelties of caste discrimination. Adherence to the *varṇa* system became a marker of national identity for Hindus, something that distinguished them from the *mleccha* foreigners. Prohibitions were imposed on travel beyond the seas to foreign lands where the Vedic faith could not be easily maintained. But the creation of an orthodox Hindu church saved the Hindu nation from extinction. Under the Guptas, Sindhusthan was a *rājñah-rāṣṭram*, a sovereign territorial nation-state encircled by the Sindhu river, the Brahmaputra (once believed to be a tributary of the Sindhu), and Sindhu the sea.

The political sovereignty of the Hindu nation was next threatened by the successive Muslim invasions beginning in the tenth century. Savarkar insists that all Hindus were equally the victims of Muslim domination – Sanatani, Sikh, Maratha, Madrasi, Brahman, Satnami, the untouchable Panchama – everyone suffered. Moreover, everyone joined in resisting to their best ability what was a foreign invasion by a warlike people. The examples Savarkar cites of Hindu resistance to Muslim rule involve the Rajputs, the Sikhs, and the Marathas, but he insists that these were all efforts to defend not only their own kingdoms or communities but the entire Hindu nation. In particular, he uses many citations from Marathi sources which describe the empire founded by Shivaji and later run by the Peshwas as *hindupadapādaśāhī*. Soon after his book on Hindutva, Savarkar wrote a whole volume celebrating the history of the Maratha Empire.[8] Despite the defeat at the hands of the invading Afghan army at Panipat in 1761, Savarkar says, the Marathas made the Hindus the *de facto* rulers of Hindusthan.

Strange as it may seem, that is where Savarkar stops recounting his version of the history of India. He does not talk about

[8] Savarkar's book *Hindu-pad-padashahi, or A Review of the Hindu Empire of Maharashtra* was first published in 1925.

the British conquests of territory and establishment of colonial rule in India, nor does he mention the many battles, including the great revolt of 1857, fought by Indians in many parts of the country to stop the British advance and later to throw them out. Even as he wants to draw from history the essential principles of nationality in India, his history stops before the arrival of the British, the immediate foreign power that was still holding Indians in subjection.

One could argue that writing as he was under the severe restrictions imposed on him, he could not afford to explicitly talk about anti-colonial politics. But that is hard to believe, because Savarkar was a very intelligent writer who could have found ways to convey his political message in the exact form in which he intended. I think there was actually a great change in his political views during his last days in prison. He had come to believe that in the context of the turn in nationalist agitations in the 1920s, Hindus were facing enemies greater than the British. As I told you before, he saw Gandhi's style of mass politics and his alliance with Muslim religious leaders as huge dangers for the Hindu nation. He was determined to fight that trend. It was this conviction that drove his politics from the 1920s.

### Defining the Hindu

His definition of the true Hindu was in line with his new politics. The Hindu must, first of all, be someone who, or whose ancestor, was born in Hindusthan. By virtue of this fact, he would share a common fatherland (*pitribhu*) with others born in Hindusthan.[9] It would make that person a Bharatiya or

---

[9] The word *pitribhu* occurs in Savarkar's English text and is quoted here in the manuscript. While the language of the manuscript does not always identify the gender of the true Hindu as male, Savarkar's English text always uses the masculine pronoun. However, this is not a reason to believe that Savarkar excluded women from the Hindu Nation. In fact, there is enough

Hindi or Indian – a citizen of the Indian rajya.[10] While this is a necessary condition, it is not, however, sufficient for that person to be a Hindu. In addition, he must also share the racial bonds of a common blood and belong to the Hindu jati. As I have mentioned earlier, Savarkar claimed that the Hindu jati was formed through the mixture of Aryans with the indigenous peoples of India. This synthesis produced the common blood shared by all Hindus. Savarkar does not believe that the rules of caste endogamy were ever a barrier to the mingling that produced a common Hindu blood. He cites the provisions in the Dharmashastra of *anuloma* and *pratiloma* marriages and insists that marrying across caste lines had always been prevalent. Not only that, even those who reject the authority of the Vedas and the varnashram dharma, such as Buddhists, Jains, and Sikhs, marry those who were born in castes within the varna order. Further, those millions of Indians who were converted to Islam and Christianity continue to share a common blood with their Hindu compatriots and hence still belong to the Hindu race (*jāti*). By the two criteria of common fatherland and common blood, Indian Muslims and Christians may belong to the Bharatiya rajya as well as the Hindu jati.

But they would be excluded by the third condition that Savarkar imposes on the identity of the Hindu: adherence to a common Hindu culture or civilisation which he calls in his English book "sanskriti". What is Hindu civilisation? It is, first of all, the common pool of the achievements and thoughts of the Hindu nation preserved in its history, literature, and art. Savarkar speaks eloquently of how Hindus all over the country, from Ceylon to Kashmir, grow up with stories from the

---

indication in his writings to suggest that he was broadly in favour of equal participation of women in public life.

[10] "Hindi" here means a person from Hindustan, which Savarkar always writes as Hindusthan.

Ramayana and the Mahabharata, or about the love of Radha and Krishna, the bravery of Prithviraj, and the martyrdom of the Sikh gurus. All the languages of India, he insists, are derived from Sanskrit, which means that Sanskrit is the mother tongue of all Hindus. The Vedas may not have any religious authority for Buddhists or Jains or Sikhs, but because of the store of wisdom and beauty contained in the Sanskrit language from its origins in the Vedas, it is as much an inheritance for them as it is for those who revere the Vedas. Because of the family relationship among the Indian languages, the literature of every part of India belongs to all Hindus. Stretching the point beyond credulity, Savarkar claims that a Hindu from Bengal will say that the Kamba Ramayana in Tamil was his but not the Persian poetry of Hafiz, or that a Hindu from Maharashtra will say "Rabindranath is mine" but not Shakespeare. Most surprisingly, Savarkar never mentions Urdu, the language of education all over northern India from Sind, Punjab, and Kashmir to the United Provinces, as an Indian language. In addition, Hindu sanskriti includes the common body of Hindu law which, regardless of regional and sectarian differences, is distinct from Muslim or Christian law. Hindu civilisation is also marked by common festivals such as Dasera or Diwali, Rakhi or Holi, common fairs such as the Rathayatra or the Kumbh Mela, common rituals and ceremonies such as at birth, marriage, or death. In sum, Hindu sanskriti, i.e. Hindu civilisation or culture, consists of the history, literature, art, law, festivals, and ceremonies which all Hindus recognise as their own.

Savarkar was keenly aware of the difficulties involved in defining a common set of beliefs or practices that constitute the religion of the Hindus. That is why he makes the ingenious move of distinguishing his concept of Hindutva from Hinduism. The latter, he says, is supposed to consist of the theological and moral principles of the Hindu religion. But every attempt to define it ends up in hopeless confusion which can only be resolved by declaring the religion of the majority of practitioners as the true Hinduism. Sometimes, this majority or dominant religion is called the Vaidik Dharma, and sometimes the Sanatan Dharma. It is supposed to consist of the Shruti, the Smriti, and the Puranas. But this defines only one part of the Hindu nation because it leaves out millions of others who are fully a part of the Hindu civilisation but do not subscribe to the Vaidik or Sanatan Dharma. Why should they be excluded from their rightful place within the Hindu nation?

## Defining Hindutva

Savarkar's solution to the problem is provided by the concept of Hindutva. He puts the onus on the prospective member of the Hindu nation: does he or does he not subscribe to a faith that originates within the territorial space of Hindusthan? That is to say, does he or does he not regard India as his sacred land (*punyabhu*)? If he does – and it does not matter if his faith conforms to Vedic rules or not, or even if it does not call itself Hindu (such as with Buddhists or Sikhs), then he regards Hindusthan as his sacred fatherland – *punyabhu* as well as *pitribhu* – and hence is a Hindu. If he does not, then he must consider some other part of the world – such as Arabia for Muslims or Rome for Catholics – as his sacred land and, therefore, will not be able to identify with Hindu sanskriti. That person, consequently, is not a Hindu and cannot be a member of the Hindu rashtra.

I have to appreciate the clever way in which Savarkar solves a problem which adherents of Hindu nationalism in his time, such as many who were active leaders of the Congress and others who had come together in the newly formed Hindu Mahasabha, had found quite intractable. How could the priority of Hindus be asserted within the emerging national formation without bringing to the fore the many conflicts between sects and castes that existed in the social life of people in every part of the country? These were not merely old conflicts; they were emerging in new forms as castes and communities were defying conventional practices and asserting new claims to dignity and social equality. A campaign by the Arya Samaj to reform religious practices would be opposed by adherents of Sanatan Dharma; a demand by untouchable castes to enter a temple or use the village pond would be fiercely resisted by the upper castes. How was a common Hindu interest to be defined in political terms?

Savarkar's solution was to define the Hindu not by the internal features of a religion but by the territorial space within which a religion is born. He takes the territorial definition of the modern nation-state as it has emerged in Europe as given. He then defines the territory of what he calls Hindusthan through a highly imaginative fictional reconstruction of Indian history. Finally, he declares all religious faiths and practices originating within the territory of Hindusthan as constitutive of Hindutva (not Hinduism, which he declares to be irrelevant in determining nationality). With these three steps, he is able to include all sects and castes among the religions born in India, irrespective of the disagreements and conflicts between them, within the definition of the Hindu nation. Even the Bohras and Khojas are admissible because, he says, they worship all of the ten Hindu avatars and only add Mohammed as the eleventh. The fact that history records many conflicts and even wars between different groups among Hindus is no reason to deny them their own national history. Did not European nations such as the English or the French or the Germans or the Italians have civil wars? If they can claim their distinct national history despite those internal conflicts, why, asks Savarkar, cannot the Hindu nation do so?

At the same time, he is able to exclude those he wanted to exclude to begin with – namely, Muslims and Christians. In the process, he does have to exclude small groups like the Parsis and the Jews.[11] He probably thought it was a small price to pay in

---

[11] Savarkar does not make any mention in his book of Parsis and Jews in India.

order to establish a robust principle of nationalism (*rāṣṭravād*). In any case, they probably did not pose any threat to the Hindu nation because they were not proselytising religions and did not try to convert people. What is curious is that Savarkar makes a special case for Sister Nivedita, the Irish disciple of Swami Vivekananda, who, he says, had adopted India as her sacred fatherland: she was to be admitted into the Hindu nation as a rare exception to the rule.

There is no question that, writing in the 1920s, Savarkar wanted to imagine India as a culturally homogeneous modern nation of the kind he had seen in Europe – nations that were proud of their military histories and reliant on national unity and armed strength to defend their interests. Discarding his earlier celebration of Muslim–Hindu unity among the rebels of 1857, he was now deeply suspicious of the loyalty of Indian Muslims who were showing such enthusiasm for the cause of the Sultan of Turkey. He wanted to define a nation that would not have to grant equal citizenship to Muslims or Christians. If you think about it carefully, Savarkar was the one who, long before Muhammad Ali Jinnah (who was then a moderate and thoroughly liberal-minded Congress politician repelled by the Gandhian turn to mass politics), first formulated a consistent two-nation theory for India, except he did not believe the Muslims deserved a separate state; they must live like a subjugated nation within Hindusthan.

Savarkar's definition of Hindutva depends on several claims that are thoroughly dubious. The imagined picture of a sovereign Hindu state, stretching from the Indus in the north to Sri Lanka in the south, under the rule of Ramchandra of Ayodhya is myth, not history. There is no evidence that anyone can show of the existence of an Indian kingdom of any great size before the Mauryas, and even that empire was confined largely to northern India. The idea of a Hindu race of common blood, based on the indiscriminate mixing of Aryas with non-Aryas, is also a myth. There was undoubtedly a mixing of the Arya people with others who lived in the country but it makes no sense to speak in any meaningful way of all those who today call themselves Hindu as possessing a common blood. Savarkar had actually adopted a pseudo-scientific language that was very common in his time in Europe. It was a language that grew out of notions of the purity and impurity of blood which produced excellence and degeneration among races. These ideas were influential among European nationalists and gave rise to the ideology of the racial superiority of Aryans preached by the Nazis in Germany. There is much evidence that Savarkar, and several of his associates, greatly admired the Nazis for their martial nationalism. It is another matter that Hitler and the Nazis had great contempt for Indians as a thoroughly inferior race which deserved to be subservient to European imperialists.

Savarkar's invocation of a common Hindu civilisation, formed by languages that are all derived from Sanskrit, and stored in literature, law, art, and festivals shared by every sect and caste in India except Muslims and Christians, is an assertion sustained only by his loud rhetoric. No serious analysis of social and cultural practices that actually exist among the peoples of India will uphold his claim. There is no ground for declaring that all Indian languages become accessible to Hindus because they are all derived from Sanskrit. Telugu or Tamil is not comprehensible to those who only speak Punjabi or Gujarati. There is some tradition of translation of literature from one Indian language to another, but it has so far made only a very tiny part of each regional literature available to readers elsewhere in India. Far more influential has been the recent circulation of stories and music through the radio, cinema, and television. But that circulation does not make all regional cultures equally accessible; there are huge biases which we must discuss later. To be fair to Savarkar, he was writing in an age when this development of audio and visual technology was still in the future. But even in his time, could he have said that Mundari or Santali was part of the Sanskrit-derived Hindu culture? His claim of a common Hindu sanskriti shared throughout India which, at the same time, excluded Muslims and Christians, is an unsustainable contention.

Most cultural communities in this country have been built regionally, even locally, around literary languages, popular festivals, and folk art and performance. There is no question that there is greater mutual understanding among the Christians, Muslims, and Hindus of Kerala than there is between a Malayali Hindu and a Kashmiri Hindu. Savarkar's insistence that Hindu sanskriti exists irrespective of divisions of caste and sect reflects his desire to reform the many discriminatory practices among Hindus, but it turns that future goal into the wishful claim that it is a permanent feature of Hindu civilisation. There are food habits or rituals practised by Dalit groups in India that upper castes would not accept as Hindu at all. Would those who claim to be leaders of Hindu culture in Varanasi or Ahmedabad accept that Hindu sanskriti allows the eating of pork or beef, as Dalits do in many parts of the country? Those who follow the Vaishnav faith are repelled by the Shakta practice of animal sacrifice which is common in Assam, Bengal, and Nepal and refuse to accept it as part of Hindu culture. And even though Adivasi groups in central India may have adopted some elements of the Brahmanical religion, they follow many traditions that are entirely their own which Hindus will never accept as belonging to Hindu culture at all.

If the question is that of regarding places within India as sacred, millions of Muslims all over South Asia consider the shrines at Ajmer Sharif or Nizamuddin in Delhi as among the holiest places of pilgrimage. You must have heard qawalis in which the singer declares that Ajmer is his Medina and the sheikh's tomb his Kaaba. Do not Indian Catholics regard the relics of St Francis Xavier preserved in Goa as supremely holy? If a feeling of sacred attachment to the land is the criterion to determine loyalty to the nation, is it justified to assert an *a priori* condition (*pūrvānumān*) to exclude all Muslims and Christians?

It is the same as saying that they cannot even be allowed to demonstrate their patriotism: they are unqualified by definition.

If you look at it carefully, you will see that while Savarkar makes such a song and dance about distinguishing the political concept of Hindutva from the religious concept of Hinduism, when he gets down to the task of defining Hindutva, he actually smuggles in religion through the back door. His idea of Hindu sanskriti cannot work without resorting to religious literature such as the Ramayana or the Guru Granth Sahib or the vachana of Basavanna, pilgrimage sites such as Varanasi or Vrindavan, festivals such as the Rathayatra or the Kumbh Mela. His political impulse is to try his best to make the criteria of nationhood as inclusive as possible so as to bring in not only those conventionally regarded as Hindus but all Dalit castes and Adivasis as well as those who follow anti-Vedic religions such as Buddhism, Jainism, and Sikhism. The criterion of holy land (*pitribhu*) allows him to do this, but only, as I have shown you, by bringing in religion in the guise of Hindu culture. What he then does is exclude Muslims and Christians from the nation by insisting that they cannot consider India as their holy land.

I must add that Savarkar was very much against the social exclusion of Dalit castes and, from the 1930s, became a strong advocate of inter-marriage and inter-dining across castes, but refused to include Muslims and Christians in that extended social circle. His first play, *Saṅgīt uhśāp*, written in 1927, is a story of two Mahar women inspired by the message of Sant Chokhamela, the Dalit Varkari saint. The two women are on pilgrimage to Pandharpur when they are lured and molested by Muslim men who try to convert them forcibly, but they survive, thanks to their unswerving faith in Chokha.[12] In other Marathi writings, he argued against superstition and caste discrimination

---

[12] This play is included in V.D. Savarkar, *Samagra Sāvarkar vāṅmaya*, vol. 7, pp. 419–538. Chokhamela was a fourteenth-century *sant* of the Varkari devotional sect. He was born in a Mahar family.

and called for greater social and personal freedom of women. He also described himself as an atheist and was merciless in his rationalist criticism of the practices of Sanatan Dharma. For instance, he called the cow a useful animal but not a mother of humans and definitely not a goddess. He asked: how can you regard an animal which eats garbage and sits on its own excrement as a goddess and treat a superbly learned man like Dr Ambedkar as unclean? If you go by the Puranas and believe that Vishnu was born as the *varāha avatār*, then you might as well worship the pig. These bitingly sarcastic articles by Savarkar on the absurdities of Hindu religious practices were put together in a Marathi book which he called *Kṣa-kiraṇe*: he was showing x-ray plates of the insides of Hinduism! I think Hindutva propagandists today are embarrassed by the atheist and rationalist side of Savarkar and prefer not to talk about these writings. You should ask a Marathi friend to find this book for you.[13]

Written in 1923, Savarkar's book *Hindutva* could not have dealt with the specific debates over communal representation, minority rights, the rights of untouchable castes and tribes, or the partition of the country that dominated Indian politics in subsequent decades. Although he was active in the Hindu Mahasabha until his death in 1966 and wrote prolifically in both Marathi and English, he did not elaborate on the implications of his idea of Hindutva for the questions of nationality and citizenship in independent India. In any case, the standing of the Hindu Mahasabha went into decline after Gandhi's assassination. A new political party, the Bharatiya Jana Sangh, emerged in the 1950s as the voice of Hindu nationalism. But the most influential organisation that carried forward Savarkar's idea of Hindutva was the Rashtriya Swayamsevak Sangh (RSS). I must now tell you that story.

---

[13] This book of essays by Savarkar was published under the title *Kṣa-kiraṇe* (Pune: Godbole Granth Bhandar, 1950).

## Hindutva and Citizenship

Keshav Hedgewar established the RSS in Nagpur in 1925. Earlier, as a medical student in Calcutta, he had come in contact with the revolutionaries of the Anushilan Samiti and went on to participate in the Non-Cooperation movement. But he was much disturbed by the Hindu–Muslim riots that broke out in parts of the country in 1923 and felt it necessary to start an organisation dedicated to the regeneration of Hindu society. The RSS was to be an organisation of disciplined volunteers who would campaign to rouse national consciousness among Hindus but stay out of politics. Although individual members did sometimes take part, the RSS did not join the Civil Disobedience or Quit India movements. Hedgewar seemed especially concerned not to involve the organisation in any activity against the British colonial government.

When Hedgewar died in 1940, he was succeeded as head of the RSS by Madhav Golwalkar. The previous year, Golwalkar had published a tract in English called *We or Our Nationhood Defined* in which he clarified the idea of a Hindu Rashtra in the context of the communal politics of the time.[14] While providing a new gloss on Savarkar's idea of the Hindu nation, Golwalkar insisted that he was not entering into the vexed subject of majorities and minorities, but only clarifying the definition of the nation. Yet in doing so, he laid out the principles on which he believed citizenship ought to be based within the Indian state.

Golwalkar was not as subtle a thinker as Savarkar. Whereas Savarkar had crafted a new and challenging concept to describe Hindutva as a national political ideology, Golwalkar, even as he followed Savarkar, resorted to a mechanical combination of factors to arrive at his definition of the nation. There were

---

[14] The original edition was published as M.S. Golwalkar, *We or Our Nationhood Defined* (Nagpur: Bharat Publications, 1939), with a foreword by M.S. Aney.

five elements, he said, all of which must be present at the same time for a nation to exist. These were country, race, religion, culture, and language.

According to Golwalkar, a nation must have its own hereditary homeland, marked by natural geographical boundaries. Interestingly, he gave the examples of the Jews and the Parsis as people who had been thrown out of their original home countries and were therefore no longer nations. The Hindu nation, he says, is old because it has a hereditary homeland, stretching from the Himalayas in the north to the seas in the south, which it has occupied for centuries.

The second factor – race – is one to which Golwalkar gives a lot of attention and calls it the most important ingredient of a nation. He was clearly much influenced by current European theories of racial purity and the superiority of some races and the inferiority of others. Thus, he heaped praises on Germany for its racial pride which had enabled it to claim its own homeland and get rid of those foreign elements which could never be assimilated into the race. He had no hesitation in claiming that the way Germany had dealt with the Jews held a significant lesson for India. Race, he said, was the body of the nation; if it degenerates, the nation dies. Golwalkar also makes a feeble attempt to argue that the idea of *jāti* is the same as race and hence the nation was a concept well known in India for centuries. To establish this, he cites the logician Gautama, author of the *Nyāyasūtra*, who defined *jāti* as *samānaprasavātmikā*, which literally means sharing a common origin or birth. Strangely, Golwalkar insists that *ātmikā* here indicates a racial fellow feeling; perhaps he thought it had something to do with the *ātmā* of a *jāti*. Hence, he argues, the sense of nationhood existed among Hindus from ancient times. He completely ignores the most common meaning of the word *jāti* in India which divides people into endogamous castes that are ranked one on top of the other in terms of status and authority. Besides, he also overlooks the fact that in the Nyāya system of logic, *jāti* is a technical term (*paribhāṣā*) which means the universal or common property (*sāmānya*) of a group or class of things. In this sense, one may speak of the human *jāti* whose universal property is humanness (*manuṣyatva*) or the animal *jāti* whose universal property is animal-ness (*paśutva*), even though individual humans or animals may differ from one another. Nowhere does this indicate anything like the race spirit of which Golwalkar was so fond.

There is no doubt that the source of his idea of race comes from modern Europe. Driven by that idea, Golwalkar insists that Hindus are an old nation whose race spirit did not die out even when they were under the domination of the Muslims and the British. The revolt of 1857, he says, was the last great attempt by the Hindu nation to defeat its racial enemies. Even though the attempt failed, the Hindu rebels have become objects of worship. He conveniently forgets that Hindus were not the only ones who rebelled in 1857.

Unlike Savarkar, Golwalkar does not bother with the problem of the variety of sects and beliefs among those who are called Hindus. He simply asserts that they have a religion which is woven into their culture and which cannot be kept out of their political life. He argues that all European nations are Christian. Indeed, a nation cannot truly exist without a religion. Even the Soviet Union, which rejects religion and claims to be atheist, actually has a religion which is Socialism. Golwalkar also made no secret of his belief that the doctrines and practices of the Sanatan Dharma, with its foundation in Vedic ritual and the varnashram system, represented the true Hindu religion. In various speeches delivered before and after independence, he claimed that the Advaita Vedanta represented the typical philosophy of the country because it declared that all particular religious doctrines were expressions of the same cosmic spirit. This philosophy of tolerance, by also insisting that individuals must occupy different social stations according to their innate qualifications (*adhikārābhed*), also ensured social harmony and prevented class war. He was against communism because it emphasised only material interests. He was also against democracy because it celebrated individual rights which, according to him, only meant the right of the few to exploit the many. The ideal state, he said, must be based on duties, not rights.[15]

He also believed that the Brahmans of northern India were the original repositories of religious knowledge and had trained and civilised people living in other parts of the country in the precepts of Hindu religion and culture. I remember him making a speech in Ahmedabad, perhaps in 1961 or 1962, in which he said that Namboodiri Brahmans went from the north to Kerala in order to have children with lower-caste women and thereby raise the racial quality of the people.[16] The caste system had, in fact, laid a solid foundation for Hindu society. Hence, in East Bengal, where the caste order was weak, there was mass conversion to Islam, whereas in northern India, where it was strong, Hindu society was able to withstand centuries of oppression by Muslim rulers.[17] There is no question that on the

---

[15] The first chapter, entitled "Our World Mission", of Golwalkar's selection of speeches and writings makes all of these points. M.S. Golwalkar, *Bunch of Thoughts* (1960).

[16] I have found one reference to a remark of this kind made by Golwalkar. Speaking at Gujarat University in December 1960, he said: "In an effort to better the human species through cross-breeding the Namboodri Brahmanas of the North were settled in Kerala and a rule was laid down that the eldest son of a Namboodri family could marry only the daughter of Vaishya, Kshatriya or Shudra communities of Kerala. Another still more courageous rule was laid down that the first off-spring of a married woman of any class must be fathered by a Namboodri Brahmin and then she could beget children by her husband. Today this experiment will be called adultery but it was not so, as it was limited to the first child." *Organiser*, 2 January 1961, cited in Shamsul Islam's Introduction to the reprint of *We or Our Nationhood Defined* (New Delhi: Pharos Media, 2018), p. 34.

[17] Chapter 10, entitled "Children of the Motherland", in *Bunch of Thoughts*, contains an argument along these lines.

subject of caste, Golwalkar's views were completely different from those of Savarkar.

On the question of language, Golwalkar insists that Sanskrit is the language of all Hindus since all regional languages of India were dialects derived from the mother language. It is a mistake, he says, to think that India is a country with many languages. He rejects the distinction made by linguists between Indo-European and Dravidian languages as a European ploy to divide Indians. Besides, nowhere in his book does he consider the people of north-eastern India who, for his purposes, are not part of the nation. He also says that Hindi had emerged as a common medium for people of different parts of the country to communicate with one another. He ignores the fact that except for a tiny group of scholars, no one in India can speak, read, or write Sanskrit.

According to Golwalkar, the combination of five elements defines the modern concept of the nation. The definition is applicable worldwide. Every true nation, even when it claims to follow religious toleration, insists that those who come from elsewhere must accept that there is a state religion, adopt the national language, merge with the national culture, and share the memories and aspirations of the national race. These "shrewd and experienced old nations", he says, like England, France and the United States, do not recognise the existence of minorities with special rights. Hindusthan too, according to him, must be the exclusive home of the Hindu nation, that is, the Hindu race with its own religion, culture, and language. Those who do not fall within this definition cannot be a part of the nation.[18]

---

[18] Golwalkar says: "Thus applying the modern understanding of 'Nation' to our present conditions, the conclusion is unquestionably forced upon us that in this country, Hindusthan, the Hindu Race with its Hindu Religion, Hindu Culture and Hindu Language . . . complete the Nation concept; that, in fine, in Hindusthan exists and must needs exist the ancient Hindu nation and nought else but the Hindu Nation. All those not belonging to the

What happens to those who live in India but cannot be included within the Hindu nation? Where Savarkar had been silent, presumably because in 1923 the question of citizenship in an independent India had not yet been formulated, Golwalkar, writing in 1939, is unambiguous. Such people have only two choices. They must merge themselves within the Hindu race and adopt Hindu culture, or they must live at the mercy of the Hindu race which has the right to throw them out whenever it wishes. There are no other options.[19] Golwalkar launched a fierce attack on the Indian National Congress for coaxing the Muslims of India to join the freedom movement. The idea that everyone who lives in India is part of the nation is tantamount to treating the country as a traveller's inn. Calling it the "serai theory of the nation", Golwalkar describes its proponents as either fools or traitors.[20] The Hindus have two enemies: the Muslims and the British. It is self-deception to believe that by making concessions to Muslims in trying to nationalise them, we are strengthening the fight against the British.

Running through Golwalkar's entire discussion on Hindu nationhood is the desire for a strong centralised state. Any recognition of the rights of minorities would, he believes, weaken

---

national *i.e.* Hindu Race, Religion, Culture and Language, naturally fall out of the pale of real 'National' life." *We or Our Nationhood Defined*, pp. 43–4.

[19] Golwalkar's exact words are: "There are only two courses open to the foreign elements, either to merge themselves in the national race and adopt its culture, or to live at its mercy so long as the national race may allow them to do so and to quit the country at the sweet will of the national race. That is the only sound view on the minorities problem." *We or Our Nationhood Defined*, p. 47.

[20] In Golwalkar's words: "Consequently, only those movements are truly 'National' as aim at re-building, re-vitalising and emancipating from its present stupor, the Hindu Nation. Those only are nationalist patriots . . . All others are either traitors and enemies to the National cause, or, to take a charitable view, idiots." *We or Our Nationhood Defined*, p. 44.

the edifice of the state. National integration, a slogan widely used in official propaganda in the 1950s and 1960s to bring minority religions and cultures into public life, was, according to Golwalkar, misdirected. True national integration could only be achieved by what he called *parākramāvād* or vigorous assimilation into Hindu national culture.[21] When demands were made in the 1950s for the creation of linguistic states, Golwalkar and the RSS were firmly against the idea which, they thought, would breed separatism. In fact, Golwalkar was against the idea of federalism itself and believed that the Indian constitution should be rewritten to create a unitary and centralised state.[22] In a similar vein, he also believed that the question of caste and other forms of social inequality and discrimination within the nation must not be confused with that of the stability and power of the state. Looking back at history, he suggested that periods when the country had a strong state, such as at the time of Harsha, were also when the caste system was rigidly imposed and illiteracy prevailed, but that did not get in the way of the power of the state. These internal problems were irrelevant to the task of strengthening the unity and stability of the nation-state which had to be given the highest priority.

### The Hindu Rashtra

You have probably been told by your friends that the RSS and the BJP do not subscribe to many of the specific positions taken by Savarkar and Golwalkar in the matter of minorities. Indeed, you may have even heard that *We or Our Nationhood Defined* was not written by Golwalkar at all. Let me tell you that that is a complete lie. I have with me a copy of the book published

[21] This argument is spelt out, for instance, in Chapter 11, "For a Virile National Life", in *Bunch of Thoughts*.
[22] A clear statement of this position is in Chapter 18 entitled "Wanted a Unitary State" in *Bunch of Thoughts*.

in 1939 in which Madhav Srihari Aney, a senior leader close to the Hindu Mahasabha, explains in a lengthy foreword his approval as well as disagreements with the author Golwalkar. There is no question that the two knew each other well. Aney could not have written this foreword to a book not written by Golwalkar. Besides, Golwalkar's views expressed in his speeches and writings after independence are quite consistent with those set out in his 1939 book. So don't get taken in by that disingenuous attempt to disclaim Golwalkar because the RSS and the BJP are now embarrassed by some of his views.

It is true that because of the compulsions of national electoral politics, both the BJP and the RSS have attempted to spread their influence and win support among Dalit and Adivasi populations. In the Northeast, even as the RSS has opened many schools and health camps, it has made adjustments with the predominantly Christian culture of the tribal peoples. But it still believes, like Savarkar and Golwalkar, that Islam and Christianity are foreign cultural influences which, unless controlled and, if possible, eradicated, will corrupt the Hindu national culture. In recent years, the Western ideologies of secular liberalism and communism have been added to the list of cultural threats that must be fought.

Politically, since the BJP has accepted electoral democracy, the effort has been to consolidate the Hindu majority in its favour, especially in northern and western India. Its claim is that in a democracy, the voice of the majority must prevail, even in matters of culture. This is the ground on which it has pressed for a ban on the sale of beef, serving only vegetarian food in official gatherings and public institutions, official sponsorship of Hindu festivals, changing Muslim place names to Hindu ones, insistence on the use of Hindi in all official communication, and so on. Alongside, it has carried out a sustained campaign through schools, textbooks, newsmagazines, and more recently social media, to spread the ideology of Hindu nationalism by circulating its own version of Indian history and culture. As you know, it has been quite successful in its effort, especially in northern and western India.

What is the Hindu Rashtra project today? I have often put this question to those who strongly believe in Hindu nationalism. Some of them have the most fantastic ideas about Akhand Bharat, stretching from Iran to Malaysia and Indonesia, and including Tibet since Kailash and Manasarovar are sacred places for Hindus. They imagine this immense territory as one over which Hindus had once exercised cultural dominance and which they should now try to reunite within some new political form. I point out that if such a single entity did emerge, Hindus would not be in a majority within it. They are not deterred by this argument, because it turns out that their imagined Akhand Bharat is not a democracy based on universal adult suffrage where each person has one vote. They imagine Bharat as an empire – a *sāmrājya* as in ancient or medieval times – where far-flung territories are conquered and brought within its sovereign jurisdiction. Hindus will be the ruling race in this imagined empire and others will be subject peoples.

Of course, not everyone is as reckless as this in describing the Hindu Rashtra. Nevertheless, they are unhappy with the existing borders of the country. They refuse to accept the finality of the partition of India in 1947, blaming Gandhi and the Congress for it. They see no distinction between Pakistan and Bangladesh: both are Muslim countries where Hindus are oppressed. They see 1971 as a missed opportunity when, instead of accepting a peace settlement with Pakistan, India should have pressed home its advantage and allowed its army to take the whole of Kashmir. In fact, occupying Pakistani lands might have even led to the collapse of Pakistan. They completely dismiss the problem of governing a population that may be unwilling to become a part of India. The territory of Kashmir is, for them, landed property that belongs to the Indian nation. Those who live there must be either assimilated or subjugated by force. When I tell them that Vallabhbhai Patel, the realist politician they admire so much, was completely aware of the difficulty of securing the willing co-operation of the people of Kashmir in 1947, which is why he was happy to give up India's claim to that state in exchange for the accession of Hyderabad, they don't believe me.

Other Hindu nationalists are more realistic in accepting that the partition cannot be undone. They argue that, in that case, the logical step is to arrange for a complete transfer of populations: Muslims must be forced to migrate to Muslim countries and Hindus living in Pakistan and Bangladesh must be rehabilitated in India. That is in fact the thinking that lies behind the amendment of 2019 to the Citizenship Act and the call for a National Register of Citizens in the whole country. Those steps are part of the realist strategy of establishing the Hindu Rashtra.

I have only told you about the project of Hindu Rashtra insofar as it is supported by political arguments. These arguments are false. But it is also propagated and acted upon by emotions of anger, jealousy, and hatred fostered by deeply held prejudices that cannot be justified by any rational reasoning. Thus, many Hindus believe that because Muslim men are allowed to have four wives, Muslims multiply much faster. The argument is logically absurd, because there is no reason why a woman should bear more children if she shares a husband with three other women rather than have one exclusively to herself. But the male-centred view of the world persuades some people that if a man has four wives, the community to which he belongs will have more children. This is a classic example of blind prejudice (*andhăpūrvāgraha*), that is, a firm conclusion drawn before looking at the evidence. Many Hindus also believe that Muslim men pretend to fall in love with Hindu women in order to convert them to Islam by promising to marry them. This is supposed to be jihad carried out by other means. Once again, apart from attributing dishonest motives to Muslim men, this prejudice completely rules out the possibility that a Hindu woman who marries a Muslim man might have a will of her own. It assumes that women are the property of their male relatives and hence of the community in which they were born.

The belief that Muslims who have no livelihood in Bangladesh are coming in their thousands into India, merging with the local population, and swelling the ranks of Muslims in India's border districts is widely held, even by leading figures in many walks of life in India. No one is prepared to examine the economic and social conditions in the receiving country that make such migrations possible. When I point to the thousands of Indians, including possibly the relatives and friends of those I am talking to, who are desperately seeking to migrate to Western countries, and ask why they are so upset if the United States or Britain imposes new restrictions on immigration, they refuse to accept that the two examples are equivalent. According to them, Indians want to migrate to the West to find a better life for themselves and a more promising future for their children; they add to the wealth of those countries. Illegal Muslim migration into India, they say, is part of a dangerous plan to bring about another partition of India.

That is how prejudice operates to motivate ordinary Hindus to regard every Muslim as an enemy and a threat to the Hindu nation. When political conditions are right, that is, when people believe they will not be punished for acting against Muslims, small groups of Hindus will fall upon a defenceless Muslim, beat him to death and boast about it on a YouTube video. The most cowardly acts of violence will turn them into heroes. This is what has been happening, particularly in northern India, in the last five or six years.

There is also the mindless obsession with Pakistan as the implacable enemy whose presence must be shunned and, if encountered, thoroughly defeated. Sportsmen, film actors, and musicians from Pakistan must not be allowed to perform in India. Cricket matches with Pakistan must be treated like lethal warfare. Since Pakistan is known to harbour terrorists, every Muslim must be looked upon with suspicion. It is useless to point out that, before independence, there were Hindus who used the method of assassination to spread terror: they are now revered as national heroes. Not so long ago, Tamil Hindu militants from Sri Lanka were the ones who first made repeated use of the method of suicide bombing a political weapon. No matter how much we may disapprove of the terrorist tactics used by jihadi militants – I don't support them at all – it still does not justify regarding every Muslim with suspicion. But prejudice thrives outside the domain of reason. A history professor once told me that when barbarians were attacking the Roman Empire, the citizens of Rome were envious of the freedom enjoyed by the invaders who were not bound by any norms of civilised behaviour. Secretly, Romans wanted to be like the barbarians. When I talk to Hindu nationalists today, not only do I see them thinking along the lines of the two-nation theory, but I also notice that they want to replicate in their Hindu Rashtra every retrograde feature of Pakistan as it exists today. Envy of Pakistan's ability to oppose India creates the desire to emulate that country and become Pakistan's bitterest and most unscrupulous enemy.

Of course, from December 2019 the project of Hindu Rashtra faced a challenge in the countrywide protests against the Citizenship Amendment Act. The protesters opposed the move to introduce religion into the definition of citizenship by reasserting the values of equality and diversity promised in the Preamble to the Indian Constitution. I don't know what your views are on the debate over the new Citizenship Act. But I am sure you were struck by the spontaneous energy behind the mobilisation of students and young people in so many cities and towns all over India. You must have also seen how thousands of women who had never before participated in a political demonstration came out to join rallies and sit for days in dharnas. Many observers remarked that no political movement has so touched the soul of the nation since the days of the struggle for independence. I think they were right. Of course, all that was overtaken and forgotten by the panic unleashed by the Covid epidemic.

But I would like to stoke your memory of those days in early 2020, because I am now going to tell you what is true and what is false about our sovereign, secular, socialist, democratic republic which promises justice, equality, liberty, and fraternity to its citizens.

# 5

# India is Not a Pluralist Secular Democracy

GANDHI AND NEHRU – these are the two names most remembered when you speak of the founders of the Indian republic. There were a lot of differences in their political views, even though the latter was, most of the time, a dutiful follower of the former in the Congress organisation. When it came to the question of how they imagined the bonds that unite the Indian nation, the big difference was that Gandhi believed the bond existed in the ordinary religious practices of Indians who had learnt to live together over centuries despite belonging to different religious groups, whereas Nehru discovered those bonds in the history of Indian empires and states. I will now show you how those very well-intentioned opinions, which they shared with many other distinguished leaders and thinkers, ended up privileging some groups over others, leading to ill-conceived and inconsistent political compromises that ultimately led to the failure of a pluralist state (*bahulātāvādī rājya*) to stop the Hindu nationalist onslaught.

### Pluralist Religious Society

I will not waste time giving you quotations from Gandhi. I am told that more than a hundred thick volumes have been published of his collected works. He never claimed to be a scholar and did not write a treatise (*śāstra*) on any subject. His writings, mostly short articles, besides his letters and speeches, have been compiled in those collected volumes. It is possible to find stray remarks by Gandhi to support almost any claim you wish to make for or against him. Let us avoid that fruitless pursuit.

In broad terms, Gandhi believed that Indians were a religious people and that Indian society was held together by religion. By religion, he did not usually mean the Sanskrit Dharmashastra texts which, he often said, contained gross untruths such as the approval of untouchability or the cruel treatment of women. What he meant was the lived practice of religion in the daily lives of ordinary people. These practices varied from region to region, from one locality to another. But everywhere, there was a common truth which was a mutual respect for the ways of living of others. This sometimes meant mutually agreed rules of separation: we will not interfere when you carry your idols in a procession, just as you will not play music in front of our mosques when we pray. Rules of separation had been worked out and were well understood. Not every space or every occasion was open to all. But there were also mutually observed rules of where and when people from different religions or sects could come together. You did not have to be a Muslim to take a vow (*mannat*) at a Sufi shrine (*dargāh*), just as Hindus would gladly offer sweets to their Muslim neighbours at Diwali. Outside the strict control of scripture and rules of orthodoxy, this was the ordinary religious life, which, Gandhi believed, contained the essential truth of religious tolerance.

Even at the level of daily life in the locality, not every rule or convention met with his approval. Gandhi had a unique ability to dismiss as untrue any evidence from history or any existing local practice that differed from his understanding of truth. If you told him that Hindus and Muslims, or Shaivas and

Vaishnavas, or Shias and Sunnis, had a long history of enmity in a particular area, he would say that history is only a record of human folly. The historical evidence of conflict was a very good reason why people should forget that past and agree to live together in peace. If the local practice in a village was that certain castes must not enter the temple or draw water from the tank, he would say that the practice was wrong; it must be changed. In other words, Gandhi held the belief that tolerance and non-violence were truths that were ingrained in every religion. If particular religious texts or rules said something else, those should be discarded as false instructions, inconsistent with true religion.

Gandhi never concealed the fact that he was an observant Hindu, adhering mainly to the practices of the Vaishnav way of life he had learnt from his family in Gujarat, even though he often famously engaged in many spiritual experiments. In his political life, even as he struggled to build alliances with Muslim leaders to fight against British rule, teach the ethics of non-violence, and eradicate the sin of untouchability, he did so as a Hindu. His location was never within some secular space of the state, unmarked by religious difference. Even as a declared Hindu, he was, surprisingly, invited by imams across the country to address the Friday *jamāt* in the days of the Non-Cooperation movement. You might say that it was because Gandhi spoke of Hindu–Muslim fraternity as a devout Hindu and not as a secular politician that he found so much friendship and trust among devout Muslims.

Then why did Gandhi fail in his attempt to keep the country together? To give you a short answer, I think it was because he put the entire burden of maintaining tolerance and harmony on the self-regulating mechanisms of society. Religious leaders and community elders, he believed, would use their authority to persuade people to avoid the path of hatred and violence. Gandhi was fundamentally against the use of government machinery or the law to influence or change religious customs, even when he agreed that those customs might be harmful or unjust. He often said he was an enlightened anarchist.[1] Whatever he might have meant by that, he certainly believed that if social practices needed to be changed, it had to be done by persuasion and not by the force of law.

It is not true, of course, that in earlier times kings or ministers never interfered in religious matters. They frequently did – not only when, as you often hear, Muslim rulers destroyed Hindu temples or Buddhist viharas, but when Hindu rulers in different parts of the country favoured one sect (*sampradāy*) over others or persecuted a particular sect. But Gandhi, true to character, dismissed these instances as aberrations that should not be repeated. What he could not avoid, however, was the effect of government policies – designed not for purposes of supervising religion but for regulating property and inheritance or securing representation in legislatures – spilling over into the daily lives of society. No matter how much Gandhi wished otherwise, local societies began to respond to political leaders who wanted to demonstrate the numbers that must be counted under this or that classification of communities. Social self-regulation of the Gandhian kind became a victim of the politics of majorities and minorities.

I will discuss later how the politics of numbers ended up converting Gandhi, the paragon of Hindu–Muslim unity in the

---

[1] The manuscript has "enlightened anarchist" in English with *aqlmand arājakatāvādī* in parentheses. Gandhi did describe his vision of the ideal state in these terms, as, for instance, in the following: "The power to control national life through national representatives is called political power. Representatives will become unnecessary if the national life becomes so perfect as to be self-controlled. It will then be a state of enlightened anarchy in which each person will become his own ruler ... In an ideal State there will be no political institution and therefore no political power." "Enlightened Anarchy: A Political Ideal", *Collected Works of Mahatma Gandhi*, vol. 68 (New Delhi: Publications Division, 1965), p. 265.

days of the Non-Cooperation movement, into a leader of the Hindus negotiating with the leader of the Muslims the terms under which the British would leave India. But the paradox of Gandhi's relation to the Hindu religion became particularly striking in his conflict with Bhimrao Ambedkar over the representation of the so-called Depressed Classes.

Ambedkar firmly believed in the need to use the powers of the modern state to change unjust social practices such as caste oppression, even when they were supposedly sanctioned by religion. As a student, he had lived for a few years in the United States and had studied the history of the abolition of slavery and the struggles of Black people to overcome racial discrimination. He was convinced that the practice of untouchability and the downtrodden condition of the *avarṇa* castes could only be removed by deploying the full force of law of a state committed to liberal reform. When British officials went about consulting Indian leaders on the proposed constitutional reforms (which would be enacted in 1935), Ambedkar strongly argued that the Depressed Classes, as the untouchable castes were then called in the census, must be treated as a minority community not included among Hindus and, like Muslims, given separate electorates and reserved representation in the provincial legislatures. Otherwise, if they were counted among Hindus, they would not have the numerical strength to influence elections in the general constituencies and so would end up without any representation in the legislature.

Ambedkar was successful in making his case. In 1932, Ramsay MacDonald, the British prime minister, announced the so-called Communal Award in which the Depressed Classes were given separate electorates and reserved seats in the new legislatures. Gandhi, then detained in Yerawada jail in Poona, went on a fast demanding the scrapping of this provision. He had always insisted that Harijans, as he preferred to call the untouchable castes, were an integral part of the Hindu community. It was the religious duty of Hindus to remove the practices of social exclusion that had prevented Harijans from fully participating in the religious and social life of the community. But on no account must the organs of the state be allowed to divide the Hindus on the basis of caste and grant political recognition to the Depressed Classes as a separate community.

Several mediators tried to bring about a compromise between Gandhi and Ambedkar. But the latter was unwilling to give up a legal protection he had won for his community after much effort, while the former was insistent that Harijans must not be recognised as a minority community similar to Muslims. But with Gandhi's health beginning to fail because of his fast, Ambedkar was put in an impossible position. Reluctantly, he agreed to a compromise by which the Depressed Classes remained within the general electorate but a certain number of seats were reserved for them in the legislature. This is roughly the position that continues into the electoral system created by the Indian constitution after independence. Ambedkar had to give up his claim that the Dalit castes were a minority community outside the fold of the Hindu religion.

I will come back later to the question of caste. What is important for you to note here is that Gandhi's faith in the self-regulating nature of social life in the localities was repeatedly shaken by the growing demand, on one side, that the new mechanism of electoral representation recognise the numerical strength of majority communities and, on the other, that the interests of minority communities be protected. As early as 1916, leaders of the Congress and the Muslim League arrived at a pact in Lucknow to accept separate representation of Muslims in provincial legislatures. I should point out that both Gandhi and Jinnah were present at this meeting – Jinnah as a member of the Congress and Gandhi as someone who had just arrived from South Africa. By 1919, when the Congress adopted the Non-Cooperation programme, the question of participating in legislatures was set aside and the Lucknow pact was forgotten. But soon, even as Hindu–Muslim amity was at its peak, there was a split in the Congress on whether or not to take part in the elected legislatures created by the constitutional reforms of 1919. The Gandhians were firmly against participating in elections in which only a tiny section of propertied Indians could vote, but the Swarajists wanted to use every institution, both inside and outside government, to mobilise support for the national cause and oppose the colonial bureaucracy. But to work as an electoral party with support from both Muslims and Hindus, the Swarajist Congress had to work out specific agreements on fair representation of the two communities. In Bengal, for instance, where the Swarajists were led by Chitta Ranjan Das, a pact was drawn up in 1923 to reserve 55 per cent of government jobs and 60 per cent of membership in local government for Muslims in Muslim-majority districts. This ensured tremendous Muslim participation in the Congress in Bengal. But after Das' death in 1925, the pact fell apart because Hindu leaders refused to abide by it. This started the drift of Muslim support away from the Congress in Bengal.

The point I wish to stress is that no matter how much Gandhi might have wanted to keep the tentacles of government classifications, representation and jobs away from the local consensus on practices of religious tolerance, they could not be kept apart. In fact, as Indian political leaders began to gain entry into local and provincial branches of government through elections, even though only a small number were given the right to vote, they began to organise themselves along lines of religion and caste to make demands on representation and jobs on the basis of numbers. The Gandhian claim of the inherent qualities of tolerance and non-violence in Indian society at its grassroots became more and more difficult to sustain.

### The Philosophy of Pluralism

Gandhi was less interested in the philosophical doctrines of religion than in the lived practices among the people. There was a different approach taken by those who were learned in the sacred texts to make the same point – that the Hindu religion taught tolerance and respect for all religions. Swami Vivekananda was one of the first among them. In his Chicago address of 1893, which you must have heard quoted many times, he announced to the world that the Hindu religion believed in universal toleration and accepted all religions as true. Using a metaphor that occurs frequently in Sanskrit texts, he described the many religions of the world as streams that sprang from different sources but flowed into the same river. But he added that toleration meant that no one should try to convert others: Christians must not attempt to turn Hindus or Buddhists into Christians, just as Hindus or Buddhists must not convert Christians to their faith.[2] Interestingly, in his speech, although he mentioned Jews and Zoroastrians as communities which had been given shelter in India, Vivekananda did not once mention Islam as a religion that was also practised by many in the country.

Many learned men followed Vivekananda in making the same argument by drawing on the Sanskrit philosophical tradition. A particular favourite was the philosophy of Advaita Vedanta which came in handy in expounding the most commonly repeated slogan about Indian civilisation: unity in diversity. Non-dualist metaphysics (*advaita darśan*) proposes that the three textual traditions of the Upanishads, the Brahma Sutras, and the Bhagavad Gita be interpreted to show their mutual consistency, despite the many differences among them.

---

[2] Vivekananda said at the opening session: "I am proud to belong to a religion which has taught the world both tolerance and universal acceptance. We believe not only in universal toleration, but we accept all religions as true." Speech at the World Parliament of Religions in Chicago, 11 September 1893. In the closing session, he said: "The Christian is not to become a Hindu or a Buddhist, nor a Hindu or a Buddhist a Christian. But each must assimilate the spirit of the others and yet preserve his individuality and grow according to his own law of growth." Speech at the Final Session, 27 September 1893.

This is the idea that was seized upon by many Indian thinkers in the early-twentieth century to argue that the essence of Hindu civilisation is unity in diversity. Vivekananda himself used the *viśiṣṭadvaita* version preached by Ramanuja. Sarvepalli Radhakrishnan, a very learned philosopher who taught at Oxford University, wrote a book called, as far as I remember, *The Hindu Way of Life*, which made the same argument based on the philosophy of Adi Sankara.[3] As I may have told you before, I am not an admirer of the Advaita metaphysics which has many other features such as the claim that the world of perception is illusory and that it is possible to attain liberation (*mokṣa*) through knowledge of the Brahman, all of which I consider ridiculous. But this is not the time to drag you into a discussion of abstract philosophy. We are discussing politics. The use of the Advaita Vedanta to claim that, despite countless differences in doctrine and practice, the Hindu religion has a fundamental unity served a clear political purpose. It asserted that from ancient times the people of India had the cultural resources in their religious tradition to respect differences while, at the same time, uniting to pursue common tasks.

The poet Rabindranath Tagore was also a renowned figure who spoke of unity in diversity. He was born in a Brahmo family and followed the monotheistic interpretation of the Upanishads preached by Rammohan Roy. The Brahmo Samaj was against the practice common among Hindus of worshipping idols. But Rabindranath wrote movingly, in numerous poems and songs, of how India had, over centuries, made room for so many different religions, languages, and cultures to thrive. Despite all its diversity, Indian society had achieved a unique spirit of harmony. Yet Rabindranath was resolutely opposed to nationalism. In fact, he argued that precisely because Indian

---

[3] Actually, the title is *The Hindu View of Life*, a short book containing the Upton Lectures delivered by Radhakrishnan at Manchester College in 1926.

society had achieved its cohesion while preserving its diversity, it must not copy Europe and try to become a nation. European nations were racially and culturally homogeneous. Indian society would be destroyed if the cultural politics of nationalism was imposed on it. In this sense, even as he sang the praises of unity in diversity, he was unlike other Indian thinkers of his time. You are probably shocked to hear that the author of the national anthem was not an Indian nationalist. If you don't believe me, read Rabindranath's English lectures on nationalism.[4] Besides, another of his songs is the national anthem of Bangladesh: what kind of nationalist does that make him?

Whether the focus was on tolerance in local societies, as with Gandhi, or abstract philosophical doctrine, as with Radhakrishnan, the political effect was to privilege the Hindu religion and its associated culture as the adhesive (*bandhan*) that held together a nation otherwise divided into numerous castes, sects, and communities. I say this was a political effect because without the new impulse to project the existence of an Indian nation that could make a rightful claim of self-government against the British colonial power, this particular vision of something called the Hindu religion would have been irrelevant. Never before had anyone thought of interpreting the metaphor (*rūpak*) of unity in diversity in this fashion. It became a political metaphor of nationalism. Even Rabindranath, who fervently argued against India becoming a nation, was turned into the poet who sang of the nation's unity in diversity.

This had two important consequences. First, other religious traditions became minor or subordinate elements that illustrated diversity while the Hindu tradition became the force that united and gave shelter to others. Religions such as Buddhism, Jainism, and Sikhism, seen as internal dissensions,

---

[4] Rabindranath Tagore, *Nationalism* (New York: Macmillan, 1917), now available in many editions.

were included within the broader Hindu tradition. Islam and Christianity were religions that came from elsewhere but had been graciously accommodated.

The second effect followed from the first. It provided philosophical and cultural legitimacy to the politics of Hindu majoritarianism. Even when the avowed intention was to encourage pluralism in public and political life, the primacy of the majority Hindu culture was assumed to promote that pluralism. At the same time, for advocates of Hindutva who rejected pluralism, the same philosophical argument could be deployed to claim that non-Hindus would be protected in a Hindu Rashtra. As I have mentioned before, Golwalkar maintained that Advaita Vedanta was the natural (*svābhāvik*) philosophy of the country since all particular religious doctrines were expressions of the same cosmic spirit. And don't forget, he used the same Advaita Vedanta to argue for the differentiation into castes as a mechanism to ensure social harmony and prevent class war. Unity in diversity would have a wonderful (*camatkārī*) political career in modern India.

## Pluralism in History

Even though Jawaharlal Nehru was not a scholar, he liked to dabble in philosophy. But it was the record of history to which he appealed when making his case for pluralism. You must have some familiarity with his book *The Discovery of India* which he wrote when he was imprisoned in Ahmednagar Fort during the Quit India movement. The book has sold millions of copies. In it, Nehru told a story in which the religious pluralism of local societies was brought together with the administrative policies of the state to picture the vibrant presence of a common culture (*milī-julī saṃskṛti*) that united the Indian nation.[5] This was a

---

[5] The manuscript has "common culture" in English, indicating that it is a phrase used by Nehru, with *milī-julī saṃskṛti* in parentheses. Nehru does use the phrase "common culture" several times in *The Discovery of India*.

theme that several Indian historians have illustrated in detail with a lot of research. But because of Nehru's prominence as the writer who made the idea popular as well as the leader who wove it into the working of government, the historical version of unity in diversity, combining culture and state policy, has become synonymous with Nehruvian secularism.

What is this historical idea? It is a story of Indian civilisation that begins with the Harappa cities and moves to the coming of the Aryans and the rise of the Vedic culture. The sacrificial practices and the varna system of the Vedic religion are challenged by Buddhism which finds patronage in the imperial formation of the Mauryas. Asoka is the first great emperor who lays down state policies of religious toleration as well as the rational principles of administration of law. The Gupta Empire which followed saw the imposition of Brahmanical orthodoxy and the strengthening of caste rules, but it also saw the flourishing of the literary, philosophical, and scientific disciplines in Sanskrit. Buddhism disappeared from the country of its birth. There was a succession of states in southern India which promoted the building of great temples at home and trade across the seas. Along with trade, Indian culture spread, entirely peacefully, in the countries of Southeast Asia.

Muslim conquerors arrived in northern India to settle and build new kingdoms. They were often violent and intolerant towards those they regarded as worshippers of false gods. But over time, they abandoned the commitment to forcible establishment of an Islamic society in India and instead adopted policies of alliance with local chiefs and toleration of non-Islamic religious practices. The reign of Akbar was the golden age of this policy. He incorporated the Rajput princes of northern India into the military bureaucracy of the Mughal state. His rule also saw the creation of a vast government apparatus for the collection of revenue and the administration of justice – a bureaucratic system that would maintain its sturdiness right into the early decades of British rule. The Mughal Empire as well as the southern sultanates of Bijapur and Golconda also promoted the introduction of the literature, arts, crafts, architecture, and music of Central Asia and Iran into the culture of the elites in different parts of India. At the same time, Sufi preachers interacted with yogis and sants of what is known as the Bhakti movement to produce the hybrid folk cultures (*miśrit lokāsaṃskṛti*) which shaped the lives of ordinary people.

The bigoted Aurangzeb, Nehru said, turned the clock back. He reversed the enlightened policy of toleration and tried to impose a rigid and puritanical official culture. It led to several rebellions. The Marathas under Shivaji created their own state which adopted, under the Peshwas, explicitly Hindu, in fact Brahmanical, ceremonies. The Sikhs under Guru Gobind Singh turned the devotional faith of Nanak into a militant religious order. The Mughal Empire began to collapse. In the midst of decay and disunity, the British emerged among the European commercial powers as the new rulers of India.

This brief outline of the historical view of India as a pluralist nation (*bahulātāvādī rāṣṭra*) is, I admit, much too sketchy. Many brilliant historians have fleshed out the details with great precision and nuance, avoiding simplifications and correcting the errors made by earlier historians. Since I don't go to libraries, I will not be able to supply you with the titles of all these books: you should ask a history professor to give you a list. But let me point out the crucial features that emerge from this history.

First, it is the history of a civilisation. How do we recognise a civilisation? From records left behind in writing, from architectural monuments, from art, coins, priceless manufactures in metal, ceramic and other durable material, and so on. All of these varied objects point to the existence in the past of elite cultures that could read, write, construct, trade, and consume in ways that were refined and sophisticated. Evidence of such elite cultures from different periods is then strung together in a story line to produce the history of a single object (*vastu*) –

Indian civilisation. Completely left out are the cultures of people who also lived, worked, ate, sang, danced, painted, and worshipped over centuries in this country but did not write down anything or construct magnificent cities or produce precious ornaments or vases that would become collector's items. The history of Indian civilisation is not the history of everyone who lives in India. On the contrary, by glorifying the culture of the powerful, the wealthy, and the learned, it produces a myopic view of what is valuable in the nation's past. If you ask me, I will strongly suggest that to obtain a true picture of the nation's history, you should first get rid of the concept of civilisation.

Second, the particular version of pluralism popularised by Nehru emphasised the fact that it was fostered not merely by cultural exchanges among different groups of people but actively promoted and enforced by the administrative machinery of the state. Hence, the history of pluralist civilisation in India is as much a cultural history as a history of state policy. This leads to the detailed study of the great state formations which, for reasons of their large territorial scale and robust administrative structures, have left behind the largest volume of records on how they functioned. As a result, the history of pluralism, or unity in diversity, in India is marked by a succession of great empires – the Maurya, the Gupta, the Delhi Sultanates, the Vijayanagara, the Mughal, the Maratha, the British. They do not cover the same territory, nor do they follow continuously one after the other. But the gaps or overlaps in space and time are covered over by a narrative in which empires and their rulers become the principal actors in creating, nurturing, and sometimes destroying the pluralist state.

What is the implication for a national idea that is pluralist? The lesson is that one must have a centralised bureaucratic state (*kendrīkṛt naukarśāhī*) claiming sovereignty over the whole territory of the country and enforcing state policies of non-interference in religious freedom and toleration of difference. But this immediately creates a problem. The territory of the country, as I have explained to you already, is, for the most part, as it was left behind by our British rulers. This territory does not coincide with those of any of the earlier empires. Consequently, the search for a historical tradition of the pluralist state inevitably privileges the Maurya Empire under Asoka or the Mughal Empire under Akbar which had both a large expanse of territory and a record of religious tolerance. This, if you think about it carefully, has the effect of focusing the geographical imagination of pluralist India on the Gangetic plains of northern India as the ground from which policies for promoting diversity must spring that could be put into practice by a centralised bureaucracy. Examples from other parts of the country where smaller kingdoms, such as in Kerala or Kashmir or Bijapur or the Tamil region or Manipur, may have also promoted pluralism but in ways that were quite different were marginalised because they did not have the imperial scale of the state that men like Nehru envisioned for independent India. It is true that Nehruvian pluralism did not, like the celebration of Advaita philosophy, give priority to the Hindu religion as the natural bond that provided cohesion to the nation. But by seeking a history of pluralist policy in the record of empires, it ignored the multiple ways in which cultural practices were tied with state policies in smaller political formations around the country.

There was yet another problem with this conception of pluralism. The historical examples of pluralist state policy involved large polities ruled by enlightened monarchs surrounded by ministers and courtiers drawn from elite circles. None of them were democracies that had to be ruled with the express consent of the people. How could such a history inform state policy in republican India? The first decades after independence saw the leaders of the Congress, drawn from the professional upper-middle classes in the various provinces, assume leadership. There were differences among them on the role of the state in matters of religion and culture. Some like Nehru held progressive views and wanted the state to act in order to modernise social practices and promote secular and scientific values. Others, influenced by Gandhi, were conservative in their social outlook and did not want the state to intervene in matters of religious practice. Some in the Congress even held views that were close to those of the Hindu Mahasabha. However, the assassination in January 1948 of Gandhi by a declared Hindu nationalist led to a period when the conservatives lost their influence. This is when, in the first two decades after independence, Nehru and other liberal-minded politicians, bureaucrats, and lawyers put in place the laws and administrative practices of what is known as Nehruvian secularism. Even though the new republic began its journey towards democracy, it was still led by an enlightened elite surrounded by the aura of being the liberators of the nation. It was relatively free to shape the policies of the state without being pressed from all sides by the demands of different groups mobilised for electoral battles.

This period did not last. By the late 1960s, it became clear that the secular outlook of enlightened pluralists would have to be modified and, some might say, corrupted in order to cope with the pressures of democracy. Let me highlight a few episodes from that story.

## The Rise of Communalism

You may have heard people – not only political leaders but also learned professors – claiming that the idea of secularism (*dharmānirapekṣatā*) has existed for many centuries in India. Don't believe a word of that rubbish. Secularism was invented in this country no earlier than the 1930s. Before that, there was no word in any Indian language to mean what is now meant by secularism. The idea emerged in the particular context of what was happening in Indian politics, especially in northern India, at the time.

I have told you that although the terms Muslim and Hindu were well understood by the seventeenth century all over India, except in what are now the hill states of the north-east, they did not mean what they mean now. Most of the time, and in most ordinary contexts, the primary community with which a person would identify was the caste (*jāti*) to which he or she belonged. But a jati was defined within a limited geographical region. For instance, there were divisions (*śreṇī*) among Brahmans of each linguistic region such that, in Bengal, Rarhi Brahmans would not intermarry with Varendra Brahmans, or in Maharashtra, Deshastha Brahmans with Konkanastha Brahmans. In fact, relations of hierarchy among castes were also defined within small regions. I will explain this later when I tell you more about the politics of caste. What is important to understand is that on occasions when a larger community was defined by the name Hindu, the castes that were included in it varied from region to region. Further, nowhere were the untouchable castes included within the category of Hindu.

Among Muslims too, although adherence to the basic practices of the religion would identify them as belonging to a Muslim community (*ummā*), they too were primarily identified in their local context as a jati. Thus, Muslim weavers in northern India would constitute the Julaha caste and Hindu weavers the Tanti caste. Muslims too fitted into a local caste structure that was hierarchical, even though its rigidities may have been less severe. In Kashmir, for instance, Brahmans who had converted to Islam often retained their Brahman family names and preferred to intermarry only with other converted Brahmans. On the other hand, there are many examples from different parts of India of Muslims whose occupations were considered polluting being excluded from prayer meetings at mosques. The story is the same with Christians in Kerala: people from untouchable castes who had converted to Christianity often formed their own churches because they would not be allowed by highborn Christians into their congregations.

There is no evidence before the late-nineteenth century of the emergence of anything like a Hindu or a Muslim community that could claim to include people over substantial regions of the country. For Muslims, the first effort in this direction was made by Syed Ahmad Khan who appealed to the British authorities for the recruitment of a greater number of Muslims to government services. One must remember that, unlike the Hindu upper castes in Bombay, Bengal, and Madras who acquired English education in the early-nineteenth century, the Muslim gentry (*asraf*) largely stayed away. They were still caught in an old world in which their landed property, knowledge of Persian and Urdu, and the sophisticated cultural skills of the Mughal court would get them positions in the bureaucracy. After the decline of Delhi as the imperial capital, many had migrated to Awadh and Hyderabad to find jobs. But after 1857, with the establishment of the new administration, law courts, and English schools and colleges, government services in northern India came to be dominated by Hindus from Bengal and Bombay. Syed Ahmad Khan complained bitterly to British officials that the traditional educated elite of north India was being overwhelmed by these newly arrived Hindus who had no respect for the old culture. At the same time, he urged the Muslim upper classes to give up their false pride and embrace the new education in English. The most lasting contribution he made to history was the founding of the Anglo-Oriental College (later a university) at Aligarh, modelled on Oxford, which would go on to produce the intellectual leaders of a new Muslim middle class with a vision that went far beyond the region.

As you can see, this early consolidation of something called a Muslim community that spanned a large region but included only the educated and propertied classes had nothing to do with religious matters. A similar movement can be seen among the Hindu educated classes of northern India. This again had nothing to do with religion. In the last years of the nineteenth century, a group of Brahman leaders based mainly in Allahabad and Banaras began to demand that the Hindustani language that was used in the courts of the North-Western Provinces (now Uttar Pradesh) be written not exclusively in the Persian script, as was the practice, but that the Nagari script be also allowed. The demand was conceded in 1900. Underlying this was the social challenge posed by a new group of educated Brahmans to the earlier dominance of a Sharif Muslim and Kayasth literati in the lower courts. Soon there emerged a larger movement, carried out through magazines, publication houses, and literary conferences, to claim that Urdu, which for all practical purposes was identical with Hindustani, was a completely separate language from Hindi. Not only that, it was argued that Urdu was the language of Muslims which had corrupted the purity of Sanskrit-derived Hindi. The movement proceeded to purge Hindi of Arabic-Persian words which had become completely naturalised in the ordinary spoken language and create a new prose language by importing and coining thousands of words from Sanskrit. This project was supposed to be far larger than merely the reform of a language: it was part and parcel of nationalism itself. The slogan of this movement was:

*cahumhum jusāmco nij kalyān*
*to sab mili bhārat santān!*
*japo nirantar ek jabān*
*hindī, hindū, hindustān*[6]

I will have much more to say later about the politics of the Hindi language. But I want to emphasise here that, first, the movement in UP to separate Hindi from Urdu in the early-twentieth century was a major step in the growth of the awareness that

[6] This popular rhyme was composed by Pratap Narayan Mishra, most probably in 1893. A rough translation is: If you truly desire your welfare, O children of Bharat! Then endlessly chant these words – Hindi, Hindu, Hindustan.

there was a Hindu majority in northern India that could be mobilised; second, it was explicitly posed as a counter to the perceived cultural dominance of an old Muslim gentry; and third, that its immediate objective was to secure a firm foothold for upper-caste Hindus in the expanding structures of the bureaucracy and the education system.

But there was another movement around the same time in the same region which did have to do with religion and which showed that the educated Hindu elite might be able to mobilise some of the more numerous peasant castes in a supposedly national cause. In the 1890s, a movement started, aimed primarily against Muslims and secondarily against low castes such as Chamars, to prevent the slaughter of cows. Gaurakshini Sabhas came up over much of northern India, with headquarters in Nagpur. In time, the movement became strong in the Bhojpur region of present-day Uttar Pradesh and Bihar. Apart from campaigns against the practice among poorer Muslims of sacrificing cows, there were numerous attacks on Muslims and sometimes Chamars engaged in skinning dead animals. At places, there was resistance by Muslims leading to violent conflicts. By the early decades of the twentieth century, what we now call communal riots became a regular feature at the time of Eid in several districts of Bihar and UP. The cow-protection campaigns were organised by upper-caste Hindus, mostly small zamindars and professionals, financially supported by wealthy Marwari merchants in Calcutta, while Ahirs, Bhumihars, and Thakurs comprised their army. They were often joined by swamis and sadhus who played a major role in stirring up crowds. On the other side, leaders from the Muslim gentry were joined by alims and imams while, in most places, Julahas were the most directly involved in armed conflicts. By 1920, a model had emerged in northern India of what is now called communalism (sāmpradāyikătā).

I have told you before that Gandhi's alliance with Mohammad

Ali and Shaukat Ali – leaders of the Khilafat movement – injected a tremendous energy into the mass mobilisation against British rule. Although the demand of their movement was the restoration of the Sultan of Turkey to the traditional position of the head (*khalīfā*) of Sunni Islam – a position the British had undermined following Turkey's defeat in the First World War – the Ali brothers were not religious leaders. Both were educated at Aligarh and Mohammad Ali went on to study at Oxford, and became a civil servant in Baroda and editor of an English newspaper. But the joint Non-Cooperation and Khilafat campaign was not a secular movement. Rather, it was understood as a deliberate coming together of the Hindu and Muslim communities in the united national cause of resisting British oppression. Every meeting, every demonstration, was marked by slogans and symbols of Hindu–Muslim fraternity, the most common sight being the new white Gandhi cap alongside the red Turkish (*rūmī*) fez. It also saw the emergence of an entire generation of popular leaders, some with a religious background and others who had modern education but were rooted in their local rural society. Most surprisingly, in regions such as UP and Bihar where Hindus and Muslims had clashed violently only a year or two before, they now joined in massive actions of solidarity.

Could this have led to a different political formation of the national movement? We will never know. In 1922, when the movement was at its peak, a huge crowd of Congress volunteers attacked and set fire to a police station in Chauri Chaura in Gorakhpur, killing twenty-two policemen. Gandhi immediately called off the movement. Even though most of his Congress colleagues criticised Gandhi, I think they too were unnerved by the energies of mobilised masses which they could not control. The movement fell apart. But once mobilised, the genie could not be put back in the bottle. The bickering over election tickets and government jobs returned with a vengeance. In province after province where they had firmly allied with Hindus,

Muslims now began to desert the Congress and form organisations of their own. The old pattern of local disputes bursting into riots not only returned but spread in many parts of the country from the mid-1920s. Thus, there were major communal conflicts in Punjab, Bengal, Bombay, Malabar, and several cities in UP among which the most horrific riots occurred in 1931 in Kanpur. This was the sequence of events that ultimately led to the partition of the country in 1947.

## The Rise of Secularism

During its heated exchanges with the Muslim League, the Congress always described itself as nationalist and condemned the other as communalist. This was how the opposition was initially posed. But with the growing visibility from the late 1930s of the Hindu Mahasabha which offered itself as the uncompromising champion of Hindu interests against Muslim demands, Nehru in particular began to sharpen the Congress position. There was, he said, a communalism of the Muslims as well as a communalism of the Hindus, against which the Congress must uphold the true nationalist ideal of keeping the political arena free from religious divisions. He began to use the English term "secular" to describe this position. He insisted that the independent India that the Congress stood for would be secular and democratic in which all Indians would have equal rights irrespective of their religion. In Nehru's thinking, therefore, true nationalism coincided with secularism and was opposed to both Muslim and Hindu communalism.

The frenzy of communal violence in Punjab at the time of partition and the subsequent conflict with Pakistan over Kashmir vitiated public opinion in northern India. Recognising the mood, senior leaders of the Congress, including Vallabhbhai Patel and Rajendra Prasad, pushed for a hard line against Pakistan. It was decided to suspend payment of Pakistan's share of the substantial reserves in pounds sterling left behind by the British.

Gandhi, who had moved to Delhi in September 1947 to stop the communal violence there, urged the Congress leaders to end their enmity with Pakistan, declaring that he belonged to both India and Pakistan. To press his point, he went on a fast in the middle of January demanding that the money that rightfully belonged to Pakistan be released. A few days later, the government relented. That is when Nathuram Godse decided to kill Gandhi.

Nathuram was born in a Chitpavan Brahman family in Poona. Since three older sons had died in childhood, his parents, believing there was an evil spell on male children in the family, brought him up as a girl, complete with a nose ring (*nath*). As a result, because his given name was Ramchandra, he came to be called Nathuram. I don't know if this childhood experience created in him a desire to carry out manly acts of bravery. In any case, from the time when Bal Gangadhar Tilak came into prominence and historians like Vishwanath Rajwade began to write on Maratha history, the idea of a vigorous and masculine nationalism under the military command of a leader like Shivaji began to attract many young Brahmans in Maharashtra. While in college, Godse participated in the Congress movement and was convinced that Hinduism had to be cleansed of practices such as untouchability and caste discrimination, but soon drifted towards the Hindu Mahasabha and the RSS. At the time of partition, he came to believe that it was Gandhi's philosophy of tolerance and non-violence which had made it possible for Muslims to break up India. Unless Gandhi was removed, he would continue to prevent the Indian government from defending the interest of Hindus. Godse resolved to kill Gandhi and thus prove that, when attacked, Hindus too could be intolerant and violent.[7]

---

[7] Godse's reasons for assassinating Gandhi are set out in his court testimony which is available as a book: Nathuram Vinayak Godse, *May it Please Your Honour* (New Delhi: Surya Prakashan, 1989); also available under the title *Why I Assassinated Mahatma Gandhi*.

Although the wider conspiracy behind Gandhi's assassination, as proved in court, did not involve too many people, many shared the broader sentiment voiced by Godse that the time had come for Hindus to overcome their sense of weakness and present a more militant face. It is in this spirit that immediately after the integration of Junagadh, Patel, with the arch-conservative K.M. Munshi by his side, took the lead in rebuilding the Somnath temple, held up as the prime symbol of a thousand years of Muslim violence against Hindus. Patel also appealed to the patriotism of the RSS and encouraged its cadres to help out with relief work among partition refugees. The Hindu Mahasabha was successful in organising large rallies in Delhi and Punjab where it blamed Gandhi and the Congress for failing to prevent the partition of the country.

However, the assassination of Gandhi produced a widespread feeling of horror. The RSS was banned and some 50,000 of its volunteers (*svayamsevak*) were put in prison. After much pleading by Golwalkar, Patel agreed to lift the ban in June 1949 when the RSS resolved to abide by the Indian constitution. The Hindu Mahasabha was not banned because Syama Prasad Mookerjee, then a member of Nehru's cabinet, intervened and tried to moderate the Mahasabha's position. He failed and left the party. But the Mahasabha never regained its influence. In 1951, a few months before the first general elections, a new party called the Jana Sangh was formed with Mookerjee as president and several key members of the RSS as chief functionaries.

Although Nehru was deeply suspicious of the ulterior motives of the RSS, Patel believed that the organisation could be tamed by encouraging its activists to join the Congress. He repeatedly urged Golwalkar – unsuccessfully – to allow RSS volunteers to participate in the activities of the Congress. Perhaps Patel was also thinking of strengthening the conservative section within his party to counter Nehru. In August 1950, Patel strongly supported Purushottam Das Tandon, a well-known conservative, against Nehru's nominee J.B. Kripalani, a socialist leader, in the election for Congress president. Tandon won. We will never know how this contest between Nehru and Patel for the soul of the Congress might have developed further, because in December 1950, Patel, who was already quite ill, died of a heart attack.

Nehru now proceeded to establish a firm grip on both the party and the government. By September 1951, Tandon was forced to resign as Congress president and Nehru was elected in his place. Despite the passions that were aroused by stories of attacks on Hindus and Sikhs in Pakistan, Nehru insisted that India's secular democracy must not be allowed to be sullied by religious divisions. He piloted a new law which prohibited the use of religious symbols in elections.[8] He also resisted persistent efforts by Hindu conservatives, not only in the Hindu Mahasabha and the Jana Sangh but also within the Congress, to block the reform of Hindu personal laws: that is a story to which I will have to come back.

The Indian constitution came into force in January 1950. It did not mention the word "secular". You will find it today in the Preamble because Indira Gandhi inserted it, along with the word "socialist", in 1976 during the Emergency and it has remained there. But in the Constituent Assembly, Ambedkar opposed the inclusion of a proposed article which would have declared that the state, being secular, should have nothing to do with any religion.[9] As you know, Ambedkar was strongly in favour of provisions in the constitution that would allow laws to be made to prohibit untouchability and caste oppression, reform retrograde religious practices, and protect the religious

---

[8] Representation of the People Act 1951.

[9] K.T. Shah proposed an amendment to this effect which Ambedkar opposed. *Constituent Assembly Debates*, vol. 7, p. 815.

and cultural institutions of minorities. Consequently, even though in his political views he was a thorough secularist, he did not want the idea to be spelt out in the constitution because, as I will soon explain, it could have come in the way of state intervention in the field of religion.

Actually, the use of the English term "secularism" has caused a lot of confusion about what it means, and should mean, in the Indian context. There are many differences in the meaning of the term in the Western world, with each language having its own word for it. I know that in the United States it means that the institutions and activities of the state must be strictly separated from religion, even though most people in American society are deeply religious. In France, not only does it mean state neutrality from religion but even prohibition on displays of religious signs in schools and public institutions. In many other countries of Europe, including Britain and Holland, as well as in Scandinavia, even though there is a national church with the monarch as its head, the government does not intervene in religious matters. In Turkey under Kemal Atatürk, secularism meant a forcible suppression of traditional Islamic institutions and vigorous westernisation of culture. In the Soviet Union too, Orthodox Christianity was thoroughly suppressed as was Islam in the republics of Central Asia. These differences are not surprising because historical and cultural conditions were not the same everywhere.

Even though India's leaders wanted the new state to be secular, it became clear at the time of making the constitution that foreign models would not work. Something different – an Indian variety of secularism – would have to be invented. What was this Indian secularism that came into being?

One of the basic realities that had to be addressed was that although the liberal idea of rights applied to individual citizens, religion in India was less a matter of personal belief than one of community practice. This had to be taken into account in the constitution. It guaranteed every person the freedom of conscience and the right to freely practise, profess, and propagate religion.[10] But at the same time, the state was given the power to restrict any economic, political, or other secular activity associated with a religious practice, and reform Hindu religious institutions and open them to all Hindus.[11] Clearly, this would mean state intervention in religion. The justification for the first restriction was that the management of religious institutions in India was a public matter and that the state must be allowed to intervene to ensure the rights of individuals even in matters of religion. The second power of intervention was limited to the Hindu religion because none of the other major religions excluded, as a matter of religious principle, any section of believers from their institutions.

Ambedkar was emphatic that the old order, where everything in life was regulated by religion, must not be allowed to continue. Religion should concern only beliefs and ceremonial rituals. In all other matters, the state must be allowed to make laws to ensure social progress.[12] Nonetheless, apart from individual freedom of religion, limited by the power of state intervention, the constitution also recognised the rights of religious communities. Thus every religious denomination (*sampradāy*) was given the right to establish and maintain religious institutions, manage its own religious affairs, and own and administer property in accordance with the law.[13] Further, it allowed religious and

---

[10] Article 25(1).

[11] Article 25(2).

[12] In a speech in the Constituent Assembly, Ambedkar said: "The religious conceptions in this country are so vast that they cover every aspect of life from birth to death. There is nothing which is not religion . . . we ought to strive hereafter to limit the definition of religion in such a manner that we shall not extend it beyond beliefs and such rituals as may be connected with ceremonials which are essentially religious." *Constituent Assembly Debates*, vol. 7, p. 781.

[13] Article 26.

linguistic minorities to establish and maintain their own educational institutions and prohibited the state from discriminating against them in granting financial aid.[14] Interestingly, while the constitution prohibited religious instruction in any institution wholly maintained by state funds, it allowed such instruction in schools and colleges set up by a religious endowment or trust even if it received government grants, provided individual students were not forced to attend such sessions against their wishes.[15] This was a complicated attempt by the constitution makers to balance state neutrality with individual and collective freedom of religion.

What emerged as Indian secularism did not fit the definitions of the secular state anywhere else in the world. There was no strict separation since the state was allowed to intervene in religion. At the same time, the state was not entirely neutral between different religions since it intervened in some religions more than in others. The argument was made that this was necessary because the social and political considerations were different. The need for progressive reform of Hindu laws to ensure individual freedom and equality and end of caste oppression required immediate action by parliament. On the other hand, the political climate following the partition violence made it necessary for the political leadership to reassure the minority communities that the Hindu majority in parliament would not interfere in their religious and cultural institutions: no changes would be made without their consent. Instead of the standard definitions in the West, Indian secularism began to be characterised by the phrase *sarvadharma samabhāv* or equal respect for all religions. Rather than shunning religious symbols, official ceremonies were marked by the presence on the same stage of all the major religions practised in India.

[14] Article 30.
[15] Article 28.

## The Troubles of Secularism

The problem of navigating a consistent path between all of these contradictory principles became clear from the early 1950s. Interestingly, disputes over secularism were settled not so much in the political arena as in the courts. Once the state decided to make laws to give itself powers to engage with religion, secularism in India became centrally concerned with the law. The basic problem was one of determining the exact line within which the state may justifiably intervene in the activities of religious institutions and beyond which things must be left in the hands of religious authorities. Judges began to define and draw this line by interpreting religious texts and customs and deciding what was essential to that religion. That which was essential must not be touched by the state, while those activities that were peripheral to religion could be reformed, taken over or even abolished by government action.

Lawsuits were filed, for instance, arguing that polygamy was sanctioned by many Hindu *dharmaśāstra* texts, just as it was by Muslim law, and yet the state had prohibited the practice only for Hindus. Was this not discriminatory? The court justified the state's action by suggesting that effective social reform depended on how far a community was prepared to accept changes in its religious practices. In India at the present time, Hindus were better prepared than Muslims to accept such changes. On the question of entry into temples, there were numerous cases in courts all over India, citing canonical texts and established custom, which argued that to allow all Hindus irrespective of caste to worship at the temple would violate the sacred rules of religion. In response, the courts sometimes asserted that these rules were not part of religion proper but were laws sanctioned by religion which could be changed by parliament, the sovereign law-making authority in the country. At other times, judges tried to interpret religious texts in order to find room for compromise, such as allowing different castes to worship the deity from different distances or at different times.

Particular sects have approached the court to claim that they be considered religious minorities and not be included within the Hindu religion. In deciding such cases, the courts have weighed the evidence of the doctrines and practices of the sect to judge whether or not they were sufficiently far removed from Hinduism to be considered a separate religion. The Brahmo Samaj passed the test whereas the Swaminarayan Sampraday and the Ramakrishna Mission failed.[16] Jains, who in their social relations are thoroughly interwoven with Hindu castes in Gujarat and Rajasthan, had been put under the jurisdiction of Hindu law by the constitution. In 2006, the Supreme Court declared that the Jain religion was definitely not a part of Hinduism, and in 2014 the Government of India recognised Jains as the sixth minority community in India.[17] More recently, some Lingayat leaders in Karnataka have launched an agitation to claim that Lingayatism is a minority religion separate from both Hinduism and the broader Veerashaiva faith to which Lingayats belong. Who knows, this matter too may be finally decided in court.

The reason why some sectarian organisations went to court to demand that they be excluded from the Hindu religion and

---

[16] Brahmoism was recognised as a religion by the Privy Council in London in 1901 and its adherents are counted separately in the census. The Brahmo Samaj was recognised by the Supreme Court as a minority religious community entitled to maintain its own educational institutions. The Swaminarayan Sampraday claimed that although its members were socially and culturally Hindu, their religion was entirely distinct. The case was finally decided against the Sampraday by the Supreme Court in 1966. The Ramakrishna Mission went to court in 1980 with the claim that its Neo-Vedantic religion was superior to and different from the religion practised by most Hindus and hence it should be recognised as a non-Hindu minority religion with the right to run its own educational institutions. It won a favourable verdict in the Calcutta High Court but lost in the Supreme Court in 1995.

[17] The others are Muslims, Christians, Sikhs, Buddhists, and Zoroastrians.

considered a minority religious community was purely opportunistic. It was to avoid interference by the government in their non-religious activities, such as running schools and colleges. The constitution allows such interference but protects the autonomy of educational and cultural institutions of minority religious communities even when they receive government aid. This is the legal window that the Brahmo Samaj or the Ramakrishna Mission wanted to use. Whatever one's position on minority rights in India, it must be admitted that religion was merely a ruse in these court cases: the motivation had nothing to do with religion.

In defining the essence of religion, judges tended to privilege an abstract philosophical conception of religion, supported by modern interpretations of religious texts, and were dismissive of popular practices that appeared to be mere superstition. When the devadasi system by which women were attached to temples and required to dance before the deity as part of the prescribed rituals was prohibited by law in Madras province in 1947, the courts declared that the institution was little more than ritually sanctioned prostitution and had nothing to do with religion. In 1949, the Bombay government passed a law prohibiting the excommunication of members from a sect or denomination. When the head of the Dawoodi Bohra community went to court, alleging that this was an illegal interference in the right of the community to manage its own affairs, the Bombay High Court decided that excommunication was a practice that was not an essential part of religion.[18] Some state governments prohibited animal sacrifice in temples on the ground that the practice represented a primitive form of worship inconsistent with true Hinduism.[19] Many judges tended to expound at

---

[18] The case was brought against the Bombay Prevention of Excommunication Act of 1949 and was decided by the Bombay High Court in 1953.

[19] The Madras Animal and Bird Sacrifices Act was passed in 1950. There have been similar laws in some other states.

length on the essence of the Hindu religion along the lines of the philosophy of Advaita Vedanta I spoke about earlier.

Why did the courts of a secular state enter into this contentious area of defining true and false religion? They could have simply followed the law and, considering the fact that they were more often than not supportive of progressive state intervention, declared that the constitution empowered the state to determine the non-religious activities of religious institutions where it could intervene. But the courts chose not to take that path. I think there are two reasons for this.

First, the High Court judges, who after all belonged to the educated upper-middle-class elite that constituted the nationalist leadership in independent India, did not want to think of their new republic as destructive of religion in the manner of Atatürk's Turkey or the Soviet Union. They wanted to steer a more liberal path where the religious freedom of citizens and communities was respected. But what happens when there are disputes over religious rights? Who arbitrates? I think our judges often thought of what ruling monarchs would be asked to do in earlier times, especially because Hindus did not have any overarching religious institution like the Christian church or recognised bodies of ulema. Religious leaders in the old days would take their disputes to the king with the expectation that he would provide an impartial resolution. Now that the British had left, our judges began to think of the court as playing the role of an impartial but socially progressive monarch.

Second, there was the more immediate precedent of how judges reasoned in such matters in the courts of British India. From the time when the East India Company arranged, in the early-nineteenth century, to compile Hindu and Muslim codes of law for use in their courts, British judges began the practice of including in their judgments their interpretation of these supposedly traditional laws so that Indian litigants would be satisfied that the foreign judges were not acting out of ignorance. As a result, by the time of independence, legal precedents on the personal and religious laws of Hindus and Muslims were full of these judicial interpretations of religious texts. Indian judges, deeply familiar with these precedents, continued the same practice after independence, to the extent of following the same linguistic idiom. If you read the language used in our court judgments these days, you will notice that most judges have read their dharmashastra in English translation and argue on Indian religions like British judges in colonial times. I often think of the *smārta* Brahmans of the past (who, of course, thoroughly detested me) chopping fine pieces of logic and weaving intricate arguments to arrive at a settlement (*vyavasthā*) acceptable to their clients. Even though they were not always impartial, they belonged to the society of their time and did not, like judges these days, pretend to speak from an abstract intellectual position up in the sky.

Although the British tried as far as possible, especially after 1857, not to involve the colonial state in matters of Indian religion, things were quite different in the princely states. Where the ruler was Hindu, he was very often the chief patron of temples, closely involved in their management and even took a leading role in religious ceremonies. After the states were integrated into the Indian Union, the question came up as to the position of the princes in religious institutions. In most cases, the ceremonial functions continued as before, as did the role of the former ruler in the management of temples, although the government often appointed its own officials to supervise the financial and administrative side. But in Travancore and Cochin states, large amounts of expenditure under the heading of Devaswom expenses were allocated in the annual budget of the state, while the properties and treasure of the temples, nominally belonging to the deities, were held in trust by the prince. After integration, the arrangement was continued. Even now, the Government of Kerala allocates funds for the temples while their management is carried out by a Devaswom Board consisting of government officials and members of the religious community. This is one instance where the finances of religious institutions are a part of state finances – a peculiar anomaly for a secular state.

The participation of government officials in the management of religious institutions through temple trusts or waqf boards is, however, much more common. This is usually justified by the constitutional provision which allows the state to regulate the economic and social activities of religious institutions. There is also considerable government expenditure in making arrangements for large religious festivals such as the Kumbh Mela in Prayag or the Rathayatra in Puri, or in assisting Haj pilgrims.

One question on which the conflict between individual and community freedom of religion continues to simmer is that of conversion. The constitution guarantees every citizen the freedom of conscience as well as the right to propagate religion. Does this include the right to persuade someone to change his or her religion? In many parts of India, there was much opposition to the activities of Christian missionaries who, it was alleged, were converting tribal people and Dalits with financial and other inducements. In fact, some princely states in Rajasthan and Gujarat even had laws regulating missionary activities. There were some members of the Constituent Assembly who did not want to include the propagation of religion in the list of fundamental rights, but they were in a minority. The matter continued to come up from time to time until 1981 when an entire village called Meenakshipuram in Tamil Nadu, consisting of more than a thousand people belonging to the Dalit castes, converted to Islam. All hell broke loose. The chief minister, Jayalalithaa, decided to pass a law prohibiting conversion, and there were moves to bring similar legislation in parliament. But since this proved to be a solitary instance and was not repeated elsewhere, the law was never enacted.

However, the activities of Christian missionaries in Adivasi areas continued to be a volatile issue. Several states with significant Adivasi populations, such as Odisha, Madhya Pradesh, Chhattisgarh, Jharkhand, and Gujarat, have laws against forcible or fraudulent conversion. Even Arunachal Pradesh in the north-east, a region where there are several states with Christian majorities, has a law of this kind. Since there have been very few prosecutions under this law and no convictions, it is still not clear what the legal standard is to determine whether force or fraud has been used to convert someone. But the political controversy over conversion continues. It reached a flashpoint in 1999 when Graham Staines, an Australian missionary, was burnt to death along with his two children by Bajrang Dal activists in Odisha. In recent times, with the proponents of Hindu Rashtra in power, there is talk once more of a law in parliament prohibiting conversion.

The conflict here is between the individual freedom of conscience and the collective freedom of a religious community to maintain its identity. The two involve very different conceptions of religious freedom. Recall Vivekananda's speech in Chicago where he spoke of India's tolerance of all faiths. This involved, he said, the obligation that a Christian would not convert a Hindu nor a Hindu a Christian. Viewed from the perspective of the religious community, maintaining its identity had to include the condition that it would not lose its members to another community. But this was completely contrary to the modern liberal idea of individual freedom of conscience. If you decide, after serious thought and due consideration of the consequences, to change your religion, why should the law stop you? In actual fact, the objection is usually not about educated individuals deciding to convert, unless, of course, she happens to be a woman, in which case her independent judgment in such matters is immediately called into question. An even bigger alarm is raised when an entire group of people, belonging to a particular jati in a particular region, chooses to convert. The assumption is that such people do not have the mental capacity to change their religion out of a call of conscience. If they do so, it must be the result of a promise of material benefit or a threat of punishment. The same assumption works when a Hindu woman converts to marry a Muslim man: the woman is not recognised as having a will of her own. The uproar against conversion shows the anxiety of Hindu elites over the loyalty of Adivasis, Dalits, and women who may be denied a place of equality in Hindu society but cannot be allowed to leave it.

Another subject on which there is continuing controversy is the possibility of a uniform civil code. The British substituted the previously existing criminal laws and laws relating to commercial transactions, taxation, and other civil matters with the comprehensive Indian Penal Code and laws regulating contracts, labour, taxation, property, etc. What they did not touch was so-called personal law relating to marriage, divorce, inheritance, and adoption which continued to be regulated by the respective religious laws of Hindus, Muslims, Christians, and other communities. There were numerous regional, caste, and sectarian variations in these laws, not only among Hindus but also among Muslims and Christians. Many of these variations reflected the fact that customary practices in different regions and among different castes bore little relation to what was written in the Brahmanical shastra or the texts of the sharia. The first major attempt to produce a uniform personal law for Muslims was made by reformist Muslim leaders who passed the Shariat Act in the central legislature in 1937. This superseded the separate laws that had existed for many Muslim communities, such as the Mapillah of Malabar, the Cutchi Memons of Gujarat, and the Muslims of the North West Frontier Province.

At the time of the making of the constitution, Nehru and other progressive Congress members, strongly backed by the handful of women in the Constituent Assembly as well as by

Ambedkar, pushed for an article to allow parliament to enact a new civil code to replace the religion-based personal laws. The opposition came from two sources: conservative Hindu members both within and outside Congress who were against modernising state legislation that would interfere with traditional Hindu practices, and Muslim members who claimed that the minority community in India was traumatised by the partition violence and would feel even more insecure if their religious laws were changed by parliament. As a compromise, the matter was postponed to the future by including the desire for a uniform civil code in the Directive Principles of state policy.

Following the inauguration of the constitution, Ambedkar, who was then the law minister, drafted a single civil code for all Hindus with a major emphasis on gender equality. He could not find majority support in the legislature, upon which he resigned in disgust. In 1955–6, Nehru, who by then had realised the difficulties of radical reform of personal laws, supported a watered-down version of Ambedkar's draft, broken up into four separate bills covering marriage, succession, guardianship, and adoption. These were passed by parliament.[20] Even though they fell short of Ambedkar's intentions, they nevertheless brought about major changes in Hindu law by legalising inter-caste marriage, allowing divorce, prohibiting polygamy, giving the daughter the same right of inheritance as the son, and permitting the adoption of daughters as well as sons. But while the goal was the secular one of disregarding traditional injunctions and enacting rational and progressive laws, when challenged in court the justification given was, as I have told you before, that they were consistent with true Hinduism.

The question of reform of the personal laws of the minority religious communities as well as the promise of a uniform

---

[20] The Hindu Marriage Act, the Hindu Succession Act, the Hindu Minority and Guardianship Act and the Hindu Adoption and Maintenance Act.

civil code were held in abeyance. However, the Special Marriage Act, which had existed from colonial times but was rarely used, was amended in 1954 to allow civil marriage outside the framework of religious personal laws. The idea was to enable a man and a woman belonging to different religions to marry each other without renouncing their religions. However, this did not necessarily create a category of citizens outside the purview of religion-based personal law, because inheritance was still regulated by the religious affiliation of each parent.

An All India Muslim Personal Law Board was set up in 1973, consisting of nominated representatives of all major Muslim sects (except Ahmadis), to supervise the application of Muslim personal law. The board is conservative and unwilling to consider progressive changes in the direction of gender equality – not even the abolition of polygamy which is prohibited in several Muslim countries, including Pakistan and Bangladesh. In 2005, an All India Shia Personal Law Board was set up to better represent the views of the Shia community, although the Muslim Personal Law Board continues to have Shia members. Marriages of Protestant and Orthodox Christians are regulated by the Indian Christian Marriage Act. They also have a National Council of Churches in India to represent them as a minority community. Catholics follow canon law as laid down by the Vatican and are represented by the Catholic Bishops Conference. Zoroastrians are regulated in their religion by the Bombay Parsi Panchayat which again remains a defender of orthodox rules of marriage and succession. Although Sikhs and Buddhists are recognised in the constitution as minority religious communities, they, along with Jains, are specifically mentioned as coming under the purview of Hindu law.

I should also point out that there is one state in India where there is a uniform civil code and none of the religion-based personal laws apply. Do you know which one? It is Goa. How did that happen? Goa under Portuguese rule was considered a part of Portugal. Its civil code is the secular family law put in place by the Portuguese republic in 1910. It may surprise you that Catholics, who constitute a significant part of the population of Goa, are governed there not by canon law as in the rest of India but by the same secular family law that applies to Hindus, Muslims, and other communities in the state.

The debate over a uniform civil code was revived in the 1980s by two sections of opinion. Hindu nationalists associated with the BJP began to call the Congress position on religious personal laws "pseudo-secular", intended to appease Muslims in order to create a vote bank. They challenged the Congress government to prove its secular credentials by enacting a common civil code for all citizens. At the same time, several feminist groups criticised all existing personal laws as patriarchal and unfair to women. They demanded a uniform civil code that ensured gender equality in all communities.

There are at least three problems that were not recognised in the heated debate over a uniform civil code. First, many seemed to assume that a uniform civil code would mean the imposition of the present Hindu code on all citizens, irrespective of religion. In other words, the Hindu code would become the universal code. In fact, these people seem to bear a grudge that Hindu men have been forced to give up their traditional right of having more than one wife while Muslim men continue to enjoy the privilege. Thus, they say, Hindus have been victimised. Besides being a thoroughly male-centred view of family law, it also ignores the fact, as numerous surveys have shown, that, regardless of what the law allows, monogamy has become the predominant norm among Muslim families in India, for no other reason than the economic one of providing a decent living standard for the family and giving children a good education. On the other hand, bigamy is widespread among Hindus because it can only be prosecuted against if the first wife files a formal complaint which, in most cases, she cannot do for economic and social reasons. It is also not clear why a uniform civil code should recognise the peculiar institution of the Hindu undivided family which is part of Hindu law now and which is a major instrument for wealthy businessmen, with the help of their expensive lawyers, to protect their properties and avoid taxes. Will the Bania community agree to give it up in the interest of a uniform code? If not, will it not remain a special privilege for rich Hindus?

Second, if there was to be a uniform civil code, would it mean an end to the existence of majority and minority religious communities? Thus, would the constitutional provisions for the autonomy of the educational and cultural institutions of minority communities continue? Would reservations for scheduled castes be restricted only to those now under the jurisdiction of Hindu law (that is, inclusive of Sikhs, Buddhists, and Jains) and not extended to Muslims and Christians? If you think carefully, you will find that when Hindu nationalists demand a uniform civil code, they think they will be able to impose the Hindu code on others, as if that would be a great victory! What they do not realise is that a uniform citizenship that does not recognise religion, which is something the present constitution does not guarantee, will remove the plank from under the claim that the Hindu majority is the true foundation of the nation (*rāṣṭra*), because if there are no legally recognised minorities, there cannot be any dominant majority community either.

Third, there is also the serious issue, pointed out by many feminist scholars and activists, of progressive changes in the law having little effect in practice because those who actually control what happens within communities and families do not necessarily abide by the law. Thus, child marriage is rampant even though the law prohibits it. Women have little protection against marital rape or sexual violence within the family, even though laws exist. There are innumerable instances where women in Hindu families are denied their share of the property or maintenance. This is not to say that laws to ensure gender equality should not be made, but that even a well-crafted universal civil code will not necessarily deliver equal justice regardless of religion, caste, and gender.

## The Decline of Secularism

While these debates were going on, the principle of secularism was further weakened by the shifting positions adopted by the Congress government after Indira Gandhi's return to power in 1980. She decided that to counter the threat from the Hindu right, she would have to shed the image of a protector of minorities and lean towards an open display of Hindu religiosity. But there was no concealing the fact that she was doing this merely as an electoral tactic. The other development was the brazen bias of the police against Muslims in the northern Indian states. When major riots broke out in Moradabad, Meerut, and Biharsharif, the police often instigated them and joined on the Hindu side.

It is in this context that the Shah Bano case became a flashpoint. Shah Bano Begum, a divorcée, had approached the court for maintenance by her husband in accordance with the law applicable to all citizens. The Supreme Court in 1985 upheld her claim to receive alimony on the ground of the fundamental right to equality which, it said, superseded the personal law of religious communities. But, as has become customary in the Indian judiciary, the court also went on to write an exegesis on religion to assert that the claim of alimony was in accordance with Islam. Muslim traditionalists were extremely upset by the judgment, questioning the competence of the judges to pronounce on the tenets of Islam. The Rajiv Gandhi government, fearing the loss of electoral support among Muslims, passed a law in parliament in 1986 to annul the force of the Shah

Bano judgment and lay down that Muslim women will only be entitled to maintenance for ninety days after their divorce.

Both Hindu nationalists and women's rights activists condemned this move by the Congress government. For the BJP, this was one more proof of the opportunist politics of Muslim appeasement by the Congress, whereas the women's movement denounced the government's political intervention to overturn a progressive court decision in favour of women's rights. Although the Supreme Court in 2001 reaffirmed the Shah Bano judgment and effectively nullified the operation of the 1986 law on Muslim divorce and alimony,[21] the issue had already set into motion an entire train of events that transformed Indian politics. The organised show of outrage by Muslim organisations following the Shah Bano judgment led to a massive mobilisation by Hindu nationalists against the appeasement politics of the Congress, culminating in the Ram Janmabhoomi movement and the demolition of the Babri Masjid. On the other side, it seriously dented the credibility of the Congress as a principled defender of secularism. Even those in the women's movement were alarmed at the way the Hindu right wing hijacked the demand for women's rights – purely opportunistically, of course, since they only directed it against Muslim personal law and refused to admit the lack of gender equality in Hindu society. By the 1990s, the terms of the debate over secularism had completely shifted.

## The Fall of Secularism

If the defence by the courts of the secular idea of individual rights to freedom and equality over religious laws had earlier led to protests from the minority community, as in the Shah Bano case, by the 2010s it was organised Hindu opinion which was defending the rights of the believer over secular freedoms.

---

[21] *Danial Latifi v. Union of India*, Supreme Court, 2001.

A particularly explosive conflict developed in 2018 over a Supreme Court judgment involving ritual regulations at the temple of Ayyappan at Sabarimala in Kerala. The temple is actually at a site where forest-dwelling Adivasi people earlier used to worship a god called Ayyanar. Ayyappan is the new deity after it was incorporated by upper castes into the Brahmanical religion. In fact, if you ask local residents, they will tell you, if they want to be truthful, that Adivasi people, including women, used to come to the temple even in the 1960s. In its present form of Ayyappan, the deity has become a young celibate who must be protected from the presence of women of child-bearing age. Hence, except for the very young and the old, no women are allowed in the temple.

Some women's rights activists went to court with the allegation that the rules enforced at the Sabarimala temple discriminate against women. The Supreme Court in 2018 ruled that those rules violated the fundamental rights of equality and freedom of religion. Following the verdict, several women, individually as well as in groups, attempted to enter the temple, but were blocked by crowds of protesters. The Left-ruled Kerala government declared that it was obliged to carry out the Supreme Court decision and so would protect those wanting to worship at Sabarimala. Both opposition parties – the BJP and the Congress – protested against the court decision and called for a series of hartals, while the Left parties organised a human chain across the entire state to support the right of women to enter the temple. The confrontation became intense over the next few weeks, with women activists trying to break the cordon to climb up the steps to the temple and protesters physically resisting them. A Dalit woman was beaten up and had to go into hiding. A Muslim rights activist was arrested for hurting religious sentiments. A few women claimed they had eluded the protesters and managed to enter the temple, a claim confirmed by the government. The temple was closed for two days in order to purify it. Finally, after repeated petitions, the Supreme Court has recently agreed to reconsider its verdict.

The Sabarimala case revealed the deep quandary into which the attempt in India to use the law as an instrument for instilling greater individual freedom and equality in religious practices had fallen. Individual rights had been balanced with the freedom of religious communities to maintain their identity and autonomy in religious matters. To achieve that balance, courts had gone to great lengths to evaluate beliefs and practices to determine the precise limits of religion within which the community should have autonomy. But did that autonomy apply only to believers? Could those who did not believe in the religion claim, on the basis of constitutional rights, to participate in deciding the practices of a religious community? Until the 1980s, these questions were raised only in relation to the minority communities and, as we have seen, the conservatives within those communities were recognised as their representative authorities. Now the same claim was being made on behalf of the faithful among the Hindus.

The question could not be avoided. Was a woman wishing to enter into the presence of Lord Ayyappan acting out of a belief in the deity or in order to exercise a civil right? If the former, then surely she would respect the deity's wish not to have women in his vicinity. If the latter, would that not be a violation of the right of believers to practise their religion in their chosen way? If the question was one of removing the stigma on menstruation or giving women the chance to worship at the temple, the matter should have been discussed and debated within the community of believers. In fact, those who know this region of Kerala will tell you that there are several other Ayyappan temples where women are allowed. Not only that, individual women have often been allowed into the Sabarimala temple by special arrangement with the trustees. As we all know, every rule in Hinduism can be broken by special arrangement with Brahman authorities. All that is necessary is the exercise of power and money and the performance of a penance (*prāyaścitt*). But once the matter turned into a political confrontation over a court verdict, positions hardened on all sides. Finally, even the court was forced to listen to the voice of the faithful – this time representing the majority community.

Nevertheless, the choice between secular rights and the rights of the religious community continued to be less a matter of principle than of political opportunity. As you know very well, the Modi government in its second term has openly advanced the cause of Hindutva and, through laws and executive action, pushed to achieve several of its demands that would pave the way towards a Hindu nation-state (*rāṣṭrīya rājya*). The abolition of Kashmir's special status was one such step. Another was the abolition of the triple talaq form of Muslim divorce. If the BJP took the side of the religious community on the Sabarimala issue, on the question of triple talaq it was for women's rights.

The practice of triple talaq has been criticised for a long time both within and outside the Muslim community in India. It is prevalent mostly in the region of South Asia where the Hanafi school of jurisprudence is predominant among Sunni Muslims. But Pakistan and Bangladesh have both abolished triple talaq by law. In India, the arch-conservatives on the Muslim Personal Law Board are neither willing to allow any interference by parliament or the courts in their family laws nor can they come to any agreement on reforms which they could recommend. Even though few doubt that the practice leads to much cruelty towards women, the situation remained unchanged. When some Muslim women approached the Supreme Court, it ruled in 2017 that the triple talaq violated constitutional rights and advised the government to enact a law to make it illegal. A bill was introduced in parliament but it was stalled in the Rajya Sabha. Following the elections of 2019, the BJP government reintroduced the bill and got it passed in both houses. Not only did it declare the practice illegal and unconstitutional but it was also made a criminal offence so that a man attempting to divorce his wife in this fashion could be tried and sentenced to imprisonment. Few will question the propriety of the act, even though some think that making it a criminal offence could lead to its misuse. Nonetheless, there is little doubt that the BJP was so vociferous in its defence of women's rights only because the religious community involved was Muslim. Only a few months before, it had taken the opposite position on the Sabarimala temple, defending the right of Hindu believers against the exercise of equal rights by women.

Perhaps the most telling example of the failing strength of secular law to withstand the mobilised assault of the Hindu communal majority was the verdict of the Supreme Court in November 2019 on the Ayodhya dispute. Five judges produced a carefully crafted judgment of more than a thousand pages to make the following key points. First, even though archaeological excavations had shown the existence of an earlier structure below the sixteenth-century Babri mosque, that evidence did not constitute proof that a temple had been destroyed to build the mosque in its place. Second, the surreptitious installation of the Ram Lala idol within the mosque in 1949 was a mischievous and illegal act. Third, the demolition of the Babri Masjid in 1992 was a criminal act of violence. Fourth, there were several instances where mutual arrangements had been arrived at for Hindu devotees to worship Lord Ram on the premises and outer courtyard of the mosque. Having made these points, and considering the facts that the mosque no longer existed and that there was a sincere belief among large numbers of devotees that the site of the mosque was the birthplace of Ram, the judges unanimously ordered that the entire site be given to the Hindu plaintiffs for the construction of a temple and that the government allot a suitable piece of land to the Muslim defendants for them to build a new mosque.

We know that deviousness (*kuṭilātā*) is a professional skill in which lawyers are trained. But it is difficult to find a more glaring example of crafty legal reasoning than what is contained in the Ayodhya judgment. After laying out in scrupulous detail the evidence that established beyond doubt that the Hindu side had engaged in a series of illegal and criminal acts to create a dispute where none had existed and inflicting serious harm on the Muslim side, the judges went on to reward the Hindu side by giving it what it wanted – to build a Ram temple on the site of the mosque – and to compensate the Muslim side by asking the government to give it an alternative piece of land. It is telling that, for the first time in the history of the Supreme Court, the judge who wrote the judgment on behalf of his four colleagues on the bench did not put his name on it. Only an appendix to the judgment bore the name of its author who undertook an extraordinary journey through mythology, folklore, poetry, travelogue, and other texts normally read only by literary scholars to make the case that Ram Lala – the child Ram – was believed by many to be a real person who was born on the exact site occupied by the Babri Masjid. This was perhaps the final stroke in the long series of exercises engaged in by Indian courts to identify religious faith as a valid ground for its interpretation of secular law.

It was indeed a political solution which the judges felt compelled to clothe in a judicial garb. Everyone knew that had the judgment done anything other than allow the building of a temple on the site of the demolished mosque, tens of thousands of activists would have descended on Ayodhya to defy the court order and start construction. Governments at the centre as well as the state would have stood by and watched. The dispute would have got a new lease of life. By giving the stamp of judicial approval to the final victory of Hindu-majority communalism, the judges applied a closure to what was perhaps the longest communal dispute in modern Indian history. Secular democracy lost its biggest battle in India.

# 6

# India is a People's Federation

I SEE YOU ARE getting impatient because all I have told you so far is what is wrong with our nationalism. What, you will ask me, is true nationalism? What are my views on how our nation should be constructed?

I understand your impatience. But I first needed to remove the cobwebs of falsehood that have obscured your view. Now that I have done that job – at least some of it – I can turn to describing the true features of the Indian nation. It is not some abstract and imaginary form that I will draw for you, like the pictures of Bharat Mata you see on posters. What I will describe is the Indian nation as it actually exists today, created in the course of a history through which the peoples who live in the territory we now call India came together to live as parts of a single political formation. As I have told you before, I am a realist. I do not, like advertising agencies and political leaders, indulge in selling dreams. What I will describe now is the Indian nation in its true form. Even though it was always in front of you, you didn't see it because your vision was distorted by years of false nationalist propaganda.

## A Federation in Crisis

Let me begin by pointing out something about the recent Covid epidemic. Have you noticed how every state government became possessive about its territory and people? Many states sealed their borders, not allowing vehicles and people from other states to move across them. Some insisted that people from states that were badly affected by the infection would not be allowed in. States negotiated with other states over the condition in which migrants were living under the lockdown and finally arranging for their return home. The Delhi government tried to shut its borders to patients from other states seeking treatment in Delhi hospitals. When did you last see every state in the country become so acutely conscious of its own people as opposed to people from other states? Mind you, this is not like Karnataka quarrelling with Tamil Nadu over the waters of River Cauvery or Manipur arguing over the status of some districts that Naga leaders want to include in a future Nagalim. This is a phenomenon that has suddenly burst into the open as a general feature of the Indian federation (*bhāratīya saṅgh*). When the very lives of people are at stake, it is the state and not the national government which comes to the forefront. Why? What does it say about the nation?

To answer that question, you must first understand how the present federal structure has emerged in India. I have already shown you that the territories and peoples that are now part of India do not have some mysterious bond of unity going back to antiquity. They have been brought together into a single political unit as a result of British conquests, Indian political movements and their internal divisions, the negotiated transfer of power and partition, and the integration into the Indian Union of the princely states and the French and Portuguese colonial possessions. There is a particular legal framework that defines the relations between the different units of the federation with the centre. That framework too has evolved since the constitution was written. You probably know the main features of that framework. If you don't, you could look up any textbook on the Indian constitution.

But there is a deeper political and social history behind that legal framework. That is what I must explain to you. The constitutional history is a history of the state structure. It describes how, after the disintegration of the Mughal Empire, the British conquered territory, subjugated the regional kingdoms, and put together a new imperial political order. That is the basic state structure, embellished by constitutional reforms in the twentieth century, which the independent Indian state inherited. True, it enveloped all that within a new democratic and republican constitution. But the basic logic by which the state machinery functioned was still imperial (*sāmrājyavādī*). This is the point you have to understand.

The tension between the logic of the state machinery and that of popular democratic politics was revealed in the early 1950s over the demand for linguistic states. Those demands have a social history which is not the same as the constitutional history. People often forget that the fundamental step towards building a democratic federation (*lokātāntrik saṅgh*) in India was taken a hundred years ago when the Indian National Congress, soon after Gandhi became its leader, decided to reorganise its provincial committees along linguistic lines, disregarding the provincial boundaries created by the colonial state. Thus, a Gujarat Provincial Congress Committee (PCC) was set up for Gujarati-speaking districts even though they were all part of Bombay province; an Andhra PCC was set up even though the Telugu-speaking region was part of Madras province; a Kerala PCC was created even though the Malayalam-speaking Malabar districts were also part of Madras province; the Bengali-speaking Sylhet District Congress Committee was put under the Bengal PCC even though it was in Assam province. The restructuring became necessary because the new Congress under Gandhi decided to give up its exclusive use of English and reach out to the masses in the regional languages. It was a crucial move that enabled the national movement to strike deep roots in different parts of the country and send its message to millions beyond the small upper-class elite which, until then, had met for the annual Congress sessions to make speeches and pass resolutions in English. Linguistic provinces, comprising districts where a single major regional language is spoken and understood, were the foundation for the coming together within a democratic organisation of the people of the country mobilised around the demand for the end of colonial rule and the creation of an independent republic. The Congress was committed to this principle and promised in the 1946 elections to reorganise the provinces on the basis of language.

The federal structure as it evolved within the colonial state followed a different logic altogether. It was imperial rather than democratic. The constitutional reforms of 1935 introduced elected ministries in the provinces. But only certain categories of property owners and taxpayers could vote, so that the electorate was only about 10 per cent of the adult population. Besides, the provinces were far-flung and multilingual, crucially held together by a bureaucracy headed by colonial officials. These were the provinces that were distributed in 1947 between India and Pakistan according to their religious composition, while Punjab and Bengal were partitioned according to the religious composition of their districts. In addition, there were parts of British India which did not come under the federated provinces but were administered separately. On top of this were added the princely states which were of varying sizes and demographic character.

If you can find a map of India from the early 1950s, or even a list of the states from that time, you will see that there were four different kinds of states listed in the constitution. The Part A states were nine former provinces of British India which included large ones such as Madras, Bombay, Uttar Pradesh, and Madhya Pradesh. Part B states were the larger princely states, such as Hyderabad, Mysore, and Jammu and Kashmir, and unions of states, such as the Patiala and East Punjab States Union (PEPSU), Rajasthan, Saurashtra, Madhya Bharat, and Vindhya Pradesh. Part C states were some of the smaller provinces and princely states, such as Ajmer, Coorg, Kutch, and Himachal Pradesh, which were put under chief commissioners. Finally, there was the union territory of the Andaman and Nicobar Islands.

It was clear that this was an arbitrary and cumbersome arrangement. Something had to be done about it. The obvious principle was the one the Congress had initiated and upheld, namely, to reorganise the states along linguistic lines. But since the leaders whose politics had been to oppose the colonial bureaucracy were now in charge of that bureaucracy, their priorities suddenly changed. They felt that the need of the hour was to preserve the state machinery; democracy could wait. It is remarkable how Congress leaders who had earlier thrived on mass movements now became apprehensive of popular mobilisation. A commission set up in 1948 with civil servants and retired judges reported that creating linguistic states would not be in the national interest.[1] A high-level committee of senior Congressmen, including Nehru and Patel, decided that even though public sentiment in some regions was strongly in favour of linguistic states, it would not be wise to pursue that course for at least ten years in the interest of the country as a whole.[2] But by the end of 1952 the agitation for a Telugu-speaking Andhra state reached a flashpoint with the death of an activist on hunger strike. The government was forced to create the state of Andhra Pradesh in 1953. This had a chain effect, with

---

[1] The Linguistic Provinces Commission, 1948, consisted of S.K. Dar (retired high court judge), Panna Lall (retired ICS), and Jagat Narain Lal (lawyer).

[2] According to Sarvepalli Gopal, Nehru's biographer, it was Nehru who drafted the report. Gopal, *Jawaharlal Nehru: A Biography*, vol. 2 (Delhi: Oxford University Press, 1979), p. 257.

agitations springing up all over the country. The States Reorganisation Commission was set up to consider the entire matter.[3] It submitted its report in 1955, in which it recommended the abolition of the distinction between Part A, B, and C states, and the merger of the smaller states with larger ones, but warned that no single principle of reorganisation such as language or culture should be followed. Instead, it suggested a balanced approach in dealing with such demands in the interest of national unity. Accordingly, while it endorsed the formation of Kerala and Karnataka as separate states on the basis of language, it recommended the separation of Marathi-speaking Vidarbha from Bombay, which was to continue as a bilingual state. It also suggested that the integration of the Telugu-speaking Telangana region of Hyderabad with Andhra Pradesh be postponed until 1961.

It is clear that the top political leaders of the new republic were taking the advice of experienced functionaries of the old colonial state machine to push back against the growing popular demand for linguistic states. The democratic logic which was so persuasive in the days of the freedom struggle now became a cause of anxiety. Men like Nehru began to see mobilisations around language as narrow and divisive, in line with caste or religious loyalty. But no matter how hard they tried to insist that the industrialisation of the country was more important than cultural politics, the agitation for linguistic states continued, especially for the division of Bombay into Maharashtra and Gujarat, and the creation of a separate Punjabi-speaking state. The former demand was conceded in 1960. The latter was something of a proxy demand. While Sikhs were mobilised by the Akali Dal in favour of a monolingual Punjabi-speaking state, Hindus were organised, most actively by the Jana Sangh,

---

[3] The States Reorganisation Commission consisted of Fazal Ali (former judge), K.M. Panikkar (former diplomat), and Hriday Nath Kunzru (former member of the Constituent Assembly).

to declare themselves as Hindi speakers. This resulted in the creation in 1966 of the states of Punjab and Haryana. It was a division along religious lines masked as a linguistic division.

Hindu nationalists in the RSS, who were not very influential in the 1950s, were, as I have told you before, in favour of a unitary state of India. Golwalkar argued against federation as well as against linguistic states. The RSS was also in favour of using Hindi as the single national and official language.

## Language and Nationalism

Why was the force of linguistic identity so powerful? Why could not the state-builders, leaders of a successful national movement, resist the demand for linguistic states by appealing to the superior claims of the nation as a whole? The answer lies in the distinction between the nation (*rāṣṭra*) as the state (*rājya*), on the one hand, and the nation as the people (*lok*), on the other. The two meanings are not the same. As I have already explained to you, the state came down to us through a history that was imperial. Regardless of our new democratic constitution, the inner principle by which the machinery of the state works is still imperial. Despite attempts to employ Hindi and the regional languages in government and the courts of law, the default language of administration in India, seven decades after independence, is still English, the imperial language. There is no principle of democracy, and thus no overwhelming feeling of collective emotion which animates the state machine. On the other hand, the democratic spirit acquired an emotional life in India with the spread of nationalism among the people (*lok*). The vehicle through which nationalist feelings were expressed was language – the many languages spoken and understood by the people of this country. The nation as a democratic union of the people was created through the deeply felt bonds of sharing a language.

But this leads to a puzzle. There are many languages used by the people of India. If the coming together of a people into a nation is enabled by a common language, then are there many nations in this country we call India? In that case, how can we speak of the Indian nation? Am I saying that the idea of an Indian nation is false?

No, I am not. On the contrary, I am saying that the truth of the Indian nation is a quite remarkable fact. Indeed, it is possibly unique in world history. I certainly don't know of any other instance like it anywhere in the world. The multilingual character of the Indian nation reflects the unique fact that the Indian nation is a federation of peoples (*lokăsaṅgh*) – many peoples, each formed by the bonds of a language. The Indian nation is the result of the fact that many peoples speaking many languages agreed to come together to form a single nation with a single democratic and federal state.

But I have still not fully solved the puzzle. If each people is united by the ties of its shared language, then the conception of the nation – its form, its history, the emotions that it evokes – will be peculiar to that language and its people. In that case, how could several peoples, each united by its own language, also share the collective feelings produced by an Indian nation? Would not the Indian nation be doomed from its birth to an impoverished emotional life? Would it not be a fragile and fragmented nation?

This is exactly the fear that gripped leaders like Nehru and Patel after independence. It is also the reason why those like Golwalkar who spoke of Hindu Rashtra argued against linguistic states and insisted that India should adopt a unitary, not federal, constitution. They put their faith in the strength of the inherited state machine and did not see the amazing political achievement of the cultural imagination of the peoples of India. The truth is that even as each people was united by the national bonds produced by poets, novelists, artists, and musicians in its own linguistic culture, each such people also created a conception of the larger federated nation called India. While each linguistic unit imaginatively constructed its own national character, it also placed itself within a larger whole which it called the Indian nation. But since the cultural content was different for each of these peoples, their conception of the Indian nation was different. In other words, while the people of each linguistic region accepted that it belonged to the Indian nation, each had a different idea of what this Indian nation meant. Those were the terms under which all of these peoples agreed to come together in a federation.

I can see that you are not persuaded by this statement of what I believe to be the truth of Indian nationalism. So I will have to give you several examples to show you what I mean. You will have to be patient with me.

## In Praise of the Motherland

Take the slogan "*Vande mātaram*" and the song of which those are the first two words. The song is known all over India as a national song. It is a particular favourite of Hindu nationalists of the BJP and the RSS. I am sure you know it was written, in a combination of Sanskrit and Bengali, by the famous Bengali novelist Bankimchandra Chattopadhyay and inserted in his novel *Ānandamaṭh*.[4] It was set to music by Rabindranath Tagore and sung by him at the Congress session in Calcutta in 1896. The song became extremely popular during the Swadeshi movement in Bengal in the first decade of the twentieth century and was adopted as a chant (*mantra*) by the Bengal revolutionary groups. An English-language daily, edited by Aurobindo Ghose, which became a mouthpiece of the movement was called *Bande Mataram*. Those two words became so identified with the spirit of resistance all over Bengal that the police would crack down on anyone shouting the new slogan. But how did it become

---

[4] This novel by Bankimchandra Chattopadhyay (1838–1894) was published as a book in 1882.

a national song and what is the nation it worships as mother?

The poem's first verse in Sanskrit praises the rivers, the orchards, the breeze, the green fields ripe with crop, the trees decked with flowers, the moon lighting up the night. That is our mother – this particular part of the earth on which we live and call our own. Our mother smiles and her words are sweet as she blesses us and grants us happiness. You must know the lines:

*sujalāṃ suphalāṃ*
*malayajaśītalām*
*śasyaśyāmalāṃ*
*mātaram.*
*Śubhra-jyotsnā-pulakita-yāminīm*
*phullakusumita drumadalaśobhinīm,*
*suhāsinīṃ sumadhurabhāṣinīm*
*sukhadāṃ baradāṃ*
*mātaram.*

These lines evoke the image of a mother who is bountiful and kind. But the next verse pictures an image that is quite different.

*Saptakoṭīkaṇṭha-kala-kala-ninādakarāle,*
*dvisaptakoṭībhujaidhṛtakharakarabāle,*
*abalā kena mā eta bale!*

Seven crore voices are shouting for her victory, fourteen crore hands are holding aloft their swords, ready to defend their mother from her enemies. With such strength, why should she feel powerless? The question is: who are these seventy million children of the mother? One has to do a little bit of research to find the answer. It could not mean all Indians, because when Bankimchandra was writing, the population of India was far more than seventy million. It turns out that seven crore was then the population of Bengal.[5] In fact, for a long time afterwards, the figure seven crore continued to be used in literature as well as

---

[5] The population of Bengal province (which then included Bihar and Orissa) in the Census of 1881 was 69,536,861. This figure comprised men

ordinary conversation to indicate the total number of Bengalis.[6] Bankimchandra was singing the praises of Mother Bengal; he envisioned her seven crore children taking the vow to defend her with their swords. In fact, after the sonorous invocation in Sanskrit, which gives the song the quality of an incantation (*stotra*), he suddenly slips in the exclamation *"abalā kena mā eta bale!"* in plain Bengali.

Are you shocked that the song *"Vande mātaram"* is not addressed to Bharat Mata? You should not be. The idea of Bharat Mata had not come into existence when Bankimchandra was writing: that occurred some twenty years later. In fact, if you ask a Bengali friend, she would know the song as *"Bande mātaram"*, which is how it is pronounced in her language. Aurobindo Ghose, who later took to a monastic life and became Sri Aurobindo, was the first to translate the song into English. He called it the national anthem of Bengal. How, then, did it become the national song of India? I will answer that question shortly. But before that I must point out another important aspect of the song.

In the first verse, the image of the mother is one of natural splendour. But the third verse in Bengali introduces the idea of the mother as a divine idol. She is knowledge, she is *dharma*; she is the life in our bodies and the soul in our hearts. It is her idol that we worship in our temples. The next verse in Sanskrit names those idols:

*Tvam hi durgā daśapraharaṇadhāriṇī*
*kamalā kamala-dala-vihāriṇī*
*vāṇī vidyādāyinī*
*namāmi tvāṁ . . .*

---

and women of all religions. The population of India in the same census was 220,654,245.

[6] At the time of the Swadeshi movement in 1905–10, the most common figure used to indicate the total number of Indians was thirty crore.

Durga, Lakshmi, Saraswati – those are the divine forms merged in the figure of the mother. She is the goddess we love and worship.

There is no doubt that the song acquired such a phenomenal power to inspire many thousands of people in Bengal because it successfully connected the familiar religious image of the mother goddess with the novel idea of the motherland. The goddess represented power, wealth, and knowledge, but as the motherland she was also the fields, forests, rivers, and skies that sustain our lives. The novel *Ānandamaṭh* was set in the context of the eighteenth-century Sannyasi rebellion in northern Bengal against the new British power. The particular scene in which the song occurs clearly establishes that for those brave sons and daughters of Bengal who take the vow to fight against the oppressors, their goddess henceforth will be the motherland. Their struggle is to liberate the mother goddess from her enemies.

As the song achieved massive circulation in Bengal following the launch of the Swadeshi or Anti-Partition movement in 1905, it began to draw attention elsewhere in India. Aurobindo's writings in English contributed to this. The annual Congress session was held in 1906 in Calcutta and delegates from all over the country witnessed the electrifying effect the song and the slogan had on the assembled crowds. Bal Gangadhar Tilak returned to Maharashtra and popularised "*Vande mātaram*" as a nationalist proclamation. The famous poet Subramania Bharathi translated the song into Tamil and made it immensely popular. Once the idea of Bharat Mata came into circulation in the second decade of the twentieth century, the mother in "*Vande mātaram*" became identified with India. Interestingly, in its travel to other regions of India, only the first verse in Sanskrit was commonly recited or sung; the specific reference to seven crore children and all the Bengali lines in the song were ignored.

But that is not the end of the story. In the 1920s, when the song became a customary item at every public meeting organised by the Congress in Bengal, objections were raised by Muslims who complained that the religious imagery in the song was too evocative of idolatrous practices and was unacceptable to them. This led to a prolonged controversy. As I have told you, by 1930 most Muslims had left the Congress in Bengal and launched their own political organisations. "*Bande mātaram*" continued as the most popular national song within the Bengal Congress, which now became predominantly identified with Hindu opinion. The secret revolutionary groups in particular had always avoided drawing recruits from Muslims, claiming that their loyalty was suspect.

However, the controversy soon caught up with the Congress at the all-India level. Muslim members objected to its use in Congress meetings. The dispute reached such a state that a committee was appointed in 1937 with Nehru, Subhas Bose, Abul Kalam Azad, and Narendra Dev to look into the matter. Rabindranath Tagore was consulted for his advice. Tagore said that the later verses of the song could give rise to objections from those who followed a strictly monotheistic religion but the first verse could be sung by all.[7] I mention this because Tagore

---

[7] In a letter to Nehru in October 1937, Tagore wrote about the first portion of the song: "I found no difficulty in separating it from the rest of the poem and from those portions of the book of which it is a part, with all the sentiments of which, brought up as I was in the monotheistic ideals of my father, I could have no sympathy . . . I freely concede that the whole of Bankim's 'Vande Mataram' poem, read together with its context, is liable to be interpreted in ways that might wound Moslem susceptibilities, but a national song, though derived from it, which has spontaneously come to consist only of the first two stanzas of the original poem, need not remind us every time of the whole of it, much less of the story with which it was accidentally associated." Prabhat Kumar Mukhopadhyay, *Rabīndra jībanī*, vol. IV (Santiniketan: Visva-Bharati, 1994), pp. 101–11. The Indian National Congress adopted the first verse of "*Vande mātaram*" as a national song in 1937. After independence, it is recognised as a national song alongside "*Jana gaṇa mana*", the national anthem.

himself belonged to the Brahmo Samaj, whose doctrine is a strict monotheism and his university at Santiniketan to this day allows no idol worship on its campus. Yet in his poetry and songs, especially those on a patriotic theme, he frequently used the abundant resources in the Bengali language of the iconic imagery of the mother goddess to evoke love and reverence for the motherland.

What is particularly interesting is that while the Muslim political leadership in Bengal found the religious rhetoric in Bankimchandra's "*Vande mātaram*" unacceptable, when Bangladesh became independent in 1971, the song chosen as its national anthem was one composed by Tagore in 1905 – "*Āmār sonār bāṃlā, āmi tomāy bhālobāsi*". Here too the land of Bengal is depicted as mother, but she is the familiar everyday mother in her village home who shelters, feeds, sings, and plays. The leaders of Bangladesh were able to tap into the same cultural resources of the Bengali language to find a national song that tied the mother icon with the motherland but without the associations with Hindu idolatry.

This is only an example I am using to show you how emotions deeply rooted in cultural memory and hidden within a language can be summoned to create, alongside or embedded within one another, multiple meanings of nationalism. Anticolonial feelings were aroused in Bengal with the decision of the British rulers in 1905 to divide the province. A song written more than twenty years earlier by a celebrated writer became the rallying cry of unity for those people in Bengal who thought it was an unjust decision. It became the national song. But soon, the same song, with the deletion of some verses, also became the national song of India. No one thought there could be a contradiction between the two incarnations of the mother.

However, the adoption of the song was not unanimous even in Bengal. It became involved in the political divisions between Muslims and Hindus. But the Bengali people held on firmly to its linguistic identity even while they were part of Pakistan. When Pakistan declared Urdu as the sole national language, the people of East Pakistan protested and, on 21 February 1952, five protesters lost their lives when the police opened fire. After forming their own independent republic, the people of Bangladesh reached into their literary heritage to find a national anthem that evoked the powerful sentiments of love and devotion associated in the region's culture with the mother figure: 21 February is observed everywhere in the world today as International Mother Language Day.

I should add that in West Bengal today, "*Bande mātaram*" continues to be owned by the Congress and the Trinamool Congress, which identify with the pluralist nationalist tradition. They have naturalised the religious imagery of the song by recalling its significance in the history of the freedom struggle and are not embarrassed by its use among Hindu nationalists elsewhere in India as an ode to Bharat Mata and, by extension, the anthem of the imagined Hindu Rashtra. How did that happen? I think the reason lies in the desire of upper-caste Hindus in Bengal to claim a line of descent from Aryavarta, revealed in the many family genealogies, called *kulaji*, which were prepared by Brahmans tracing their origins to five Brahmans, accompanied by five Kayasthas, who were supposedly brought from Kanauj to Bengal by a certain King Ādiśūra.[8] This desire was also expressed in the way nationalist poets and novelists in Bengal sought to identify with the martial history of Rajputs and Marathas, something they could not find in the history of Bengali Hindus. For castes lower in the hierarchy, regions outside Bengal have recently become destinations for migrant workers seeking to improve their lives and secure the future of their children. Nationalism in Hindu-majority West Bengal is

---

[8] King Ādiśūra is supposed to have reigned in western Bengal in the tenth or eleventh century, but no historical evidence has been found of such a ruler.

fully invested in the idea of the Bengali people united by language but integrally a part of the Indian nation.

## Celebrating Fatherland

If love of motherland is the dominant emotion in the Bengali language which gives life to the idea of the nation – whether that nation is Bengal or India or Bangladesh – Maharashtra provides a striking contrast. You must have noticed that when Savarkar speaks of attachment to the national territory, he calls it *pitribhumi* (*pitrubhu* in Marathi) and translates it as "fatherland" in English. Grammatically, this is a little odd because *bhū* and *bhūmi* are both Sanskrit words in the feminine gender. Of course, *pitṛbhūmi* could also mean the land of one's forefathers in which case the land could still be referred to in the feminine. But one must remember that *mātṛbhūmi* clearly means the land that is one's mother and is translated as motherland in English. Actually, in using *pitribhu* and fatherland synonymously, Savarkar was following an established tradition in Marathi of depicting the nation as male. Let me tell you a little bit of this interesting history which casts its shadow far beyond the field of the Marathi language.

Any talk of nationalism in Marathi ends up getting tied to something called Maharashtra Dharma. There are at least two versions of this idea that have gained prominence since the late-nineteenth century. The first is associated with Vishnushastri Chiplunkar and Vishwanath Rajwade, two pioneering scholars on the history of Maharashtra.[9] Both were Brahmans – and that is not an incidental fact. Both took pride in the glory of Maratha political and military power in the seventeenth and eighteenth

[9] Vishnushastri Krushnashastri Chiplunkar (1850–1882) was a leading Marathi essayist who shaped the "high Marathi" prose style in the language. Vishwanath Kashinath Rajwade (1863–1926) was a pioneering historian of Maharashtra.

centuries but emphasised that the source of this power was to be found in Maharashtra's social history and especially the history of the Marathi language. Rajwade carried out a massive effort to collect and preserve an archive of documents from all over Maharashtra describing the local history of settlements and leading families of the region.[10] Maharashtra is possibly unique in India in the richness of such written historical accounts, called *bakhar* in Marathi, outside the Persian tradition of chronicles which, of course, was very well established in many parts of India. In fact, the only other regional tradition which is similar can be found in – and this may surprise you – the north-east of India where the Ahom rulers introduced the practice of compiling chronicles called *buranji* in the Tai-Ahom language, probably from as early as the fourteenth century; the practice was later continued in the Assamese language by leading families and religious establishments. For Rajwade, the *bakhar* collections became the source for re-creating the social history of Maharashtra in its own language.

Rajwade claimed that the Old Marathi in which the earliest *bakhar* prose accounts were written as well as the verses of the famous thirteenth-century text *Dnyāneśwarī* reveals a linguistic form directly derived from Pāṇini's Sanskrit grammar.[11] This, he said, was the pure urbane language spoken in Maharashtra at that time, free from contamination by foreign influences. It shows the spirit of a comprehensive dharma which united the religious, social, and political life of the people. Then came the invasions by Alauddin Khalji and the occupation of the region, first by the Turks and then by the Portuguese.[12] In three hundred

[10] He founded and led the Bharat Itihas Sanshodhak Mandal in Poona as a forum for the collection, discussion, and publication of documented history.

[11] *Dnyāneśwarī* is the verse commentary on the Bhagavad Gita by Sant Dnyaneshwar, composed in 1290. It is a canonical text of the Varkari sect.

[12] Prince Alauddin Khalji invaded and plundered the Yadava kingdom of Devagiri, near present-day Aurangabad, in 1292. Sultan Alauddin Khalji's

years of assault by foreigners (*mleccha*), religion was in jeopardy, the caste structure was broken, and political power was snatched from the people. But the spirit of Maharashtra Dharma was not extinguished. Despite corruptions, it survived in the Marathi language which preserved the precious compositions of the Varkari poets and the *bakhar* histories of the community. Finally, the combination of Ramdas Swami, a Deshasth Brahman ascetic, and his disciple Shivaji, a Maratha warrior, launched in the seventeenth century the political revival of Maharashtra which culminated, in the next hundred years, in the Maratha Empire establishing its dominance over most of India.[13]

What was Maharashtra Dharma as re-established in its full glory in the Maratha Empire? According to Rajwade, it included Hinduism as it was known in the rest of India. But it was much more. It was the establishment of righteous rule, namely, the rule of *dharma*, which meant the protection of the Brahman and the cow. It also meant brave leadership by the ruler and the freedom and unity of the people. The entire Varkari tradition, for Rajwade, represented the consolidation of all jatis in Maharashtra within the Brahmanical social order of varnashram. However, faith in Vithala, the deity worshipped in Pandharpur, produced a weak and passive sectarian tradition that turned its face away from politics. The Varkari tradition emphasised devotion and collective worship but did not resist the oppressors. It took the combination of Ramdas, who did not belong to the Varkari sect, and the warrior Shivaji to lead Maharashtra to martial glory. Marathas, under the guidance

---

army under the command of Malik Kafur invaded and incorporated the Konkan region into the Sultanate between 1311 and 1313. The Portuguese conquered Goa, then ruled by Sultan Yusuf Adil Shah of Bijapur, and established a settlement there in 1510.

[13] Sant Ramdas (or Ramdas Swami) (*c.*1608–1681) was the founder of the Samarth sect and is famed in Maharashtra as the spiritual guide of Shivaji.

of Brahmans, were the first nationalists of India who fought to protect Hindu identity against Muslim rulers. Maharashtra Dharma was superior to the Hindustani dharma of the Rajputs which was limited to a narrow military ethic and did not have the broader vision of Hindu political rule, which is why Rajput princes became subordinate allies of the Mughals. In Rajwade's view, Maharashtra Dharma encompassed Indian nationalism but was also something more.

This view of Maharashtra as the birthplace of a martial Indian nationalism intent on establishing a state free from foreign rule became firmly rooted in Brahman-dominated public culture. It was represented most dramatically in the historical personality of Shivaji on horseback with sword in hand. The nation was masculine, armed to defend itself against aggressors. The theme was repeated endlessly in popular history, historical novels, theatre, and, in the twentieth century, cinema. But, despite the claim that Maharashtra Dharma was the most developed form of Indian nationalism, it always retained its distinctly Marathi character. Tilak started the Shivaji festival as a nationalist mass ceremony and tried to introduce it in other provinces but failed. In the rest of India, Shivaji was undoubtedly revered as a national hero but remained too closely tied to Maratha history to occupy the entire space of the Indian nation.

This Brahman-inspired view of Maharashtra Dharma was strongly challenged by anti-caste activists such as Jyotirao Phule, Savitribai Phule, and Vithala Ramji Shinde, besides Dalit leaders such as Bhimrao Ambedkar.[14] They did subscribe to the idea of Maharashtra Dharma as embodied in the Varkari tradition

---

[14] Jyotirao Govindrao Phule (1827–1890) was an anti-caste reformer who founded the Satyashodhak Samaj to fight against the oppression of women and lower castes. His wife, Savitribai Phule (1831–1897), was a pioneer in women's education. Vithala Ramji Shinde (1873–1944) campaigned against untouchability and set up the Depressed Classes Mission for the education of Dalit students.

but refused to associate it with the Maratha Empire under the Brahman Peshwas. Indeed, anti-Brahman activists questioned the role of Ramdas Swami as Shivaji's spiritual leader and argued that the true legacy of Maratha valour was snatched away from Shivaji's successors by devious Brahman ministers.

Ambedkar and other Dalit activists even located the independent spirit of martial resistance in the Mahar soldiers of the East India Company who fought for the British to bring down Peshwa rule. You must have heard of Bhima Koregaon over which there has been much controversy recently and several prominent civil rights activists have been held in prison. Koregaon, on the bank of River Bhima, is where a small Company contingent which included many Mahar infantrymen was attacked by soldiers of Peshwa Baji Rao II's army in 1818. The attack was repulsed and was followed by a series of battles which eventually led to the defeat and fall of the Maratha Empire. Ambedkar organised in 1927 a celebration of the Mahar victory over the Peshwa army at Koregaon. It has since become an annual event organised by Dalits. This version of Maharashtrian bravery completely rejects the nationalist story told by Brahman historians.

But the multiple versions of the nationalist idea in Marathi culture have had significant impact on politics both inside and outside Maharasthra. The celebration of Shivaji as the foremost nationalist warrior and statesman continues unabated, as exemplified in numerous statues and lavish performances such as the monumental theatrical production called *Jānatā rājā* depicting his life.[15] Following the formation of Maharashtra state, the Shiv Sena was formed in 1966 to assert – using violence, if necessary – the priority of *marāṭhī māṇus* (the Marathi people) over others at home and aggressively flaunt Indian national power

---

[15] This play by Babasaheb Purandare was staged in an open arena in Pune in 2007 in five parts, three hours each, with a cast of more than 150 actors as well as camels and elephants. It was performed again in 2019.

outside, especially against Pakistan. In this sense, the Shiv Sena, whose top leadership consists of Brahmans and Chandraseniya Kayastha Prabhus, but whose supporters come mainly from the middle castes, follow the Brahmanical nationalist tradition of claiming militant Marathi nationalism as the true Indian nationalism. You may have also noticed that with the BJP increasingly claiming to represent the project of India as a Hindu Rashtra, the Shiv Sena has recently retreated to defending the interests of Maharashtra.

The Brahmanical tradition of militant nationalism is also carried on from Nagpur where Marathi Brahmans founded and ran the RSS. This leadership adopted the *bhagvā dhvaj*, the saffron-coloured flag of Shivaji's army, and instilled military discipline among its cadre, even as it promoted Hindi as the national language and set up units in all parts of the country. At the other end of the spectrum, Dalit intellectuals and activists from Maharashtra, following the lead of Ambedkar, have been at the forefront of the Dalit movement in India and several of them urge Dalits to give up their degrading status among Hindus and embrace the egalitarian practices of Buddhism.

### Language as Mother

Speaking of nationalism, whether majoritarian or pluralist, I have told you earlier that the myth of Aryavarta as the centre of Indian civilisation, the history of successive imperial states, and the emergence of Hindi as a language of public discourse have combined to create the widely held impression that the upper-caste North Indian Hindu male speaking Hindi, whether as mother tongue or an adopted language, is the typical representative Indian. But this impression has not gone without challenge, even within the main tradition of national politics, even though many would like to forget that history. I am speaking of Tamil Nadu which occupies such an important position in so many fields of national life.

Like Bengali, Marathi, and Hindi, Tamil too had its early moment of literary nationalism. But curiously, it was the Tamil language rather than the land which was deified as the mother goddess Tamil Thai.[16] Tamil was a classical language which could rival Sanskrit, reaching its golden age of the Sangam literature in the Buddhist period between the fourth century BCE and the first century CE. The canonical collection of sacred verses on ethics called *Thirukkuṛaḷ* by Thiruvalluvar does not have any particular theological content and is claimed by Tamils of every sect and denomination, including Christians and Muslims.[17] The song "*Niraarum kadai udutha*" in the famous 1891 play *Manonmaniyam* by Manonmaniyam Sundaram Pillai first depicted Tamil as *thaai* or mother.[18] So persistent has been this iconic representation that the song is now the official Tamil anthem, while a statue of Tamil Thai stands in Madurai and her temple in Karaikudi.

The idea of India as motherland made its entry into Tamil in the early-twentieth century through the poems of Subramania Bharathi. Bharathi travelled extensively all over India, attended Congress sessions, and spoke for the freedom of India from British rule. In one of his poems, he suggested that the Kurukshetra war was the Indian freedom struggle in which the Pandavas were like Indians today fighting for their legitimate rights against the Kauravas who, like the British, had usurped power.

But by the 1920s, the Non-Brahman movement, represented in politics by the Justice Party, attacked this version of nationalism as a Brahman-led attempt to impose Aryan dominance over the Dravidian peoples of southern India. The Justice Party opposed the Congress and demanded that the colonial

---

[16] The Roman transliteration is Thamizhth Thaai.

[17] This collection of 1330 couplets is variously dated between 300 BCE and 500 CE.

[18] Manonmaniyam Sundaranar (1855–1897) was a historian and playwright.

authorities provide greater representation and reserved jobs for non-Brahmans. But the cultural side of the movement proved far more influential. Maraimalai Adigal, who was also the proponent of a neo-Shaiva religious revival within the Vellala caste, led the campaign for pure Tamil shorn of Sanskrit words.[19] This was, you will notice, linguistic reform in a direction totally contradictory to the one taken by Hindi, Marathi, or Bengali, where Sanskrit words were borrowed or coined to produce a new vocabulary suitable for modern administrative, scientific, and philosophical discussion. The literature, oratory, and performance inspired by the Dravidian movement shunned the Brahmanical Tamil of the nineteenth century and went back to classical Tamil roots to shape a new public language.

The towering figure in the Dravidian cultural movement was E.V. Ramasamy, commonly known as EVR, who later came to be revered as Periyar, which means "the great old leader" (*buzurg netā*).[20] Under his leadership, the Self-Respect movement vigorously campaigned for the removal of untouchability and the end of degrading hereditary occupations such as scavenging. It also tried to put a stop to child marriage and encouraged widow remarriage, romantic marriage, and marriage across castes and religions. Significantly, the movement asked couples not to get married in temples and instead have their marriages registered under civil law.

But EVR's criticism of Brahmanism went much further. Upholding a very different identity of the Tamil-speaking people, he equated Brahman dominance in the Tamil region with the racial superiority asserted by Aryans over Dravidians and the imposition of Sanskrit on Tamil. He also criticised the Brahman dominated Hindu religion for assigning value and prestige to

---

[19] Maraimalai Adigal (1876–1950) was a prominent writer on Tamil literature and Shaiva philosophy.

[20] E.V. Ramasamy (1879–1973) was the founder of the Self-Respect movement and the Dravidar Kazhagam.

the most unproductive group in society and reducing women to abject subjugation. He urged people to give up religious rituals which were nothing but superstition. EVR himself was a thorough rationalist and atheist and preached against religion in the strongest possible language. In fact, he did not stop with merely speaking his mind; he acted on his beliefs. He went around towns and villages, often accompanied by his younger colleague Annadurai, burning copies of the Manusmriti and pulling out idols from temples and throwing them into a pond or river. To add a personal note, I myself saw him organise events at fairgrounds where highly satirical and scandalous presentations were made of stories from Hindu mythology. I was sceptical of the way he ridiculed gods and goddesses and the fantastic tales told about them. But he would stroke his flowing white beard and insist that people had been lulled into sleep by the opium of religion. They had to be shocked in order for them to realise that they had been fooled all these years. Although I fully agreed with his views on religion, I was not convinced by his tactics. I believe this was one of the reasons why he later fell out with Annadurai, who was more interested in building a broad base of support for his party in order to fight elections. But I could not deny that EVR was able to persuade lots of people to take the vow of atheism.

In EVR's view, the Tamil people were Dravidian and non-Brahman; the Brahmans in their midst represented the Aryan imperial forces of North India. The conflict was sharply posed when the provincial Congress ministry led by Rajagopalachari decided in 1938 to introduce the compulsory teaching of Hindi in Madras schools. EVR and other leaders of the Justice Party launched widespread agitations with the slogan "Tamil Nadu for Tamilians", arguing that the teaching of Hindi, with its religious baggage of Aryan and Brahmanical culture, would destroy the rationalist culture of the Tamil people. The movement drew massive support and more than a thousand agitators went to prison. Of course, with the onset of the war in 1939, the Congress ministry resigned.[21]

But the anti-Hindi movement became even stronger after independence when there were attempts to replace English with Hindi as the official language of the country. The background to this was the political demand made by the Dravida Munnetra Kazhagam (DMK), formed by Annadurai and Karunanidhi in 1949, to establish a separate federation called Dravida Nadu, the Dravidian nation consisting of the non-Brahman peoples of southern India. With the anti-Hindi agitations of the 1950s, the focus on language turned the movement into one of Tamil nationalism. Tamil Thai was now the violated and endangered mother, threatened by an aggressive Indian nation located in the north. Both EVR and Annadurai condemned Hindi imperialism which, they said, represented Aryan Brahmanical dominance.

The agitations were quite frenzied: the Indian map and copies of the constitution were burnt and, in some cities, shops owned by North Indian traders were attacked. In 1964–5, thousands took to the streets shouting slogans against Hindi, hundreds went to jail, and at least ten burnt themselves to death. I happened to be in Madras at the time and saw the outburst of emotion displaying love for Mother Tamil and hatred for the witch Hindi. The latter was called *arakki* or *pey* (*rākṣasī*) meaning a demoness, *potuppen* (*veśyā*) meaning a whore, and much worse. At this point, the idea of Tamil as the mother language of the Tamil nation allowed no room for Indian nationalism. I should point out that this was no uncommon sentiment held by a fringe group; it was shared among very wide sections of Tamils. This was proved in 1967 when the DMK led by Annadurai swept the Congress from power. Two years later, Madras state was renamed Tamil Nadu, meaning Tamil country (*tāmil deś*).

---

[21] Actually, the order for the compulsory teaching of Hindi in secondary schools in Madras was withdrawn in 1940.

I also remember that because of the protests, All India Radio stopped broadcasting the national news in Hindi from all stations in Tamil Nadu. This continued for many years.

Of course, the DMK gave up its position of separating from India and decided in the 1960s to accept the Indian constitution and participate in elections. After splitting from the DMK, M.G. Ramachandran (MGR) even named his party the All India Anna DMK to show that it represented more than the Tamil people. Under Jayalalithaa, the party also gave up the atheistic cultural ideology of the Self-Respect movement and embraced popular Hindu religious practices. Nevertheless, even though Tamil nationalism based on its linguistic identity has taken its place within the Indian nation, it has done so by engaging with the Indian state on the terms of this inclusion. The Dravida political and cultural struggle, from the Non-Brahman movement, the Self-Respect movement, the anti-Hindi agitations, the demand for a separate Dravida Nadu, to the continued position in power of the two Dravida parties for more than half a century, represents the history of this negotiation.

### The Ignored Northeast

Bengal, Maharashtra, Tamil Nadu – these are all major constituents of the Indian nation with extensive association with the history of Indian nationalism. But even in these cases, as I have shown you, the relation to the Indian nation of the Bengali, Maharashtrian, or Tamil people, each united by language, was not the same. Not only that; in each case, the relation was a matter of controversy and even conflict. I could give you more examples to make the same point – from Andhra, Kerala, Karnataka, Goa, and Odisha, for example. You have already heard enough about Jammu and Kashmir and the thwarted national aspirations of the people living there. Punjab too, you might remember, saw a prolonged and violent separatist movement in the 1980s, even though it is a region that figures prominently in the story of Indian nationalism.[22] Assam too had a similar experience in the same period when militants of a Liberation Front carried out a violent campaign to separate Assam from India.[23]

But let me not multiply examples. Instead, I will take you to a part of the Indian mainland about which you probably know the least. These are what used to be called, at the time of Indian independence, the hill districts of Assam. You will see how much the Indian state was forced to concede in order to negotiate special terms for the inclusion of the peoples of this region into the Indian nation. Those negotiations remain inconclusive. In fact, in my view they will never reach a satisfactory resolution unless the dominant opinion within the Indian nation recognises the distinct national character of the peoples of the north-eastern hills.

I have already told you that the British treated the hill districts of Assam as an exceptional case. Unlike the agrarian regions of India where the colonial state thoroughly reorganised the legal, administrative, commercial, revenue, judicial, and police systems, the presence of the state was very superficial in the north-eastern hills. The region was not considered valuable either for its revenue or its natural resources. British officials generally preferred to exercise their authority as "Bor Sab" (*baḍe sāhab*

---

[22] The Khalistan movement which aimed at creating an independent Sikh state reached its peak in the late 1970s and 1980s with many violent actions of terrorism and assassination. The most dramatic action by the Indian armed forces against the movement was the storming of the Golden Temple in Amritsar in June 1984, which was followed a few months later by the retaliatory assassination of Prime Minister Indira Gandhi. The movement was crushed in the early 1990s by massive counterinsurgency operations in Punjab by the security forces.

[23] The United Liberation Front of Assam (ULFA) was founded in 1979 and launched its most sustained spell of violent activities in the early 1990s. The Indian state suppressed the movement by military action.

in Assamese pronunciation) by recognising, and sometimes creating, local chiefs who were supposed to maintain peace and enforce their customary practices. The British also projected an image of being the protectors of what they called the tribes against commercial and political encroachment by the more economically advanced people of the plains. For this reason, they drew territorial lines to regulate the entry of outsiders into tribal areas and prohibit them from acquiring property there. When a provincial ministry was set up in Assam under the constitutional reforms of 1935, the hill districts were left out of its jurisdiction and kept under the direct charge of the governor.

The reason why the British found it so difficult to administer the Assam hills in the same way as the plains has to do with a much more fundamental truth about the people of this region. Historically, there were many attempts by powerful states like the Ahom and the Kachari, or the Manipuri kingdoms, or indeed the Burmese rulers, to establish dominance over the hill peoples and extract tribute and slaves. The struggle of most of these hill peoples was to avoid coming under the domination of states and retain their autonomy as stateless societies. In this sense, the peoples of the north-eastern hills have a historical experience that is very different from that of the agrarian societies of most of India. It is also different from the experience of the Adivasis of central and western India who, even while retaining their cultural distinctness, have had much closer connections with large state formations and, in some cases, even created their own kings and developed their own tax systems. The autonomy of the hill peoples of the north-east has its foundation in the desire to remain out of state control.

This is not to say that the hill peoples lived in some pristine state of nature. They had their own social organisations which were quite complex but entirely different from those of the caste societies of the plains. To mark the distinction, the British called them tribes.[24] What they meant was that instead of *jāti*, the society was based on relations of clan (*kul*) and lineage (*vaṃś*). The hill people developed agriculture and crafts. Their social organisation varied. Among the Khasi, for instance, there were settled villages and even chiefs, called Siems, who had something like royal status and were accorded a position by the British that was similar to that of the rulers of princely states. Others, such as the people of the Lushai Hills, periodically moved their settlements and seemed to be in a constant state of migration. Besides, individuals often migrated from one village to another and took up membership of another clan (*kul*). Not only that, the practice of *jhum* – shifting cultivation on hillside terraced lands – made it impossible to apply to the hill communities the rules of agrarian property that prevailed in the plains. In short, the absence of a state was accompanied by a resistance to being fixed to a permanent habitation which is what the kingdoms of the agrarian plains wanted in order to make it easier for them to impose land taxes and police the population.

The region also had a vast number of languages, mostly belonging to the Tibeto-Burman family but each spoken by people of only a few neighbouring villages. I once heard an amusing story from an Angami schoolteacher who was explaining to me how the different dialects spoken by the Naga people differed from one another. She said that the first human being was called Ukepenofu who had many children and grandchildren. When she died, she went to heaven. Her descendants thought that to maintain contact with her, they would build a tower reaching all the way up to heaven. But Ukepenofu did not want all these people to come to her to ask for gifts. So she made everyone speak a different language. When someone asked for a stone, they brought him a stick; when someone needed a plank of wood, he got a bucket of water. All was confusion. In the end,

---

[24] The manuscript uses the English word "tribe".

they had to give up the idea of building the tower. But they were left with their many languages. The teacher who told me this story also added half-jokingly that this was probably how the Naga people made sense of the Biblical story of the Tower of Babel.

The observation is not without significance. The British colonial officials may have decided not to interfere too much in the affairs of the hill tribes, but they did allow Christian missionaries to set up churches and schools, and to teach people to read, write, and become Christians. By the 1930s and 1940s, there emerged, especially among the Khasi, Garo, Naga, and Lushei people, a small but significant middle class that was educated in English. If I remember right, the 1951 census found that the literacy rate in what was then called the Lushai Hills was 30 per cent and in the Khasi-Garo-Jaintia Hills 20 per cent, both higher than the average literacy rate in India at the time. Today, the literacy rate in Mizoram (the former Lushai Hills) is above 90 per cent, one of the highest among Indian states.[25]

Arunachal, Meghalaya – these are names that conjure up poetic images from Sanskrit *kāvya*. But in actual fact, the nationalist movement in India had virtually no connection with the north-eastern hills, not even with the middle class there. You may have heard of Rani Gaidinliu as a fearless Naga freedom fighter. She was a Kabui Naga whose cousin Jadonang founded the Heraka religious movement which wanted to revive the traditional religion of the Naga people and drive Christian missionaries and Christian Kukis out of the Naga regions of

---

[25] According to the 1951 Census, the relevant literacy rates as percentages for districts constituting the present north-eastern hill states were: Mizoram 31.14, Meghalaya 19.21, Manipur 12.56, Nagaland 10.52, Arunachal Pradesh 4.11. The average literacy rate for India was 18.34. The corresponding rates in 2011 were: Mizoram 91.58, Meghalaya 75.48, Manipur 79.85, Nagaland 80.11, Arunachal Pradesh 66.95. The average for India was 74.04. Mizoram has the third highest literacy rate among Indian states, after Kerala 93.41, and Lakshadweep 92.28.

Manipur. After clashes with the police, Jadonang was arrested and executed in 1931. Gaidinliu then became the leader and declared war on the British. For several months, she and her followers were hunted by the Assam Rifles through the hill regions until she set up camp in the North Cachar Hills, where her forces were overpowered and she was arrested. Jawaharlal Nehru met her in Shillong jail in 1937, greeted her as a brave freedom fighter, and addressed her as "Rani". The title stuck to her name after independence when, against the background of the insurgency in Nagaland, Rani Gaidinliu was celebrated as an Indian freedom fighter. In actual fact, her struggle was against British rule but she had nothing to do with Indian nationalism.[26] And Nagas have never had any kings or queens. In the 1970s and 1980s, the RSS tried to present her as a defender of the Naga indigenous religion against the secessionist Christian political movement.

I don't think the Indian National Congress passed a single resolution relating to the hill districts of Assam before independence.[27] Even Congress leaders in Assam rarely said anything about the hill peoples. The fault was not entirely theirs. British officials were determined not to allow politicians from the plains to have anything to do with the hills. After provincial ministries were formed in 1937, even elected premiers like Gopinath Bardoloi and Muhammed Saadulla had to take the governor's permission to visit the hill districts.[28] In the months

---

[26] Gaidinliu (1915–1993) was awarded the Padma Bhushan in 1982.

[27] Actually, there was a Congress resolution at its Faizpur session in 1936 condemning the exclusion of the hill districts of Assam from the purview of the reformed provincial ministries as "yet another attempt to divide the people into different groups . . . and to obstruct the growth of uniform democratic institutions in the country."

[28] Gopinath Bardoloi (1890–1950), a leading Congressman, was briefly premier of Assam in 1939 and chief minister from 1946 to 1950. Syed Muhammed Saadulla (1885–1955) of the Muslim League was premier of Assam in three spells between 1937 and 1946 and member of the Constituent Assembly of India.

before Indian independence, some British officials in Assam suggested to their favourite tribal chiefs that the north-eastern hills might be clubbed together and merged with Burma as a crown colony or declared an independent state under British protection. But this proposal was not approved by authorities in Britain who made it clear that the region must remain part of the Indian province of Assam.

That is when Indian leaders in the Constituent Assembly turned their attention to the place of the hill districts of Assam in the Indian Union. It would be unfair to summarily condemn them for their lack of sympathy for the people of the north-eastern hills. National leaders like Nehru who took an active interest in the region, or Assam Congressmen like Gopinath Bardoloi or Bimala Prasad Chaliha, were not unsympathetic. They realised the need to respect the demand for autonomy of the hill tribes, for otherwise their entire way of life could be threatened, causing unrest and revolt. On the other hand, the ideology of progressive nationalism convinced them that efforts must also be made to modernise and develop the economy of the region and integrate it with the rest of the country. The trouble was that they thought of this dual approach as the magnanimous policy of a state that still saw the region as the frontier of its imperial territory. It was impossible for them to regard the hill peoples or their representatives as equal partners in the making of the new Indian nation-state.

The constitutional solution to the problem of reconciling the tribes' demand for political autonomy with the urge expressed by Assamese politicians to integrate the hills with the plains was devised by a committee headed by Bardoloi.[29] It drafted the Sixth Schedule which, with substantial modifications over time,

---

[29] The Bardoloi Sub-committee of the Constituent Assembly had two other members: J.J.M. Nichols-Roy (1884–1959), a prominent Khasi leader, and B.N. Rau, constitutional adviser.

still remains a part of the constitution. The Schedule enabled the formation of district councils in the hills with legislative and administrative powers over land, forests, agriculture, village management, chiefs and headmen, tribal law, social customs, and primary education. This would be the domain where elected tribal representatives would have political autonomy. As it happened, this compromise crafted by the Sixth Schedule satisfied nobody. The traditional chiefs did not like an elected council being foisted on them, while the middle class found the autonomy offered to them thoroughly insufficient.

Naga leaders rejected the district council proposal and instead formed the Naga National Council (NNC) in 1946. At this time, the organisation was dominated by Ao representatives. But in the weeks before Indian independence, Angami Zapu Phizo took a small team to Delhi to meet Gandhi and other leaders and press the Naga claim to independent nationhood.[30] On 14 August 1947, Phizo declared independence of Nagaland. To this day, even though parties and leaders in Nagaland participate in electoral politics and join governments within the framework of the Indian constitution, no Naga leader or organisation has openly rejected this declaration. The day is still observed by many in Nagaland as their independence day.

Phizo, who had collaborated with the Japanese in Burma during the Second World War, started campaigning for Naga independence soon after his return in 1946. It is important for you to remember that in addition to the role of the Christian religion in transforming the traditional social and cultural practices of the people of this region, the fact that it was also an active theatre of war, with the Japanese army advancing from Burma to the Naga hills to be ultimately stopped at Kohima, had the effect of infusing a modern military culture among the

---

[30] A.Z. Phizo (1913–1990) was the leader of the Naga independence movement in its earlier phase.

people. There was active recruitment by the British of young men from the Naga and Lushai hills during the war, most of whom were demobilised when the war ended.

To get back to my story, Phizo took over the NNC in 1949 and called for a plebiscite on the question of joining India. This unofficial plebiscite was held by the NNC in 1951 in which an overwhelming majority is supposed to have voted for an independent Nagaland. You do not have to be sceptical about this result because, when Phizo called for a boycott of the 1952 general elections, there were no candidates and no polling in the Naga Hills. Phizo had not yet given up the hope of a negotiated settlement with the Indian government because he met Nehru several times in 1952 but could not get a satisfactory assurance. In 1954, he went into the forests to prepare for a guerrilla war but, faced with an onslaught from the Indian security forces, decided to flee to East Pakistan and look for international support. Neither Pakistan nor China was keen to help him with his military preparations. Finally, after a long and hazardous journey through Europe, he reached London sometime in 1958. Helped by Michael Scott, an Anglican missionary who had earlier been in India, Phizo sought to publicise the cause of Naga independence as the struggle of indigenous people in India. From his distant base in London, he also tried to direct the Naga resistance against the Indian state.

Despite the sympathetic gestures from Indian political leaders towards the demand for autonomy of the hill peoples, the machinery of the state came down hard on any show of resistance. Following the boycott of the general elections in 1952, leaders of the NNC were harassed and protest gatherings dispersed by force. The Naga Hills were declared a disturbed area and special regulations introduced to allow for tough administrative action. All foreign missionaries were prohibited in the region. When Phizo went underground and tried to organise an armed resistance, the Assam Rifles were deployed. In 1954, Phizo formed the People's Sovereign Republic of Free Nagaland with the help of the Chang chiefs of Tuensang near the Burma border. The army was sent in to crush the uprising. In spite of that, there were some 15,000 rebel fighters in 1956. Even after leaving the scene, Phizo continued to be active in Naga politics. When the resistance in Tuensang was crushed by the Indian army, Phizo formed a Federal Government of Nagaland with the help of several Sema leaders. The counterinsurgency operations by the army were extremely bloody, with massacres, rape, and the burning of entire villages. In those days, there was virtually no media presence in such remote areas. Consequently, it is impossible to get independent accounts of what happened. But I have heard so many Naga men and women speak in harrowing detail of the terror unleashed by the Indian army in the 1950s that I have no doubt that it was unspeakably violent and brutal.

After the insurgency was crushed, the Indian government decided to make a political gesture and give Nagaland the status of a separate state in 1963. The temporary provisions of Article 371, designed, you may remember, to accommodate Mysore and Travancore at the time of the adoption of the constitution, were now put into use to grant several special powers to the new state to protect its political and cultural autonomy. Central laws were not to apply to Nagaland in matters of the religious or social practices and customary civil and criminal law of the Nagas, or for the ownership and transfer of land. Elections were held to the Nagaland assembly in 1964 and, by the following year, the Naga National Organisation led by Shilu Ao emerged as the main electoral party in Naga politics. Since then, political parties have never been very stable in Nagaland, with frequent splits, coalition governments, and legislators switching from one party to another.

But the spirit of rebellion and the demand for Naga independence did not die. Like most underground movements of resistance, the Naga armed organisations too went through dissention and splits. The National Socialist Council of Nagaland (NSCN) was formed in the early 1980s by a younger generation of militants who claimed to have a Maoist ideology of socialism but adopted the slogan "Nagaland for Christ". The NSCN rejected the peace agreements that various Naga leaders had earlier signed with the Indian government and repudiated Phizo for being a reactionary tribalist.[31] It sought help from China which, however, refused to do much more than offer some operational training to its guerrilla fighters. In 1997, it entered a peace agreement with the government to halt the insurgency. Currently led by T. Muivah, the NSCN is in negotiations with the Indian government for a new peace agreement which, it says, must recognise Naga sovereignty and unify all Naga areas within and outside Nagaland into a new state within India called Nagalim.

If you turn from Nagaland to the history of Mizoram, you will find that the role of the educated Christian middle class is even more prominent. While the Lushei (also called Kuki) took the lead, they organised themselves across tribal divisions in the Mizo Union, captured the district councils, launched a non-cooperation campaign against the chiefs, and, in 1954, successfully abolished the chief's office throughout the Lushai Hills. This laid the foundation for a democratic reordering of cultural and political life. There was a severe famine in the region in 1959. A popular organisation formed to provide famine relief became in the 1960s the Mizo National Front (MNF) which demanded independence and separation from India. The repression from the Indian armed forces was severe, including bombing from the air of populated settlements in and around the town of Aizawl in 1966 and the forcible relocation of entire villages the following year – events that spread intense hatred for India among the people and marked a turning point in political relations.

---

[31] The manuscript has *trāibalvādī* in quotes.

The MNF insurgency, led by Laldenga, continued for more than two decades until a peace agreement was signed in 1986. Mizoram became a state in 1987 and Laldenga was its first chief minister.

Nagaland and Mizoram show how language and religion came together among peoples who had no historical connections with Indian nationalism to produce a national feeling that was intensely conscious of its distinct identity and claim to legitimate sovereignty. They were small in number – less than a million Nagas and half a million Mizos in 1951. But they suddenly found themselves in the Indian Union and were conferred Indian citizenship by the constitution without ever asking for it. As people in the region will tell you, they are only accidental Indians. In this sense, the position of the people of Nagaland and Mizoram is quite different from that of Kashmiris or Goans or Sikkimese who either had historical links with Indian nationalism or expressly voted to join the Indian Union. The national consciousness of the Naga and Mizo peoples was quite different.

I have told you about the many languages in this region, some spoken by only a few hundred people. But this situation has changed in the course of the last century. A language called Nagamese arose as the language of the marketplace – a mixture of Naga words with Assamese – to facilitate interactions with the plains. The mission schools taught English, but only a small section which became fluent in the language had access to middle-class occupations. In recent years, although English is the official language of Nagaland, Nagamese has emerged as the common vernacular with a standardised written form in Roman script.

The languages spoken in Mizoram were tonal languages, like Chinese. The same word spoken in a high or low tone could mean different things. The Mizos also have a very musical culture. I do not know of another people among whom musical ability is so universal. When missionaries preached the gospel in the Lushai Hills, they chose to translate the hymns into Lushei in order to be sung in church. I have heard funny stories of how Mizos found it difficult to observe the solemn atmosphere of the Protestant church when they were asked to sing, because it was unthinkable for them to sing without dancing. But preaching in the Lushei language facilitated the emergence of a standardised vernacular in print. The political movement of Mizo nationalism has, in recent decades, taken this forward to produce what is now called the Mizo language which is taught in all secondary schools and is, along with English, an official language of Mizoram.

I must also tell you a little bit about the role that Christianity plays in Naga and Mizo national consciousness. The spread of the religion had significant effects in transforming the traditional institutions and cultural practices of the region, creating an educated middle class with an awareness of its place in India as well as the world. It facilitated, as I have told you, the emergence of a public culture of books, magazines, pamphlets, speeches, and musical performance that became the vehicle of strong political emotions. Christian practices were selectively combined with features of traditional culture to produce Naga or Mizo modernity. In this respect, the process is not too different from what happened in the rest of India. But with the rise of a national feeling that includes an acute awareness of its marginal, indeed neglected and often despised, place within the Indian political formation, Christianity has become a major marker of the distinctiveness of the Naga and Mizo people against an Indian nationalism that celebrates its Aryan-Hindu civilisational heritage. Christianity offers the hill peoples the ground to reject the charge of being sunk in a primitive tribal culture, while their new common languages give them the means to forge the political unity of the Naga or Mizo people. This is shown by the fact that even the NSCN, which upholds a socialist and secular ideology, endorses the slogan "Nagalim for Christ".

The combination of language and religion makes the Naga or Mizo people equal to the rest of India, but different. If this strikes you as strange, just remember what the combination of the Dravidian race with the Tamil language did for the Tamil people.

You must also know that given their high literacy, and particularly literacy in English, young men and women from the north-east are now increasingly visible in the cities of India as students in universities and white-collar employees in both private and government sectors. The idea of armed resistance against the Indian state, regardless of the legitimacy conferred on it by the memory of atrocities by the Indian security forces and the national resolve to assert a claim to sovereignty, is no longer seen as a realistic political option. It is my impression that there is a much greater willingness now, especially among the young, to find a place of worth and dignity within the Indian system. An interesting pointer to this is the fact that in past decades, in several parts of Nagaland, Mizoram, and Manipur, there was a system of parallel taxation by underground militant groups that was not only accepted by the local populations but also tolerated by the government. This indicated that the people recognised the legitimacy of the demand for their sovereignty voiced by the militant nationalist groups. The government too, like all imperial states, chose to look the other way as long as it helped maintain a balance of forces. In recent years, however, the people show their impatience when they say that the underground groups engage in extortion. There is a much stronger feeling than before for a peace settlement that recognises the autonomous national character of the hill peoples while giving them a satisfactory place within the Indian federation.

But the experience of young people from the north-east who live in Indian cities is a bitter one. Every mark of distinctness – their looks, their food, their language, their manner of social interaction – is looked upon with suspicion and contempt.

They are stereotyped as primitive forest-dwellers belonging to some foreign race. This experience does not reassure the youth of the north-eastern states that they will find a place of equal respect in the Indian federation. It is significant that the youth culture of this region looks for inspiration not to the popular cinema of India but to music videos from South Korea.

The examples of the Naga and Mizo peoples illustrate a general truth. The situation in the other north-eastern states, such as Meghalaya, Manipur, Arunachal Pradesh, and Tripura, may have their own distinct features – it would take too long to go into them now – but they too share this truth. Not only that, I have shown you that even in the case of Bengal or Maharashtra or Tamil Nadu, there is no one conception of nationhood. That is the general truth. The Indian nation undoubtedly exists in every part of the country. But in each region, the people with a shared language developed a specific conception of their nationhood while, at the same time, defining their place within the larger Indian nation. This truth demands that the Indian state grant a legitimate and equal political place within the Indian national federation to each of these constituent but different peoples. That is the truth which has been denied so far by the Indian state, regardless of which party has held power.

How will this truth be recognised?

### A Just Federation of Peoples

During the debate over linguistic states in the 1950s, Bhimrao Ambedkar made an important intervention which, sadly, was not noticed at the time. Endorsing the principle that each state in the Indian federation should have one main language, he pointed out that this did not necessarily mean that each language should correspond to only one state. In other words, while each state should be monolingual, each language region need not be constituted into a single state. Just as multilingual states must be broken up, there could also be several states where the same language is spoken. This was because, along with language, Ambedkar also introduced the criteria of equitable size and viability. I think his argument needs to be considered seriously.[32]

The reason why states should be monolingual was simple. Recognising that the vehicle of democratic communication and solidarity was language, Ambedkar pointed out that if a state had sizeable populations speaking different languages, conflict would be inevitable. This had been shown in Madras in the dispute between Telugu and Tamil speakers and in Bombay between Marathi and Gujarati speakers. The most rational solution was to divide these provinces into monolingual states. Of course, this might still leave each state with small populations that speak a different language. They must be regarded as minorities and offered special protection of their language and culture.

The subject of minorities was one to which Ambedkar had given much thought. From the 1920s, he argued at length with British officials that Dalits (then called the Depressed Classes) must be considered a non-Hindu minority like the Muslims and given constitutional protections such as separate electorates and reserved places in the legislature and government service. In general, he referred to the fact that any territorial demarcation of state boundaries, no matter how homogeneous a population it tries to produce, will necessarily include some minorities. Any just constitution that respects the aspirations of the people must make special provisions for the protection of minority interests. Otherwise, a communal majority – in this case, that of a linguistic community – in an electoral democracy is likely to coerce the minorities into a condition of miserable submission.

[32] The reference here is probably to Ambedkar's pamphlet "Thoughts on Linguistic States" (1955) in *Dr. Babasaheb Ambedkar Writings and Speeches*, vol. 1, ed. Vasant Moon (Bombay: Government of Maharashtra, 1979), pp. 137–204.

Ambedkar's first principle was, therefore, monolingual states with adequate protection of linguistic minorities. But that could not be the only criterion. It was very important, he said, that the states were roughly of equal size. If there were a few states that were much larger than the others, they would become an oppressive power within the federation. That is why he insisted that large states like Uttar Pradesh, Madhya Pradesh, Maharashtra (then part of Bombay but claiming separation from Gujarat), and Bihar, while remaining monolingual, should each be divided into two or three parts. That way, not only would their inordinate weight within the federation be reduced, but each of the parts, while remaining monolingual, could also develop their own political character in accordance with their local needs. For instance, regions like western UP, Rohilkhand, Awadh, Bhojpur, Mithila, or Chhattisgarh, while remaining Hindi-speaking states, could emerge as distinct political entities without being forcibly submerged within large states like UP or Bihar or Madhya Pradesh. One could say the same thing for Marathwada or Vidarbha or Konkan in Maharashtra. Ambedkar did not say this, but we could even imagine the emergence of a Bhojpuri- or Chhattisgarhi-speaking state. In other words, Ambedkar qualified the linguistic principle with that of balanced size in order to achieve a federation that was both democratic and equitable.

It is interesting that Ambedkar pointed out that the combined weight within the federation of large Hindi-speaking states such as Uttar Pradesh, Madhya Pradesh, and Bihar was producing among the southern states a sense of apprehension of North Indian domination. He was clearly referring to the separatist position of the DMK and the anti-Hindi agitation brewing in Madras. Ambedkar suggested that these genuine fears might be allayed if large states were broken up.

Ambedkar also added a further criterion of the viability of states. He was a thoroughly realist thinker who believed in the importance of constitutional mechanisms to ensure the rights of the people. He also believed in the beneficial effects of good laws. By viability, he meant not only the financial and administrative adequacy of a state to carry out its tasks but also its demographic and social capacity to participate equally in a federal system. Viability would thus require a state not to be so deficient in its own resources that it must become perpetually dependent on aid from the central government. It must also have a demographic structure that is not so unequal that a tiny ethnic minority can exploit the majority of the people without facing any political resistance. Once again, Ambedkar's intention was to arrive at a federal system that was balanced as well as sensitive to claims of equal respect and dignity.

You will easily notice that several of Ambedkar's arguments have turned out to be true. Arguments of size and viable equity have led to the creation of new states such as Uttarakhand, Chhattisgarh, and Jharkhand. In each of these cases, there was an argument about the unduly large size of Uttar Pradesh, Madhya Pradesh, and Bihar. But there was also the demand that culturally distinct population groups such as Adivasis that were regionally concentrated would have greater political weight in the new states. This too was a perceptive observation that Ambedkar had made when arguing for smaller states. Small minority groups tended to get thinly distributed in a large state and so had little political influence. But if they lived in a smaller state, their local concentration in areas where they were relatively more numerous could give them a much more prominent political role. The principle of division in these cases was not linguistic, but of disparities within a linguistic region that could be usefully addressed by a territorial solution.

A similar argument was made when, in 2014, the Telugu-speaking state of Andhra Pradesh was split to form a separate state of Telangana. The claim here was a regional disparity caused by the influx of powerful business interests from coastal

Andhra into the city of Hyderabad, thereby accentuating the backwardness of the rural Telangana districts which used to be in the nizam's dominion. The regional disparity argument was also used recently in 2019 when Ladakh was controversially separated from Jammu and Kashmir, although there was a clear ethnic, religious, and linguistic dimension as well. I don't know if Ladakhi, written in the Tibetan script, will now become the official language of Ladakh, even though most people there speak Bauti or Purkhi, neither of which has a written form.

Ambedkar's arguments suggest a federal structure in which states are mainly monolingual, reflecting democratic solidarities produced in each case by the sharing of a common linguistic heritage, but also roughly equal in their participation and influence. You must remember that federalism operates with territorial units. This means that it has the capacity to accommodate differences and resolve disputes through territorial adjustments. Differences that cannot be resolved territorially require special constitutional mechanisms. In all this, Ambedkar's basic emphasis was always to respect the aspirations of the people. He insisted that a democratic constitution can work only if the people agree to live within the same constitution. If a section of the people refuses to do so, as the Muslim League declared in its Lahore resolution in 1940, Ambedkar's view was that it should be allowed to form a separate state with its own constitution. Forcibly keeping an unwilling minority within the same political formation would make matters both undemocratic and unstable.[33] The principle applies to federal units too. If a section of a state's population is unwilling to live together with others within the same state, it should be allowed to form a separate state within the federation. But if a separate state is not viable,

---

[33] Ambedkar expressed this view in his book *Pakistan, or the Partition of India* (1945) in *Dr. Babasaheb Ambedkar Writings and Speeches*, vol. 8, ed. Vasant Moon (Bombay: Government of Maharashtra, 1990).

as is the case with Dalits who are too thinly distributed to form a viable territorial unit of their own, then they must agree to live within the same constitution provided they are given special constitutional protections.

If you consider a demand such as that of Gorkhaland, the linguistic principle would immediately suggest that the Nepali-speaking people of the Darjeeling hills have a legitimate claim to a state of their own. But the question of viability cannot be brushed aside. Would such a state become permanently dependent on central assistance or could it, like Goa, for instance, flourish by further developing its tourism sector and tea gardens? I don't think the people of the Darjeeling hills have been given a chance to make their case as an equal part of the Indian nation. In other cases, such as the demand for Bodoland, viability may be a more difficult issue to settle. The difficulty is not in finding a workable institutional arrangement to protect the rights of the Bodo people within Assam but in accepting that the Bodo people are equal to the Assamese in belonging to the Indian nation.

I do not wish to go on with a list of outstanding disputes over state boundaries or regional claims and propose solutions to each of them. I do not have such solutions. But I do think that there are guiding principles that can be found from the way such claims are made and solutions proposed. Ambedkar suggested such a set of principles more than sixty years ago. Since then, Indian federalism has evolved further. I believe we can now develop Ambedkar's principles to express the underlying truth of the federal system as an arrangement that links the state machinery with the people constituted as a nation. This is a truth that frequently shows itself, even though those in power within the central organs of the Indian state refuse to recognise it.

The first truth is that the states came into the Indian federation in ways that were often quite different. These differences mark variations in the manner in which the people of a region have thought of their own unity as a people as well as their relation to the Indian nation. I have described to you how the various princely states or states like Goa, Sikkim, Mizoram, and Nagaland joined the Indian federation. Each case was different. For most princely states, the people were not even consulted, even though in some cases – for instance, where there were strong States People movements – there was some indication of what the people wanted. In a few cases, such as Junagadh, a plebiscite was held, although for Jammu and Kashmir it was not. Even for the provinces of British India, which passed into the Indian Union with the transfer of power, there were some cases where a plebiscite was held, as in the North West Frontier Province and Sylhet. But more significantly, if less visibly, the relation to the Indian nation of the people of the main linguistic regions of British India was not the same everywhere. I have shown you how the conception of the nation as a people and its belonging to the Indian nation varied from Bengal to Maharashtra to Tamil Nadu. You would not see this if you only consider the formal machinery of the state where all the provinces are bound by the same laws. But, as I keep reminding you, the state (*rājya*) is not identical to the nation (*rāṣṭra*). The former has been inherited from our imperial rulers; the latter is constituted by the people (*lok*) themselves. The people of each state have agreed to live together with the people of all the other states within the same Indian constitution because they have, each in their own way, negotiated the terms of the union. This is, therefore, the first principle: each constituent people of the Indian union is different and must be recognised and respected as such.

The second principle is that while the people of each state is different in quality (*guṇ*), in its status (*sammān*) within the federation each is equal to the others. This is not merely a matter of being formally equal in law. It must be an active principle in the functioning of the federation. This is precisely the reason why it is unwise to have some states that are so much larger than the others that they can wield a degree of power that causes resentment within the federation. But relative size is only one aspect of the problem. Even greater is the problem of perception. If some people feel that they are the original and permanent members of the nation and others have been admitted only as a gesture of goodwill or perhaps by political necessity, then the rule of equal respect is violated. This is what happens when the North Indian Hindu looks upon the Kashmiri Muslim as a troublemaker who should be sent to jail or the student from Nagaland as an uncivilised forest-dweller whose food habits are obnoxious. The gentleman or lady in Delhi conveniently forgets that when Indians face the same treatment in Europe or the United States, they make indignant complaints about it in the Indian media. It is not an irrelevant comparison. Kashmiri or Naga students in Delhi have exactly the same feeling. Thinking of the comparison is a good way to achieve a condition of equal respect – by putting oneself in the other's position and feeling what the other feels. It is a basic requirement for a just federation.

The third principle is that the people must have priority, not the state machinery. I have given you numerous examples where the perceived need to preserve the stability of the state and follow established ways of functioning of its machinery were given greater importance than the demands of the people. The demand for linguistic states was opposed on the plea that it would disrupt the stability of the state. Policy in Jammu and Kashmir has been driven most of the time by giving priority to the Indian state's relation with the Pakistani state: the wishes of the Kashmiri people have played almost no role at all. The Indian government's policy in the north-east in the last seventy years has been similarly dictated by the urge to secure a border region: the people who live there have been considered too few in number and too insignificant in influence to matter. No surprise, therefore, that Kashmir and the north-east are regions where it is considered legitimate to deploy the armed forces against Indian citizens. Despite numerous atrocities and the incredible bravery of women like Chanu Sharmila in Manipur in resisting it, the policy has not changed. In the end, after a hunger strike lasting sixteen years, Sharmila gave up.[34] But the Armed Forces Special Powers Act is still in place. Nowhere in India except Kashmir and the north-east is the army permanently deployed in this manner.

Why is the state given priority over the people? Who gives it this priority? It is those who think they have primary ownership of the Indian state because, as representatives of the essential core of the Indian nation, they have inherited the state from the British. They believe it is their duty to protect and preserve the state against people who they see as newcomers who don't share the same view of nationalism and whose loyalties to the nation are questionable. Those who hold this view are not just a handful of patriarchal politicians and stuffy bureaucrats. The equation between the preservation of the existing state machinery and the interest of the core of the nation is assumed by an influential part of the Indian people. Let me explain.

I have told you earlier how, from the late-nineteenth century, the idea of an Indian nation originating in ancient Vedic society took hold among educated Indians. It was solidified into a fully developed nationalist ideology in northern and western India in the early-twentieth century through the claim that the Hindus of this region were the first and most genuine Indian nationalists. In Maharashtra, this took the form of the celebration of Shivaji and the Brahman-led Maratha Empire. In northern India, the key elements of this nationalist ideology were the Sanskrit

---

[34] Irom Chanu Sharmila (b. 1972) was on hunger strike from November 2000 to August 2016 demanding the withdrawal from Manipur of the Armed Forces Special Powers Act, 1958, which gives the armed forces the power to search, arrest, and use deadly force against anyone on suspicion of anti-state activities.

tradition, memories of Rajput resistance to Muslim conquest, and the rise of Hindi instead of Urdu as the language of education and government. From the mid-twentieth century, these two streams have converged to form a nationalist ideology which emphasises the need for a strong state machinery, centralised as far as possible, that is able to display a nation unified in its tradition and culture. In the first three decades after independence, this ideology was able to accommodate the idea of a pluralist democracy. In more recent times, however, it has been swamped by waves of nationalist propaganda that declares India to be a Hindu Rashtra whose tradition and culture are genuinely represented only by upper-caste Hindus who also speak Hindi.

Earlier, the precedence claimed by this group within the nation was subtle. It was exercised by the weight within the federation of large states such as Uttar Pradesh, Madhya Pradesh, and Bihar, and periodic attempts, resisted in different regions, to push Hindi as the common language of political discourse – a new imperial language in place of English. But the thrust was necessarily moderated because the ruling Congress Party was in power in almost all regions of the country. As a result, all or most regions had to be represented in its decision-making bodies. In recent years, the ruling BJP is localised in northern and western India. The overwhelming part of its leadership is drawn from those parts of the country. In addition, the present generation of politicians from Maharashtra and Gujarat are far more fluent in Hindi than used to be the case earlier. Consequently, Hindi has become, for all practical purposes, the sole language of Hindutva politics, its functionaries are overwhelmingly drawn from the north and the west, and the upper-caste Hindu culture of the north is projected as the national culture of India. Dominance within the state has been converted into dominance within the nation. How else could vegetarianism be claimed as the national cuisine and Ram the national god?

This shift in the cultural content of nationalism can also be seen in the way the idea of Indian citizenship has changed. In 1950, Articles 5 to 11 of the constitution declared that anyone living in India who did not claim citizenship of another country was an Indian citizen. There was no question about one's religion or language nor was the nationality of one's parents relevant. This declaration by the constitution recognised the fact that Indian citizenship was a completely new idea. Indians who lived in British India were not citizens but subjects of the British Empire. Citizenship was given to Indians by Indians through the constitution. No one had priority there. It was not as if some were already citizens and extended the benefit to others through an act of charity. It is important to remember this because it confirms the first principle of democratic federalism, namely, that people living within the territory of India became Indian citizens because they agreed to live together under the same constitution. The people came first, the state came later, because it is the people who gave themselves a constitution that defined the form of the state.

This idea of citizenship was strengthened by the Citizenship Act of 1955 which declared that anyone born in India was entitled to Indian citizenship. Even someone born of foreign parents on Indian soil could become an Indian citizen. This is, of course, the rule in many countries including the United States and, until recently, the United Kingdom. But this enlightened idea of Indian citizenship was cast aside in 2003 when the Vajpayee government amended the Citizenship Act to bring in a completely different idea – that of being descended from Indians. Citizenship was modified by conditions that required proof of the citizenship of parents and grandparents. It also brought into the law a new concept of the illegal migrant as someone who was living in the country without valid documents that authorised his or her stay. This meant the possible exclusion from citizenship of lakhs of people who have lived in this country for years and even generations, as was shown in Assam in course of compiling the National Register of Citizens. Recently, in 2019, the citizenship law was again amended to exclude Muslims from the category of people from neighbouring countries who could be given Indian citizenship.

At the same time, the 2003 amendment granted overseas citizenship to people of Indian origin who had left the country to become citizens of other countries. Remember, this privilege was not meant for those millions of Indians who work in the Gulf countries and send back crores of rupees. No, it was meant to flatter the nationalist egos of those who had abandoned their country to grab the chance of bringing up their children in the West. They are given a red carpet welcome as honorary citizens when they come to India for their holidays.

The truth of Indian nationalism has been either distorted or concealed. To recover it, the ground must be laid for a regeneration of the Indian state as the democratic federation of peoples. The just federation can be based on the three principles I have laid out: that the people of each state be recognised as different; that they be recognised as equal; and that the people have priority over the state.

While a just federation would go a long way in establishing a proper relation between the state and the nation, it would still leave untouched the problem of unequal relations within each state. These might be inequalities of wealth and income, caste discrimination, gender inequality and the oppression of women, or discrimination against religious, linguistic, and cultural minorities. A more effective federation would not get rid of these problems. But if states had more power and influence within the federation, they would be in a better position to address these problems because politics within the states are in general far closer to the ground than at the central level. If you look carefully, you will find that the actual business of addressing the people's needs and settling disputes is done by their representatives at the state and local levels. Even central policies have to be implemented there. That is where a proper connection must be established between the state machinery and the people.

But I am not ignoring these other problems within states with which the nation must also engage. Let us now talk about them.

# 7

# People's Alliances Strengthen the Nation

### Educating the Nation

A NEW NATIONAL education policy was announced by the Indian government in July 2020. After several aborted attempts and many piecemeal changes over the years, this is the first time since 1986 that a comprehensive overhaul of the country's education system, from pre-primary to doctoral research, is being attempted. Needless to say, it has provoked a lot of debate. I was shown a copy of the policy by a college professor. She complained that it was a piecemeal imitation of the education system of the United States. Since I know nothing about education in other countries, I cannot tell if she is right. But I found much in the new policy to interest me.

In fact, there are some excellent suggestions in it which, if properly implemented, will do a lot of good. The objective of promoting multilingualism and respect for diversity and local custom is most welcome. So is the recommendation that, up to Class 8, the medium of instruction should be the language spoken at home or the local language. Thereafter, the medium could be the regional language but, if the home language happens to be different from the regional language, there should be bilingual teaching, as far as possible. The three-language formula should continue. I saw no explicit attempt to foist Hindi on the non-Hindi-speaking regions: obviously, a lesson has been drawn from the protests that greeted a suggestion in 2019 from the Union home minister that Hindi should be a required language. The policy recommends that for science and mathematics there should be bilingual textbooks in English and a regional or local language.

All of these are admirable recommendations concerning the basic modalities of primary and secondary education in a multilingual country like India. As far as higher education is concerned, since I have never had the misfortune of attending a college or university, I am in no position to quibble with the claim that they need a thorough overhaul. But suspicions begin to appear when one listens to the nationalist rhetoric in which the recommendations are wrapped. We are told that the guiding light of the policy is the heritage of ancient and eternal Indian knowledge and thought. Education must be rooted in the Indian ethos and foster pride in being Indian in spirit, intellect, and deed. Higher education in India must recall the example of large multidisciplinary universities such as Nalanda, Takshashila, Vikramshila, and Vallabhi. Further, since there is a remarkable unity among the major Indian languages because of their common origin in Sanskrit, that classical language must be taught at all levels in order to introduce students across the country to the enormous riches contained in what the policy calls "Sanskrit knowledge systems". Emphasising the need to supplement scientific and technical education with an exposure to the humanities, the policy points out that ancient Indian education was not complete without training in the sixty-four *kalā* or arts.

I must confess I am trying very hard to suppress a laugh as I mention this last item. But let us not be distracted. Why do I say that these statements in the new education policy are suspicious? Because it confirms once more what I explained at length when talking about pluralist democracy – that whether secularist or Hindu nationalist, every policy that adopts a single, uniform, and integrated view of national culture inevitably gets reduced to a justification in terms of the dominant Sanskrit-based elite tradition of northern India. Many of the detailed proposals in the policy were suggested in the 1970s. They were then presented as elements of a policy to promote pluralist secularism. But the rhetoric was for the most part exactly the same. Let me show this to you.

If you look at the detailed proposals, a major objective seems to be to create a population trained to supply the emergent economy with its varied needs for personnel at different rungs of production, distribution, commerce, finance, and services. These needs are changing fast with the introduction of new technologies. You have seen before your eyes the changes brought about in daily life by the mobile phone, internet, and computers. In days to come, you will see many more new machines that will use artificial intelligence or non-traditional energy sources. It is hardly surprising that the government will try to equip the country's school and university system to cope with the changing requirements for producing, managing, and using these technologies effectively. If nothing else, business lobbies are demanding it. Then why not plainly state the perfectly valid objective of modernising the education system without clothing it in all that talk of ancient Indian tradition?

I think I have given you the answer already. But let me reiterate it. The technological conditions of modernity have a certain universal global quality. They seem to be the same everywhere. If that is so, the search for education systems that might be appropriate in creating those technological conditions also leads to countries whose schools and universities have produced those technologies. The college professor may well be correct when she says that the Indian policy tries to replicate the education structure of the United States. One should not be surprised by that. But it makes the nationalist educator deeply anxious. If all we are doing is copying formulas that have worked in other countries, what happens to the distinctness of our culture? How is the next generation to be educated in it? That is the reason why even the most ambitious modernising effort must be presented as nothing other than an affirmation of ancient Indian heritage.

This nationalist reasoning is not only false but pernicious. It is false in this case because the proposed structure of school and university education, its essential curricula, its interdisciplinary orientation, have nothing in common with education in ancient India. In the first place, while it is true that there do exist treatises (*śāstra*) in Sanskrit on music, architecture, metallurgy, and medicine, these were neither produced nor taught in places like Nalanda or Vikramshila, which were *vihār* for *śramaṇ* monks, nor in the Brahman's *gurukul*, but in the families and workshops of master specialists in those occupations. In fact, it was quite unheard of for an apprentice in architecture or metalwork to study Nyāya or Mīmāṃsā. So the claim that Nalanda or Takshashila were large multidisciplinary universities like the great universities today is ridiculous.

Second, the suggestion that every student, no matter what his or her specialisation, was trained in the sixty-four arts is hilarious. If orthodox Brahmans were told that Buddhist monks in Takshashila or Nalanda were being taught the art of making a bed of flowers (*puṣpāstaraṇ*) or gambling with dice (*dyutaviśeṣ*), it would have only confirmed their deepest suspicions that the *vihār* was a den of vice. On the other hand, they would have been scandalised if they heard that a brahmachari in a *gurukul* was being taught the art of needlework (*sucivāṇā-karmāṇi*) or putting on perfumes (*sugandhayukti*). These are all included among the sixty-four arts, as are *hastalāghav* (sleight of hand), *aindrajāl* (magical tricks), *prahelikā* (solving riddles), *vastragopan* (concealing clothes), *kaucumār* (fancy dress), and *meṣākukkuṭālāvakāyuddhavidhi* (lamb, cock, and bird fights).

Leaving aside specialised crafts such as *dhātuvidyā* (metalwork), *vāstuvidyā* (architecture), and *takṣaṇ* (carpentry), these fine arts were mostly taught to the *nāyikā* who you will find in Sanskrit *kāvya* in the role of a princess or a courtesan. It should come as no surprise that the most well-known account of the sixty-four *kalā* occurs in Vātsyāyana's *Kāmasūtra*. They had nothing to do with the curricula of the Buddhist or Jain monasteries. Why is this being proposed as an example for engineering students to emulate?

If you ask me, these random insertions of elements from the so-called Sanskrit knowledge systems occur because even the slightest similarity is believed to be sufficient to justify the claim that modern education is nothing, and indeed must be nothing, but the elaboration of a pedagogical ideal well established in India's ancient past. The superficial scattering of Sanskrit names and concepts fosters a vague spirit of reverence for a particular cultural heritage without encouraging its critical appraisal. When students are taught philosophy, they will probably be told of the six schools of *darśan*.[1] Perhaps they will also hear a mention of the *nāstik* Jaina, Bauddha, or Ajivika schools. But will they be told the reasons why Buddhists and Jains reject the Vedas or the theories of matter held by the *āstik* schools? Will students be encouraged to look into those vigorous philosophical debates of the past and decide for themselves which were the better arguments? When they are told about *jyotirvidyā*, will the students know that while astronomical calculations of the movement of stars and planets, based on algorithms constructed from years of observation, were accurate in varying degrees, the theories of planetary motion on which ancient Indian astronomy was based were mostly false? Will they be told that astrology (*jyotiṣ*) is entirely unscientific? When they learn about *āyurved*,

---

[1] The six schools of philosophy are Nyāya, Vaiśeṣika, Sāṃkhya, Vedānta, Mīmāṃsā, and Yoga.

will they also learn that while specific herbs, salts, minerals, and oils are often quite effective in treating particular illnesses, the physiological and chemical theories of traditional medicine are false? I doubt very much that ancient knowledge will be presented to students in a critical spirit. That is not the function it serves in India's education system. The knowledge that students are expected to master is the knowledge of modern science and technology. The Sanskrit knowledge systems, presented as a seamless, placid, and harmonious whole, are intended to produce reverence and docility.

This is confirmed by what the policy says about the ethical ideals that must inspire young students. They must be taught traditional Indian values such as *sevā*, *ahiṃsā*, and *niṣkām karma*. While lip service is paid to local and tribal knowledge, there is no doubt at all that the student's ethical world is to be defined by the dominant values of Brahmanical patriarchy. One of the most astonishing features of the policy is its repeated insistence on teaching the Fundamental Duties as listed in Article 51A of the constitution. This is probably the least-known article in the founding document of the republic – for good reasons. First of all, it did not exist in the original constitution and was introduced by Indira Gandhi's government in 1976 during the Emergency, along with the terms "secular" and "socialist". As far as I know, no liberal constitution in the world describes anything called the fundamental duties of citizens – it is a concept that belongs to the authoritarian state. A lawyer friend tells me that it was first introduced in the constitution of the USSR under Stalin in 1936: that constitution, of course, no longer exists. It is also mentioned in the constitution of China. The constitution of Japan, written by American lawyers after Japan's defeat in the Second World War, also has a section of this kind, because the Americans were worried that the Japanese might not be loyal to the new state that was being imposed on them. Anyway, Article 51A, inserted into the constitution by the Emergency regime in India, reeks of the authoritarian atmosphere of the time.

In fact, the committee, headed by Swaran Singh, who until then had served on every Congress ministry at the centre, proposed this constitutional amendment by arguing that the citizens of the country, in return for the rights that the state had given them, must be required to perform certain duties for the state. If a citizen did not care for the duties, he did not deserve the rights. The duties included respect for the national flag and national anthem, defending the country and rendering national service when asked, preserving religious and linguistic diversity and India's composite culture, developing a scientific temper, protecting public property, and avoiding violence. If you remember what I told you about pluralist secular democracy, you will recognise these as elements of Nehruvian secularism packaged in the authoritarian rhetoric of Indira Gandhi's Emergency.

The concept of fundamental duties is truly pernicious. It suggests that the constitution is a transaction between citizens and the state in which rights are offered in exchange for the promise of duties. This is patently false. It suggests that the state that existed prior to the constitution – a state supervised by officials who were not appointed according to the constitution – entered into a contractual exchange with citizens. This makes nonsense of the declaration on the first page of the constitution that it had been given by the people to themselves: it was most definitely not offered to them by a pre-existing state. But this was the mentality I described to you of the rulers who took power in Delhi after independence. They thought of themselves as successors to the British, and perhaps even the Mughals and the Mauryas – rulers of an imperial state. That is the spirit in which Article 51A listing the Fundamental Duties was inserted into the constitution, even though, like the Directive Principles, it cannot be legally enforced. This insidious article needs to be removed as soon as possible.

But if the duties were indeed an attempt to boost Nehruvian secularism by Indira Gandhi's authoritarian regime, why are the present rulers of the country insisting that they should be taught in schools today? The answer is the same one that I suggested earlier: the details don't matter; all that matters is that students learn to be dutiful towards the state. It is the authoritarian temper of instruction that is crucial. Recall that the chief ideologues of the Hindu Rashtra – Golwalkar, for instance – explicitly argued against the idea of fundamental rights which, he said, promote selfish individualism; he emphasised duties to strengthen the collective spirit and national unity. Consequently, when the student is told of *jyotiṣ* or *āyurved*, she must receive the knowledge as the timeless truth of ancient wisdom, while learning at the same time how a spacecraft flies to Mars or a heart can be transplanted from one human body to another. In the spirit of Advaita Vedanta, the deepest contradictions must be interpreted as contained within a harmonious unity. That, hopefully, will produce meek and contented citizens who will not feel entitled by the constitution they have given to themselves to question those in positions of authority.

### The Citizen as an Obedient Subject

Perhaps I am being too charitable, because there is a deeper suspicion I have that may not be unwarranted. It is entirely possible that the ideal relation between the citizen and the state that inspires this policy of educating the next generation of Indians is not the one that is elaborated in the constitution. Instead, despite all the genuflections towards that document, the vision of the ideal state that actually informs the education policy is that of the righteous *rājā* ruling his *rājya* according to the precepts of *daṇḍanīti*. You probably think *daṇḍa* means punishment. You are right, because that is indeed the core of *daṇḍa*. But when elaborated as an ethical framework of governing a kingdom, it is much more. Let me tell you a little bit about this interesting subject, because if I am correct in my suspicion, then the statements about inculcating Indian ethical values in the minds of young students are not just traditional window dressing on a modernising plan but expressions of a serious intent to revive and reinstate a political ideal that the freedom movement and the constitution had decidedly discarded.

What is *daṇḍa*? Manu describes a frightening figure – a powerful man with glistening dark skin and bloodshot angry eyes. That is whom the king must deploy to prevent miscreants from causing harm and disorder. Fear of *daṇḍa* is the key to a well-governed *rājya*. Without it, no one would be able to enjoy what is rightfully his and the strong would torment the weak. *Svāmya* or *svasvāmitva* – the sense of one's rightful claim (*adhikār*) within the varna order – would vanish. Actually, Manu had a very low opinion of the moral quality of ordinary people: *sarvo daṇḍajito loko durlabho hi śucirnarah*, he said, which means that it is so rare to find an honest man in this world that *daṇḍa* is the only way to rule. Otherwise, he warned, using some picturesque language, the strong will devour the weak like skewered pieces of fish over a fire, crows will feed on the sacrificial bread, and dogs lick the sacrificial ghee. Complete chaos will descend on the world: *svāmyanca na syāt kasmiṃścit pravartetādharottaram*. Only the fear of punishment can ensure protection of the king's subjects.

Several centuries after Manu, Kautilya in his treatise on *artha* provided a far more complex account of *daṇḍanīti*. He had accumulated the wisdom drawn from the history of several large kingdoms, including those founded by Greek rulers who had entered the north-western parts of India. He knew that whereas the force of punishment was essential, its excessive use led to oppression, enmity, and revolt. The judicious king, he said, must be wary of *prakṛtikop*, that is, the anger of his subjects. Consequently, he must soften his *daṇḍa* with sweet words and gifts, cultivate the virtue of *vinay* (courtesy) through self-discipline and learning, and take advice from elders and wise men. If opposition persists, he must sow discord among his enemies. Only if all of these steps fail should he resort to decisive force. *Daṇḍa*, we might say in today's language, is an ethical policy to be used with skill and judgement.

But even though it may not be signified only by the policeman's stick (*daṇḍā*), it is nevertheless far removed from any notion of liberty and equality. The subjects of Kautilya's *rājya* had no rights against the state. The *adhikār* which the rule of *daṇḍa* was supposed to protect was the claim of each to what legitimately belonged to him or her according to law. What was the law? That which was laid down in the Dharmashastra. The king could not make law: the law was already given for him to enforce. Brahmans had compiled the laws from past authorities; they interpreted them and adjudicated disputes over conflicting interpretations. These laws of the Dharmashastra assigned varying *adhikār* to different people according to caste, gender, and age. Freedom and equality as universal rights were inconceivable in this hierarchical world of dharma.

*Daṇḍanīti* as the ethical framework of ruling a polity (*rājya*) was firmly rejected when the people of India adopted their constitution in 1950. Remember, there were many rajas and nawabs in India at the time, many of whom claimed to rule according to traditional ideals of good kingship. They were all made to give up their sovereign claims and accept the constitution embodying the fundamental rights of all citizens. There were no subjects (*prajā*) any more because the former rajas were now citizens with the same rights as you or me. Who will apply *daṇḍa* in a *rājya* governed by a liberal constitution?

This is where those who have ruled India since independence have repeatedly performed the *kalā* of sleight of hand (*hāth kī safāī*) to usurp sovereign-like powers that do not belong to them. Those elected to office pretend to be little sovereigns with their own fiefdoms where they distribute gifts and extract loyalty, much like Kautilya had advised the king. Even the babu in a government department or the police constable standing at a traffic light is a miniature wielder of *daṇḍa*. If you ask those who run the system, they will tell you, some with a knowing wink and others with a tired shrug, that that is the only method which works. People have been used to being commanded for generations: it is deeply ingrained in their habits. So they will only observe the law if they have a genuine fear of punishment. Education in liberty and equality is fine in elite institutions where both teachers and students belong to privileged groups that do not fear the state; it is a wasteful luxury when applied to populations who must be taught habitual obedience to the nation-state. They must be educated in their fundamental duty to obey authority.

The ethical policy of *daṇḍanīti* as expounded by Kautilya was, of course, an ideal. In actual fact, there were, as is well known, good kings and bad kings, wise kings and foolish kings, kind kings and tyrants. *Daṇḍa* was sometimes applied whimsically and fiercely, often to help one party against another. At other times, it was not applied when it should have been. When people were oppressed in this manner, they accused the king of *adharma* and protested. If that did not work, they looked to other powerful figures to help them in their resistance, perhaps even to remove the ruler and replace him with another. Every region in India has histories of revolt against oppressive rulers. These revolts prove that the people possessed a strong sense of their legitimate rights (*haq*) – rights that were not necessarily limited to the definitions declared by *sarkārī* Brahmans or ulema. At moments of protest, the people believed they were the ones upholding *dharma* or *insāf*, not the errant king.

This was the spirit that inspired the mass movements against British rule. Don't forget that ordinary people fought against British rule long before the Indian National Congress was born. They had local leaders, some of whom were chiefs or princes, others were religious leaders. Sometimes the people found leaders from among themselves. During the great revolt of 1857, even though there were several prominent leaders, and the Mughal emperor himself was made the symbolic head of the rebellion against the British, in most places it was the rebel soldiers who mobilised the people. They refused to obey the *daṇḍa* of an unjust ruling power.

The Indian constitution formalised this idea of people's rights as the foundation of justice in independent India. It rejected the old idea that the ruler's *daṇḍa* was the only secure guarantee of justice. Instead, only those who were elected by the people would have the power to run the government, and only as long as the people kept them in office. The laws were now to be made with the approval of the people. This would create a much better system in which the people would themselves participate in maintaining order and delivering justice. Even punishment must be according to laws made by the people's representatives. *Daṇḍa* was to be replaced by citizens' rights.

I have told you that not everyone was happy with the constitution. Golwalkar explicitly argued against fundamental rights, claiming they would promote individual selfishness and destroy social cohesion. In fact, this is not true even in relation to the law. While liberal ideas in the West do speak only of individuals as having rights, the Indian constitution in several places recognises the rights of groups, as with scheduled castes and tribes or religious minorities. In actual politics, movements are launched all the time to claim or defend group rights and governments often recognise them. As I said earlier, even when people speak of their fundamental constitutional rights, they act in the belief that they are protesting collectively to defend what they know to be the true *dharma*.

But the RSS suspicion about rights flows from a deep anxiety that new claims over unjust relations of caste, gender, class, or language would destroy what they view as the essential cohesive force of traditional Indian society built around an idealised *varṇāśram* order. Their belief in the cultural identity of the nation from ancient times is justified by the persistence of this cohesive moral force. Any movement that questions the moral authority of this tradition is viewed with disapproval by the votaries of Hindu Rashtra. The most recent outburst of faith in constitutional rights occurred during the protests against the Citizenship Amendment Act in which, as you know very well, students and young people played a very visible role. I have no doubt that this is one of the immediate reasons that prompted the inclusion of lessons on Fundamental Duties in the proposed educational reforms. Future citizens, it was decided, must be trained in obedience, not rights. If you want evidence, you need look no further than Uttar Pradesh, where the *mahānt* of a *math* rules the state by openly displaying the ferocity of his *daṇḍa*.

There is one more aspect of the new education policy that I should point out. Despite all the talk of teaching through local languages and respect for the local environment, there is a strong and clear centralising move operating within the policy. Thus, there is to be a single authority that will supervise higher education in the entire country. While state education boards may have their own curricula and textbooks, those laid down by the NCERT, a central body, must act as the model.[2] In general, the policy reminds everyone that, because education is a concurrent subject on which both the centre and the states may legislate, in case of a conflict the central policy must prevail. If you didn't know it already, let me point out that, like Fundamental Duties and the secular and socialist republic, this was one more contribution of Indira Gandhi's Emergency regime. That is when education, which used to be an exclusively state subject because it was believed to be intimately tied to the regional

---

[2] National Council of Educational Research and Training (NCERT).

linguistic cultures, was brought into the concurrent list. Once again, the proponents of Hindutva, for all their diatribes against the Nehru legacy, have shown their secret fondness for Indira Gandhi's authoritarianism. It fully conforms to their ideal of a strong nation-state ruled by a *cakravartin*, the universal emperor eulogised by Kautilya. You would not be wrong in thinking that the ceremonies performed at the recent consecration of the Ram temple at Ayodhya was a dramatic representation of this ideal.

## The Persistence of Caste

The subject of centralisation of powers brings me back to the question I raised earlier about Indian federalism. Why am I arguing that in order to defend people's rights, which are under serious threat, we must urgently turn our attention to revitalising the federal system? Because I believe that by bringing back the main focus of political life in the country from the centre to the states, we will be able to address contentious issues closer to the level where policies are actually implemented. That way, there will be much greater opportunity for the people to make meaningful and effective alliances among themselves that will actually strengthen, not weaken, the nation. It is a completely false idea that a centralised nation-state displaying its force of unity at the top in a strong party or a strong leader is the sign of a strong nation. The strength of a nation of such diversity as India can only be built on the basis of strong alliances among the people (*lokămitratā*) at the state and local levels.

Will the caste question be more effectively addressed, even if it is not entirely resolved, if it is allowed to be tackled more decisively at the state level? I believe so. There are two crucial dimensions of the caste question that are relevant here. First, caste conflicts, when they appear in the political arena, are no longer tied to religious conceptions of varnashram. No one argues any more, like they used to in earlier times, with citations from genealogies and caste puranas, about who is purer than whom. That is not to say that people have necessarily forgotten those stories that combine history with legend. If you talk to any landowning Thakur in Uttar Pradesh, he will probably tell you that his family is descended from a certain Ganesh Rai Rajput who supposedly conquered all the territory surrounding his village at the time when Alamgir Badshah was on the throne. Some years ago, there would even be a *bhāṭ* in the area who could be called upon to recite a whole ballad with all kinds of miraculous events describing the glorious family lineage of the Thakur landlord. That was a means not only of maintaining his prestige but also his claims to the land. But those sorts of stories are no longer relevant in political disputes over caste. The latter are now fought entirely in terms of economic demands and political mobilisation. Second, the central issue in caste disputes now is reservations. Everything boils down to that. I believe that for both of these reasons the opportunity to negotiate solutions at the state and local levels has a much better chance of success than the present situation, in which every local solution becomes entangled with its implications for central policies whether or not it is consistent with what prevails in other states.

Since I have had to get involved in caste matters all my life, I know how the effect of politics on caste has changed over the years. You should know that no matter what the Dharmashastra said about the four varnas, actual jati structures varied from one region to another, sometimes even from one set of villages to the next. Some regions had many more jatis than others. Even when a jati existed over a large province or perhaps even the whole country, marriages and other social relations would occur within the jati only over a few neighbouring districts. Sometimes the same jati was regarded as higher in the caste order in one region but lower in another. Because of changes in economic or political conditions, a jati could rise or fall in status. There were occasions when one section of a jati which had changed its traditional occupation or acquired political power broke away from the rest of the jati and declared itself a separate jati with higher status. These changes were often sanctified by Brahmans who invented genealogies or wrote a new *purāṇ* to justify the change in status. Thus, politically powerful lineages (*vaṃś*) among Sudra or tribal communities in some regions came to be regarded as Kshatriya. In some districts in southern Bengal where a large section of the Kaibarta caste changed its occupation from fishing to farming, it separated itself from other Kaibartas, called itself the Mahishya jati, and claimed the status of a clean Sudra caste. Very often, such a rise in status was supported by the participation of the jati in a devotional movement led by a *sant* or a Sufi sheikh preaching the message of the equality of all human beings in the eyes of god and the unjustness of caste discrimination. For instance, Narayana Guru carried out a powerful movement against untouchability in Kerala by consecrating a Siva idol which, he said, was an Ezhava Siva as opposed to a Brahman Siva: his religious movement provided a major spurt to education among the Ezhava caste. That is how religion remained implicated in settling new claims about relations between jatis.

Things began to change from the late-nineteenth century. Alongside the old methods, the new method for pressing a claim for higher status of a jati was to embrace the new system of school education. Middle- and even lower-caste groups in different parts of the country urged their young men (it was still only men) to go to school, pass examinations, and enter white-collar occupations. Once that began to happen, there were changes in lifestyle and the adoption of social practices prevalent among the upper castes. It was actually a form of cultural rebellion, as if they were telling the upper castes, "Don't feel so superior because we can be as good as you." In time, as more and more people from the agricultural and artisan castes got school and college education, they began to demand jobs. That was the beginning of the politics of reservations which started in the princely state of Mysore in the early years of the twentieth century and spread to Madras province in the 1920s when the Justice Party took up the campaign. Numerically strong agricultural castes such as the Vellala and Gaunda, and prosperous trading castes such as the Chetti, took the lead in the Non-Brahman movement in Madras which transformed the social and political scene in the Tamil region in the twentieth century.

I should also tell you that the Brahmanical ideology – which justified the caste system as rooted in a religious tradition that separated different social occupations and assigned one's birth in a particular jati according to one's karma in past lives – succeeded in exerting its influence even within the various bhakti sects that had a large following among Sudra castes. Thus, the Vaishnav movement, which was extremely popular among the agricultural and artisan castes in Assam, Bengal, and Odisha, was nonetheless dominated by Brahmans and caste rules were maintained. But untouchable communities in most regions, even when they adopted Puranic gods and goddesses, rejected the Brahmanical justification of caste. They often invented their own origin myths which explained their present condition either as the result of some misfortune or, more commonly, the nefarious designs of Brahmans or other powerful figures. And needless to say, Brahmans did not preside over their ceremonies or festivals. As a result, the religious life of the Dalit jatis existed in a zone of relative independence.

Sometime in the 1890s, Iyothee Thass, who was born in the untouchable Paraiyar caste but had taught himself Tamil and English and become a practitioner of Siddha medicine, declared that the untouchables were not Hindus.[3] In fact, he claimed

---

[3] Actually, Iyothee Thass made the declaration in 1886. In 1891, he set up the Dravida Mahajana Sabha to urge members of the untouchable castes

that the Paraiyar caste was originally Buddhist. A few years later, he went to Ceylon and formally converted to Buddhism. On his return to Madras, he set up the Sakya Buddhist Society to spread the religion among Dalit groups. His newspaper *Oru Paisa Tamizhan* (One Paisa Tamilian), which I have seen, was quite remarkable for its strident but well-argued articles.

The anti-caste movements carried out by E.V. Ramasamy (Periyar) and Bhimrao Ambedkar are, of course, very well known. Ambedkar took the religious justification of caste seriously, studied various Brahmanical texts, and severely castigated them for their cruelty and inhumanity. Alongside, he fought relentlessly for the legal protection of the rights of Dalits as a minority community outside the fold of Hinduism. After his crucial contribution to the making of the Indian constitution, he seemed to lose his faith in the effectiveness of legal methods to eradicate the evil of caste discrimination. Towards the end of his life, Ambedkar became a Buddhist, initiated a religious order called Navayāna Buddhism, and encouraged Dalits to break out of their condition of slavery within Hindu society by embracing the new religion of equality. Many have done so, especially from the Mahar jati in the Vidarbha region of Maharashtra: they are known as neo-Buddhists. EVR, on the other hand, as I have already told you, campaigned against all religions, especially Hinduism, as full of irrational superstition and spread the message of atheism.

In the course of the freedom struggle, especially the mass movements after 1920, the Congress gained the support of several large landowning agricultural castes such as the Maratha in Maharashtra, the Patidar in Gujarat, the Jat in Uttar Pradesh, and the Reddy in Andhra. But the central leadership of the Congress which took power after independence consisted

---

to declare their religion as "casteless Dravidians" in the Census. His name is written in the manuscript as Ayodhī Dās.

almost entirely of upper-caste Hindus and elite Muslims with an education in English. This was also the social character of the bureaucracy, the judiciary, and those involved in higher education at the time. The Congress created a new electoral machinery with which this central leadership mobilised the dominant landowning castes in the villages to secure the votes of other, less powerful, castes. Dalit castes at this time had little political experience and few effective leaders of their own: they were mostly dependent on the infrequent and modest benefits offered to them by Congress governments at the centre and the states.

The years between 1967 and 1977 saw a critical period of change. In 1967, the Congress was defeated in several states, revealing the fragility of the old caste alliances on which its election machinery was built. In particular, the large landowning castes in northern India, boosted by the ongoing green revolution in agriculture, felt they were being denied a greater share of political power by the upper-caste elite at the centre. But the opposition parties in the states were fragmented. Following the split in the Congress in 1969, Indira Gandhi centralised power, especially during the Emergency. With the defeat of her regime in 1977, the floodgates were opened for popular mobilisation in the states. The large landed castes, such as the Jat, the Yadav, the Patidar, the Kamma, and the Vokkaliga, launched their own political parties in various states, often with charismatic leaders. The landed castes in Tamil Nadu had, of course, already come together under the DMK. This was the beginning of the rise to prominence of the regional parties, several of which formed state governments in the 1980s. It also produced caste alliances of a kind unimaginable within the religious conception of varna and jati. Motivated by the political compulsion of building electoral majorities, castes of varying ranks came together under the leadership of a party. Thus, when the dominant Patidar caste in Gujarat deserted the Congress for the Janata Party and later the BJP, the Congress under Madhav Singh Solanki brought the Rajput, the lower-caste Koli, and the herdsmen Rabadi into a Kshatriya group which formed an electoral alliance with scheduled castes, Adivasis, and Muslims. This came to be known as the KHAM (Kshatriya, Harijan, Adivasi, and Muslim) coalition. The new caste alliance was produced by politics, not religion.

This was also the decade when demands for greater representation of the lower castes in government, the services, and education became louder. Social justice was the new slogan in which these demands were expressed. There was, without doubt, a huge churning in society when people who had earlier quietly accepted the commands of the upper castes now felt bold enough to stand up and refuse. It was also the period when the grip of the central government over the states was loosened, the arbitrary powers of the governor were curtailed, and state governments acquired greater capacity to respond in their own way to local demands. Many observers think this was the period when the federal system was most responsive to the needs of the states and most open to innovation.

The backlash began in 1990. The occasion was the implementation by the V.P. Singh government, itself on the verge of collapse, of a seven-year-old report by a commission headed by B.P. Mandal which had recommended a 27 per cent reserved quota in central government services for the Other Backward Classes. The OBC, as you probably know, is a census category from the colonial period which listed a number of Sudra castes who were not included in the Depressed Classes category of untouchable castes (the latter are now the Scheduled Castes). There is actually a mystery surrounding the actual number of people in the OBC category because, since independence, caste populations have not been counted in the census except for the Scheduled Castes. The Mandal report used figures from the 1931 census to estimate the OBC population. V.P. Singh's announcement led to consternation among the upper castes. All hell broke loose after a student in Delhi set fire to himself in protest and died in hospital. All across northern India, upper-caste young men came out on the streets, often using the ugliest of casteist language and symbols, to claim that merit was being sacrificed at the altar of vote-bank politics. Incidentally, you should notice that whenever there is a charge of vote-bank politics, it is always about lower-caste or minority votes, as if upper castes, by definition, cannot constitute a vote bank. Actually, this charge reflects a deep-seated fear of the consequences of democracy itself, because the entrenched power of a small minority is threatened by the mobilisation of a majority of the other castes.

The BJP responded to V.P. Singh's announcement by launching a *rath yātrā* in support of a movement already started by the Viswa Hindu Parishad for building a Ram temple at the site of the Babri mosque in Ayodhya. Lal Krishna Advani led the journey, along with tens of thousands of enthusiastic followers, from the Somnath temple in Gujarat through hundreds of towns and villages of northern India towards Ayodhya. He generated a wave of support – a mixture of religious devotion to Ram and political sympathy for Hindu nationalism – but also provoked a series of communal clashes. The rath yatra was stopped by Lalu Prasad Yadav's government in Bihar and Advani was arrested. The BJP withdrew its support from the central government and V.P. Singh was forced to resign.

This episode is very significant because it marked the beginning of a successful BJP strategy to counter the effects of the political mobilisation of the lower castes by the regional parties. The strategy was for the upper-caste elite to call upon all Hindus, irrespective of caste, to join in the fight to restore Hindu pride and glory and support a party that did not, unlike the Congress or the regional parties, depend on the votes of Muslims. The strategy was relevant only in western and northern India where, as I have explained to you, the long memory of conflict of Rajput and Maratha chiefs against Muslim rulers and the recent history of partition were still fresh. But over the next thirty years, the BJP persisted with this strategy in order to build a permanent communal voting bloc that could give it enough parliamentary seats in the western and northern states to allow it to form a majority government at the centre. It succeeded in 2014 and again in 2019.

How? At one level, there was an acceptance by upper-caste political leaders that greater representation of the lower castes was to some extent inevitable. I have looked at the list of parliament members over the last three decades. From 1991 to 2009, the number of OBC members increased significantly, not only in the Janata Party, the Samajwadi Party, and the Rashtriya Janata Dal, but even in the Congress. My guess is that the same thing happened in most state legislatures as well. Within a few years, state governments which had not already done so implemented OBC reservations in state government services. When the Congress came to power at the centre in 2004, it ordered OBC reservations in higher education. Although various organisations protested, no political party, whether the BJP, the Congress, or any Left party, moved to undo the OBC reservations. Of course, the demand for government jobs became less attractive for the educated upper castes with the expansion of the private sector from the 1990s. Nevertheless, there was an attempt on their part to absorb the initial impact of the democratic force represented by the popular mobilisation following the adoption of the Mandal report.

But that is only one part of the strategy. The other part was to devise a campaign of Hindu unity which specifically addressed disaffected OBC groups in various states. As a matter of fact, the push for OBC quotas had definitely resulted in the more numerous and organised castes, such as the Yadav in UP and Bihar, cornering most of the reserved jobs. This caused resentment among other OBC castes such as the Kushwaha or Teli

## PEOPLE'S ALLIANCES STRENGTHEN THE NATION

in UP and the Kurmi in Bihar. Even when the Bahujan Samaj Party under Mayawati moved energetically to empower Dalits, it was the Jatav caste that secured most of the benefits, leaving the other Dalit castes unhappy. The BJP, without disowning its core support among the upper castes and the Bania trading community, skilfully exploited these resentments to gain votes to secure an electoral majority. The effort was not restricted merely to elections, but extended to gestures of inclusion of marginal low-caste groups into the larger Hindu fold. I have seen how Valmiki sanitation workers in UP cities now display images of Brahmanical gods and goddesses in their houses, organise pujas and festivals to which they invite upper-caste BJP leaders, and claim with a lot of enthusiasm that they feel proud to be part of the Hindu nation. In a small corner at the back of the house, however, hidden from public view, they still have a small shrine of Lal Beg, the Sufi saint who had sheltered this untouchable community for centuries.

You might say that the BJP is doing something all parties are expected to do in an electoral democracy. But there is something else in the BJP strategy that the regional parties lack. With their organised strength from Gujarat and Maharashtra in the west to all the states in North India and the loud and visible presence of Hindutva proponents in the Hindi media, the BJP can project the image of a party that can hold power on its own at the centre. On that image is superimposed the image of Narendra Modi as a self-made OBC who has risen above caste identities to become a national leader rivalled by no one else. Yet, at the same time, the upper-caste representation in parliament has increased substantially in 2014 and 2019 while Muslim representation has fallen to the lowest point ever, almost entirely because of the caste composition of BJP members. It is its identification with central power that characterises the BJP today in every state and distinguishes it from all other parties, including the Congress, which no longer retains a position even as the main national opposition. When people vote for the BJP in state elections, they do so with the knowledge that it controls the immense resources of the central government.

There is no surprise, therefore, in the recent spate of centralisation of powers by the BJP government under the unusual conditions created by the Covid pandemic. It is said that a crisis is also an opportunity. The BJP has seized the moment to push through a decisive consolidation of central powers by, for instance, declaring a national lockdown, assuming powers over state governments under the little used Disaster Management Act, issuing central health guidelines which states must obey, insisting on holding university examinations even when the states are reluctant to do so, and, of course, not paying the promised financial compensation to the states for the losses they have suffered because of the poor collection of revenue under GST.[4] In addition, the centre has introduced, without any discussion in parliament, significant structural changes in conditions of the employment of labourers, participation of corporate houses in purchasing agricultural commodities from farmers, and, as I have mentioned already, education. In all of these, the central government has assumed greater powers of direction and monitoring without taking any responsibility for the implementation of policies.

What I have tried to show you is that the core support of the BJP among the upper-caste urban sections of the middle class has been retained by strengthening its power at the centre, because it is the central government which makes policies regulating the institutions that most affect the interests of this class – business houses, banks, financial institutions, central services, elite colleges and universities, private hospitals, etc. Even as it has reached out in its election campaigns to disaffected OBC

[4] Goods and Services Tax. In the face of stiff resistance by opposition-ruled states, the central government was forced in October 2020 to offer some compensation to the states.

and Dalit groups, its policies have diligently followed the path of supporting big business and an expanding middle class. The spread of popular democratic mobilisation which began in the 1980s has been definitely halted. The continuing centralisation of powers is a sign of the crisis of the federal system, itself a manifestation of the crisis of democracy.

This drift towards a centralised authoritarian system must be reversed. This could begin with a refusal by the states to accept the unjust usurpation of their powers by the centre. But more than that, a sustained stand on restoring the federal balance could create the opportunity for many innovative solutions to the intractable problems of caste, language, religion, gender, and class. It is worth remembering that in the 1990s and 2000s, when the states had much greater flexibility and resources, several state-level attempts were successfully made within the existing reservations framework to meet the demands of castes that continued to be deprived, such as by sub-quotas within the SC or OBC quotas, or including Muslim castes among the OBC. There is even the possibility of legal innovations to allocate more reserved quotas beyond the maximum of 50 per cent allowed by the courts. After all, there are many more jobs at the state level than in the central services, even if they are less lucrative; greater resources in the hands of the states will only increase the possibility of a fairer distribution of benefits, and hence of resolving many outstanding disputes.

I told you earlier the story of how, in the 1950s, the Congress leaders who had just come to power held on to the colonial structures of provincial administration because they were afraid that a reorganisation along linguistic lines would create new popular mobilisations and destabilise the state machinery. The BJP leaders are in a similar situation today in relation to caste. As I have explained to you, castes are not frozen entities: they change in size, location, status, and power along with demographic and social change. Curiously, no one knows the exact number of people included within the different castes in each state, because every census carried out after independence has counted only scheduled castes and not the others. The Mandal commission used figures from the 1931 census to calculate the number of OBC in each state. Everyone knows that, after seven or eight decades that have seen massive demographic changes caused by post-partition migration and the movement of millions from rural to urban locations, the 1931 caste figures could hardly be valid today. But there is great resistance to counting caste populations because of the new popular mobilisations and political equations that might emerge. Following persistent demands from regional parties, a caste enumeration was included in the 2011 census. The results were ready in 2014, but the BJP government has refused to publish them, claiming that they require further verification.[5] As preparations for the 2021 census begin, indications are that only scheduled castes and tribes will be enumerated and not the other castes. This only shows that the Hindu upper-caste political consolidation feels seriously threatened by the prospect of new caste mobilisations backed by up-to-date census numbers and prefers to cling to the familiar power equations created by outdated colonial classifications.

I am not for a moment suggesting that by bringing the primary focus of both policies and politics to the state level all outstanding problems will be resolved. That would be a foolish claim. The caste question, for instance, cannot be resolved without sustained attention to two crucial dimensions – one, expanded and more equitable economic opportunities, and two, ending social practices that continue to reproduce caste discrimination in daily life in both cities and villages. I will, at some point, have to tell you more about those topics. But at least in relation to caste politics, I do believe the possibilities of

[5] The Socio-economic Caste Census 2011 was completed in December 2013. The BJP government decided to refer it to the Niti Ayog for verification. The caste figures have not been published yet.

greater equality and democratisation have been blocked by the centralising politics of Hindutva. New avenues will be opened by a more vibrant and resourceful politics in the states.

## What About Language Disputes?

I have explained to you how the regional languages of India lie at the foundation of the democratic composition of the states within the Indian federation. This was recognised by the Indian National Congress a hundred years ago and has been confirmed by developments since the 1950s. But a state within the federation has a territory with defined boundaries. Not everyone living within that territory will necessarily have the same mother tongue. In other words, every state within the federation, like the nation-state itself, will have linguistic minorities – one cannot avoid it. The question is: what should be the place of linguistic minorities in monolingual states? How are their rights to be negotiated? I believe that if states had both the responsibility as well as the resources, the question of linguistic minorities would be better answered at the state rather than the central level.

To show this, let me consider the example of perhaps the most difficult of these cases: Assam. The dispute over the Bengali-speaking minority in Assam has been a huge problem since at least the 1960s and has still not been solved. Why has it proved so intractable?

You must first remember that even though the western part of Assam – historically known as Kamrup – was subjected to Mughal authority for some time, the Assamese heartland in the Brahmaputra valley, ruled for several centuries by the Ahom kings, was never part of any Indian empire until the British annexed it in 1826 after defeating the Burmese occupiers. Thus, Assam shared with the rest of the Northeast the sense of political distance from the rest of India, even though Brahmanical cultural norms were quite well established there, solidified by a powerful Vaishnav movement in the sixteenth century.[6] Following the conquest, the British administered Assam, including the Khasi, Garo, Naga, and Lushai hills, as a part of Bengal until 1874 when it was made into a separate province under a chief commissioner. The language problem began from this period in the middle of the nineteenth century.

Being a part of Bengal, Bengali became the official language of bureaucracy and education in Assam. The argument was made that Assamese was just a regional dialect of Bengali: the latter had a standard literary form which the former did not. The first generation of English-educated Assamese, mostly educated in Calcutta, bristled at the suggestion that they could have no distinct linguistic identity. It so happened that a group of American Baptist missionaries were at this time publishing an Assamese journal called *Orunodoi* and printing books in the Assamese language. They joined prominent Assamese cultural figures in demanding that Assamese be officially recognised as a language of education in Assam. There was some resistance to this from Bengalis who were already filling up the expanding lower bureaucracy and professional occupations in colonial Assam. The government finally gave in and agreed in 1873 that Assamese would be a language of education and the courts. But the seeds of bitterness were sown.

The second, much more consequential, dimension of the problem was opened at the turn of the century by the colonial policy of encouraging peasants from Bengal to settle in the relatively underpopulated Brahmaputra valley, and especially in the fertile *char* islands formed on the riverbed. The intention was to increase agricultural production in Assam and lower the population pressure in the Bengal countryside. The result was a dramatic spell of immigration into Assam for the next six or

---

[6] The movement led by Srimanta Sankardev in the fifteenth and sixteenth centuries created a network of Vaishnav monasteries or *satra* all over Assam.

seven decades, unmatched anywhere else in India, and possibly in the world. The population of Assam increased in some decades by as much as 35 per cent when the average for India was about 20.[7] The partition of Bengal in 1947 and the troubles in East Pakistan in 1971 led to further waves of refugees. The Assamese people began to fear that they would be turned into a minority in their own homeland.[8]

This sentiment was strong within the Congress party in Assam. In the 1946 elections, it wanted Assam to be reorganised on the basis of Assamese language and culture. It demanded that the Bengali-speaking Sylhet and Cachar districts be separated from Assam and the settling of Bengali immigrants be stopped. There was also a strong feeling of the distinctness of Assam as a part of India. Ambikagiri Raichoudhury, a leading literary figure and Congress leader, described the Assamese as a *jati* (nation) within the Indian *mahajati* (great nation) and wanted an Indian federation in which the people of each linguistic state would have dual citizenship.[9]

Matters came to a head in 1960 when a law was passed to make Assamese the official language in all government institutions all over Assam. Soon after that, Gauhati University declared Assamese as the medium of instruction in all colleges in Assam. The opposition came mainly from the Bengali-speaking Cachar district. The dispute erupted into ugly riots in several towns in 1960–1 in which the slogan was "*bongal kheda*" (throw out the Bengalis).

---

[7] The census figures of population growth in Assam (with all-India averages in parentheses) are as follows: 1901–11 16.99 (5.75); 1911–21 20.48 (-0.31); 1921–31 19.91 (11.00); 1931–41 20.40 (14.22); 1941–51 19.93 (13.31); 1951–61 34.98 (21.51); 1961–71 34.95 (24.80).

[8] According to the 2011 census in Assam, Assamese is the mother tongue of 48.38 per cent and Bengali of 28.91 per cent.

[9] Ambikagiri Raichoudhury (1885–1967) was a major poet and essayist as well as a prominent leader of the Congress. He founded the Axom

Unless you were a party to this dispute, you would find it hard to blame any side. Given their history of living in an independent kingdom until the British conquest and the humiliation of their language being subjected to the domination of Bengali, Assamese cultural and political leaders were understandably concerned about the demographic threat posed by continued Bengali immigration in a democratic age in which population numbers had political significance. On the other hand, how could one blame poor Bengali peasants from populous districts like Mymensingh for trying to build a better future by bringing new lands under cultivation and settling down in new villages? As far as they were concerned, they were not taking away other people's lands; on the contrary, they were, through their hard work, making the land more productive. If existing political arrangements created the conditions for bitter conflict between the Assamese and the Bengalis, the fault was not on either side; the fault lay in the political arrangement.

There were two distinct groups of Bengalis in Assam. One lived in Cachar district which was adjacent to Sylhet and was long an administrative part of Assam. In addition, Karimganj subdivision, which had a Hindu majority, was separated from Sylhet in 1947 and added to Assam. After 1947, many Hindu refugees from Sylhet moved into Cachar and Karimganj. Bengali Hindu refugees who came from East Pakistan in later years mostly merged with this group. This was, in other words, a Bengali population, predominantly Hindu, that had lived in Assam for generations and was also prominent in government services, education, and the professions, especially in Shillong, the capital city.

The other group consisted of Bengali peasants, mostly Muslim, who settled in various rural districts of Assam through the

---

Xomrokhwini Xobha in 1926 and the Axom Jatiyo Mohaxobha in 1936 to promote the cause of Assamese national identity.

twentieth century. The partition of the country in 1947 did not put a stop to this historically established process of agrarian expansion. The charge is that, despite the international border, people have continued to enter Assam from Bangladesh and swell the ranks of the Bengali population.

Perhaps it was this international element that supplied the reason for the crucial turn in the language dispute in Assam. From the early 1980s, a reorganised Assamese movement not only directed its demands towards the central government but in fact put the responsibility of solving the problem on New Delhi. The trouble is that no central intervention in a particular state can be dissociated from its implications for other states and political groups. As a result, the path was opened for a spate of promises, agreements, and laws that, instead of resolving anything, have only complicated matters.

In 1979, the All Assam Students Union (AASU) launched a movement demanding the expulsion of millions of "foreigners" who had, over the years, infiltrated Assam. What was earlier a campaign against the presence of the *bongal* – an ethnic minority – was now turned into a call for action against the *bidexi* – the illegitimate foreigner. In seeking to avoid the taint of narrow chauvinism, the AASU framed its concern as one that involved the security of the country's borders. Surely, its leaders said, all of India should be worried that illegal migrants were changing the demographic balance of a strategically crucial border state. The central government must ensure that all foreigners were removed from the voters' lists in Assam.

As the movement gained steam, state assembly elections became due in 1983. When it was announced that voting would be held according to the existing lists, the movement led by the AASU declared a boycott of the elections. It was one of the most violent elections ever held in India, with more than three thousand being killed, including the massacre of more than a thousand Bengali Muslims at a place called Nellie. The

Congress government was sensitive about its national image of protecting religious minorities and so would not easily concede the Assam movement's demand which would obviously affect the Bengali Muslim community the most.

Following Rajiv Gandhi's massive election victory in 1984, the central government entered into negotiations with the leaders of the Assam movement and signed an accord in 1985. The agreement laid down that a National Register of Citizens (NRC) would be compiled for Assam which would include only those who were legally in the country before 1971. The AASU leaders reorganised themselves into the Asom Gana Parishad (AGP), a regional political party, which then won a massive victory in the 1985 elections.

But the work of compiling a register of citizens proved to be a hugely difficult administrative task. How was a person who may have entered the country several decades ago to prove his or her credentials? In many cases, people were required to prove that their deceased parents had legitimately entered the country. The matter was complicated by a law which put the onus of proof on a person whose citizenship was said to be doubtful. In other words, such a person would be presumed to be an illegal migrant unless he or she could produce documents that proved otherwise. As the process went ahead in various NRC tribunals, it emerged that no document – ration card, voter card, PAN card, Aadhaar card, even a passport – was a reliable proof of citizenship because of the suspicion that it might have been procured by making false claims. The Assam case even led to important changes in the law of citizenship which applied to the whole country – such as the cut-off date of 1986 after which new conditions were to apply for the grant of citizenship in order to accommodate the provisions of the Assam accord, or a definition of the illegal migrant as someone who was living in the country without a valid entry permit.

The work of the NRC proceeded extremely slowly. Militant elements within the Assam movement blamed both the state and central governments for not taking the question of Assamese national identity seriously enough. Declaring its intention to separate from India, the United Liberation Front of Assam (ULFA) began in 1990 a series of violent attacks against rail and road transportation, the security forces, and political leaders. Initially, ULFA enjoyed considerable popularity among the Assamese people. But as often happens with such underground organisations, its cadres began to extort money from ordinary people and indulge in indiscriminate violence. When the security forces hit back, the leaders took shelter in the Burmese highlands. In a few years, ULFA was no longer a significant force.

The register of citizens in Assam was published in November 2019. It satisfied nobody. It declared 19 lakh persons as illegal migrants, of whom 12 lakh were Hindu (mostly Bengali and some Nepali) and 7 lakh Muslims (mostly Bengali). The AGP declared that there had been a massive undercounting of illegal migrants, because it believed there were many more. The BJP, which was then in power both at the centre and in the state, was faced with a difficult political problem because so many Hindus had been declared illegal. Its position was that Hindu migrants were refugees and should be welcomed whereas Muslims were infiltrators who must not be counted as citizens. The result was the hurried passing of the Citizenship Amendment Act in December 2019 which declared that Hindu immigrants from neighbouring countries had entered India because of religious persecution and so could be given citizenship even if they did not have valid documents.

You know what happened after that with the protests all over the country against the NRC and the CAA. In Assam and other north-eastern states, on the other hand, there were massive protests for the opposite reason – that the NRC had not been strict enough in identifying illegal immigrants! What I want to point out is that this intractable situation was created largely because, instead of trying to resolve a local dispute locally, the central government was invited to intervene and take responsibility for the solution. It resulted in a complete mess.

Could it have been different if political leaders in Assam had persisted with the difficult task of finding a compromise solution among themselves? I have to speculate here, because I cannot prove something that conditions did not even allow to happen. As I have explained to you earlier, those like Ambedkar who thought deeply about this problem suggested that the basic democratic principle of monolingual states would work only if the minority languages were given enough protection for their autonomous growth. If you remember the situation in colonial Assam when it was a part of Bengal, the Assamese leaders had made a perfectly legitimate demand that Assamese be recognised as a medium of instruction in schools and colleges in Assam. The same principle should hold today in Assam districts with large Bengali populations. But there is a corresponding responsibility on the part of the minorities too. They must accept the democratic principle that Assamese continue to be the principal official language. From my travels in Assam, I know for a fact that most Bengalis of the younger generation who have gone to school there are fluent speakers and readers of Assamese. How could it be otherwise? Younger members of immigrant peasant families do not want to be stuck in their traditional rural occupations; they want to find a future in the cities. This they can do only by learning the language used by most people in the cities and towns of Assam. If the political situation was conducive, the immigrant Bengali population could become an assimilated part of Assamese culture which has traditionally included both Hindus and Muslims.

The Assamese cultural elite, it seems to me, is still haunted by the memory of Bengali cultural domination. That is why it does not trust the official figures of Assamese speakers, claiming that they include millions who are not ethnic Assamese. To assert the priority of the ethnic Assamese, it keeps pushing back the date before which one must prove one's domicile in Assam in order to count as a citizen. The Assam accord had fixed that date as 1971. Assamese cultural leaders are now demanding that the central government push the date back to 1951. The problem cannot be resolved this way. The question of infiltration across international borders must be dealt with separately; it should not be allowed to interfere with the process of finding a mutually acceptable settlement among the majority and minority linguistic communities in Assam.

Democratic negotiation and compromise within the framework of a monolingual state that protects minority languages is the only workable method by which a solution to such problems can be found. Resort to the force of central law, intimidation, and the threat of internment or expulsion only creates unrest and panic and deepens the sense of distrust on all sides. Negotiated solutions have been found in other states where there are sizeable linguistic minorities. There is no reason why, with goodwill and imaginative cultural leadership, Assam cannot find its own forms of alliance (*mitratā*) among the people.

The Assam case, as indeed the rest of the Northeast, also clearly shows that there can be no single principle of cultural politics, whether based on religion, caste, or language, valid for all of India. Regional cultural formations are necessarily varied, producing different political equations in different states. Thus, even though Hindu nationalists as well as secular pluralists believe that the Hindu–Muslim division is the biggest political question in the country that must be resolved, Assam shows that it does not have the same significance as elsewhere. Similarly, divisions of language have different political consequences in different states. No single great national formula will work everywhere. That is the reason why states have evolved their own party systems with different patterns of alliances. Any party – such as the Congress, the BJP, the CPI, or the CPI(M) – which claims to have a national perspective often finds it difficult to justify why it is aligning with one party in one state but opposing it in another. They would be spared these ideological gymnastics if they were simply to admit that state politics has its own sphere of autonomy.

## The Oppression of Women

This is not a subject on which I can tell you much that you don't already know. Not only are you aware from your own life experience of discrimination against women but you have also discussed this subject on many occasions with your friends. Let me just point out one or two things that might help you connect the condition of women with issues of caste and minorities.

Very recently, there was much agitation about a horrible incident of rape and murder of a young Dalit woman in Hathras in Uttar Pradesh.[10] The UP government denied that there had been rape; it had the victim's body burnt in the middle of the night, pressurised the victim's family to change its statement, and cracked down hard on opposition leaders and the media. It became a matter of much political dispute between the BJP government in UP and opposition opinion all over the country. You will also remember the so-called Nirbhaya incident in Delhi in 2012, when the ghastly gang rape and murder of a young woman caused widespread agitation. However, on that occasion there was no real dispute because no one stepped up to support the alleged rapists. What do you think is the difference between the two cases?

The victim in the Delhi incident was a college student who was travelling by bus with a friend. Her assailants were migrant workers of a lower caste and social status. The horrifying details of how the young woman was tortured and serially raped and her friend severely beaten shocked all middle-class residents of

---

[10] The incident was reported in October 2020.

Delhi who saw in Nirbhaya, as the victim came to be called, someone who could have been their daughter or sister. It suddenly brought home to them the ever-present threat lurking round the corner for women in the city who travel in public transport to go to study or work. Inevitably then, the threat was identified in the thousands of migrant male workers, mostly single, who also move around in the same spaces. The difference in education, caste, class, and cultural background between these men and their potential victims was plain for all to see. What was the punishment whose very thought would strike fear in the hearts of these reckless men such that they would refrain from the ghastly crime?

The situation seemed to remind people of *daṇḍanīti*. Many insisted that the accused be shown no mercy and hanged. Others thought that hanging as a punishment was not specific enough: they must be castrated. A lot of people thought that the judicial process was too slow and riddled with loopholes: the criminals must be summarily shot dead. As it happened, public pressure did result in the judicial machinery acting at great speed in this case. Except for one accused who was a juvenile, the other four were sentenced to death. The legal process of seeking mercy for the convicted persons did take time but all four were finally hanged in March 2020.

In Hathras, on the other hand, the violence against a Valmiki woman by a group of young men from a Thakur family was rooted in long-standing relations of domination by upper-caste landlords over poor Dalit families in UP villages. There was a time when such incidents were so routine that they would not even have been brought to the notice of the police or reported in the media. That situation has changed. The Dalits are now more vocal; there are laws that provide for severe penalties for caste atrocities. The electronic media is now more enterprising in covering such stories from rural India. In response, the landed elites are also using caste and political networks to hold on to their power in the villages and put down the disobedient Dalits. The Hathras case revealed this ugly feature of the complicity of caste and landed power with the exploitation of women. It also showed how, despite the existence of laws protecting the rights of victims of sexual and caste violence, the legal and administrative process can be subverted by powerful groups at the state and local levels of government.

This raises a legitimate question. Is the cause of women better served by the central government making effective laws and actively intervening in specific cases so that women's rights are protected or should one allow the forces of state and local opinion to find an acceptable solution? On the face of it, the answer would seem to lie in central intervention. That was the understanding that drove leaders of the women's movement in the 1970s and 1980s to push for central legislation to severely penalise sexual violence against women, recognise the right of abortion, and prohibit sex-determination tests before birth. Since then, many other laws have been made by parliament to reduce discrimination against women in education and employment. Although attempts to reserve a minimum proportion of seats for women in parliament and state assemblies have not succeeded, there is such reservation in municipalities and panchayat bodies. Indeed, it is sometimes said that India has some of the most progressive laws on women's rights in the world.

But what is the result on the ground? As far as middle-class women in the cities are concerned, the situation has certainly improved in the last few decades. Think of yourself or your friends and compare your lives with those led by your grandmothers. Fifty, seventy, or a hundred years ago, girls in the family would have had much fewer material opportunities than boys: the latter would have been given better food, healthcare, and education. That kind of overt discrimination is no longer common in middle-class families. Women have access to the highest levels of education and professional training. Most families are as proud of the achievements of their daughters as they are of their sons'. With greater education and, in many cases, independent incomes, women now have greater say in family decisions. What is even more significant is that as the size of the middle class has expanded in the country, this aspect of the middle-class lifestyle which values women's education is being adopted by more and more people. All this undoubtedly indicates a change for the better.

But there is another side to this story about which, I am sure, you are also aware. While educated women in middle-class families are allowed, even encouraged, to take up professional jobs and public responsibilities, that gift of freedom does not in any way lessen their primary task of taking care of their homes and children. As a result, women are saddled with a double burden: they have to prove themselves equal to men in the outside world as teachers, doctors, administrators, scientists, and dozens of other professionals while, at the same time, retaining their essential quality as mothers or wives or sisters or daughters.

The fact that women's education and employment outside the home have been widely accepted among the middle class has created a new anxiety among men. Can women be trusted not to misuse their freedom? What if girls meet boys, get into romantic relationships, and marry men not approved by their families? What if they forget that, while they must compete with men in education and professional training, they must also remain true to the traditional virtues of Indian womanhood? They must be modern for sure, but not too modern! When your mother went to college, it was rare for women to wear jeans and sunglasses. That was considered too modern, something worn by film stars and fashion models, not ordinary women. Now, of course, you and your friends wear whatever you please. But isn't there something else you are told you must not do because it is too modern and therefore not appropriate for decent women? Drawing attention to your modern clothes and behaviour, you must have been warned, will only signal to men that you have a Westernised lifestyle that encourages free mixing between men and women; hence, they will assume that you must be available for sexual advances from men. In other words, while becoming modern may be desirable for men, there is always a limit on the degree to which women could be modern. Why? Why is there a difference between men and women on what is acceptable behaviour?

The reason is not far to seek. For all their embrace of modern values, middle-class men still think of the family as something they own; women and children are under their charge and so have to be protected like property. No matter what the constitution or the law says, men are reluctant to acknowledge that women have equal freedom to make decisions. No matter how educated, women are believed to be driven by irrational impulses, emotions, and passions. They are susceptible to manipulation by unscrupulous people. Consequently, every choice made by a woman must be approved by a man who can act as a responsible guardian. This is a sentiment that prevails even in the most progressive middle-class families. When women act in defiance of their male protectors, the latter regard it as a violation of their authority – something that others will see as a failure in their role as guardians. Hence, disciplining women becomes a matter of preserving the honour of the family or caste or community. This is the feeling that drives the *khāp* panchayats in Haryana to restrain women from wearing jeans or using a mobile phone. It is the same feeling which feeds fears over what is called "love jihad" which is supposed to be an organised plan under which Muslim men pretend to fall in love with Hindu women in order to convert them. Note that there is a similar resistance among Muslim men when women from their community marry Hindu men. In neither case is there an acknowledgement that women have an equal right to choose their marriage partners.

The fact that women in middle-class families are now encouraged to take up jobs and contribute to the family income has also introduced a new dimension of commercial transaction in marriage alliances. Marriage as a social relation had always offered an opportunity to families and groups to move up or down the jati ladder. The usual method was to secure the marriage of a daughter with a groom from a jati or clan of a higher standing. This method was often used by groups which had acquired wealth or political power and, having done so, wanted to gain recognition as a superior jati. Many powerful groups and clans belonging to lower jatis all over the country were recognised in this way as Kshatriya through marriage alliances with Kshatriya families. This practice reached bizarre proportions among Brahmans in Bengal where a man from the highest-ranking *kulīn* category would marry dozens of women from lower-ranking Brahman families in order to give the latter the chance to rise in social prestige. But the commercialisation of the marriage alliance has acquired a different character, especially among the rising middle classes in India today.

This involves the creation of the so-called marriage market. Families compete with one another to give their daughters in marriage to grooms who have promising professional careers by offering massive dowries. Indeed, the dowry has become a matter of competitive bidding. You must have heard stories of the amount of dowry an IIT engineer or IAS officer could fetch in the marriage market. What is particularly striking is that jatis among whom even a few years ago the prevailing practice was for men to first secure gainful employment to pay a bride price in order to find a woman he could marry, have, with their entry into the urban middle class, shifted to the dowry. Upper-caste cultural norms have an overwhelming influence on the culture of the middle class in India. The result is the addition of a new dimension to the oppression of women – the harassment of brides to extract a bigger dowry, leading at times to what are called "dowry deaths". The shocking thing is that this happens most often in educated middle-class families where the marriage alliance has become entangled in a commercial transaction.

The situation in rural society is different but also changing. First of all, the traditional patterns of landholding and agriculture have changed enormously in the last few decades all over India. The old landed families are in decline; most of the younger members have moved into urban occupations. Dominant peasant castes have become politically mobilised and exert much influence in local affairs, using their political muscle. But Dalit and other lower-caste groups, who are still mostly landless, are also more politically conscious and do not accept their subjugated condition without protest. This has meant repeated clashes, often violent, by upper and dominant peasant castes against lower castes. And women often become the immediate victims. This is what happened in Hathras.

So you could say with some justification that, unless there is strong intervention by a higher authority, the growing conflicts at state and local levels may play themselves out, but, no matter which side wins, women will be among the principal victims. There has to be, you will say, central intervention to protect the rights of women. I can see your point. But I will ask you to think about the matter once more. Why is it that the laws that already exist cannot be implemented? Why is it that organisations and activists defending the cause of women, in spite of getting a lot of support from national leaders and the national media, are frustrated in their efforts at the local level? They are blocked, even harassed, by local politicians, administrators, and the police. The district courts, they find, are not sympathetic and frequently avoid the responsibility of enforcing the law. Why is that such a common experience?

The reason is that the powers that sustain the traditional domination of men are rooted in relations between castes and families at the local level. These are deeply embedded in local social practices, supported by local cultural traditions, and enforced by authorities representing local communities. That is where the task of social change still remains to be carried out. For the last several decades, the progressive women's movement has achieved many significant results through their campaigns for better laws and regulations for the protection of women. Opinion among the urban middle classes is now much more sensitive than before to the need for better legal protection of women's rights. But the task of changing practices in regional and local cultures still remains to be accomplished. There is no shortcut to that objective.

If you accept that, you will have to admit that if the focus of politics around the country shifts more to state and local levels, the struggle for equal rights for women will have to be resumed with new vigour – this time in the regional languages, with an eye to regional and local practices, directed at regional power structures that prop up the domination of men within families and communities. One would have to confront both traditional institutions and novel practices at the local level that have escaped attention so far because of the focus on legal reform at the top. The task will not thereby be made any easier, but it could lead to more effective steps to end the perpetual oppression of women in this country.

# 8

# The Nation Belongs to the Entire People

## The Changing Middle Class

WHO RULES INDIA today? You will probably say, "Why, of course it's the BJP which rules India today, just as the Congress used to rule it at one time." Your answer would not be wrong but it would be superficial. Because I could tell you about villages in Bihar, for instance, where the leading landlord family continues to dominate village life just as it did a hundred years ago. The patriarch of the family might tell you that one of his sons is in the BJP and another in the RJD, while his nephew hobnobs with the Congress. "No matter which party is in power," he will tell you with a chuckle, "I run things here." I could also tell you about a businessman in Pune who claims to finance the Shiv Sena, the NCP, and the BJP. "Every political leader here owes me something, and so no matter who runs the government I can always get things done." In other words, political parties and leaders may win elections and form governments, but they are able to do so only because they are supported by powerful groups in society which in turn expect to be rewarded by policies that favour them. So one could say quite truthfully that it is not the BJP or the Congress that actually rules. Rather, certain groups that are already powerful in society rule through parties such as the BJP or the Congress.

But then, you might ask, what about us – the people who vote in elections to throw out a ruling party and bring the opposition into power? How can we be acting on behalf of landlords and businessmen? Surely that can't be true.

Well, think again. Imagine a situation in which people are fed up with the government and want to change it. How do they come to that decision? Perhaps because prices are high, or there is too much crime, or ministers are accused of corruption, or the government is seen to be too heavy-handed and arrogant – there could be many grievances of this kind. But then, such grievances are around all the time, no matter which party is in the government. Why is it that the complaints suddenly become so strident that masses of people decide to vote out the government? How does the public mood change? This is where money and organisation come in.

There was a time in the decades after independence when the Congress ran governments in every state in India. They had strong state-level leaders who presided over party machineries that were good at gathering votes. Some of those who were elected to state assemblies or parliament were veterans of the freedom movement. They were widely known and respected. Others were rich and influential patricians who could mobilise their own workers to campaign for them and had enough money to bear the expenses. In either case, the Congress relied on powerful landowners in the villages and wealthy magnates in the cities who had the local resources to organise enough voters to ensure the victory of the party's candidates. Needless to say, these powerful people expected Congress leaders to help them in return to preserve their properties and increase their wealth. In other words, Congress rule until the 1960s was built on the basis of a reciprocal relationship of power between the party leaders, on the one hand, and wealthy and propertied groups in city and countryside, on the other.

But if these were the only forces acting on the Congress party, there would not have been all that government investment in building power plants and steel towns, dams and bridges, railway lines and airports. Remember, huge resources were raised by the government in those days for the development of infrastructure and heavy industry. For this, the savings of the people had to be mobilised and taxes imposed on the rich. In fact, except for the consumer goods sector which was left to private companies, all other manufacturing, banking, insurance, mining, rail and air transport, even hotels, were dominated by the public sector. What was the force behind this?

It was the educated middle class. The political leaders of the Congress as well as bureaucrats, judges, journalists, scientists, teachers – people who shaped opinion and framed policies – were from the urban middle class. They were the personnel who ran the government. Motivated by lofty nationalist sentiments, they wanted to overcome the backwardness of traditional Indian social practices and the economic poverty that colonial rule had left behind. They wanted the new nation-state to take the lead in introducing progressive laws and bold economic policies to build a more egalitarian society with a modern industrial economy. The middle class was the key political force that held the political balance in the heyday of Congress rule.

But this middle class with a bilingual college education in English and a regional language was, as I have told you before, a very small group, numbering no more than two or three per cent of the population. How could it have wielded so much influence over the policies of the government? The answer lies in the history of nationalism and the freedom movement. I have told you before how the Congress began in the nineteenth century as an annual meeting of eminent lawyers and public figures from different parts of the country. They came together for a few days in the winter and delivered speeches in English. I also told you how, after Gandhi took over the organisation, the Congress carried out mass campaigns, mobilising not only a wider middle class but also peasants in the villages and workers in the cities. At the same time, writers from the bilingual middle class used the printing press to spread the message of nationalism in the various regional languages. They not only published newspapers and wrote political pamphlets, but also poetry and novels and plays for the theatre. They criticised British rule and called for an independent nation-state that would be free, modern, and prosperous. The message of nationalism reached millions who, in their own way, began to make sense of the idea of the nation as a united people. I have already explained to you how, in this process, the people in each language region of India became aware of belonging to the nation. Middle-class political and cultural leaders played a crucial role in generating and spreading these ideas of freedom, modernity, and nationalism.

After independence, men and women from the middle class took the lead in framing and carrying out government policies. They were the leaders of every political party. They also ran the bureaucracy, the judiciary, the armed forces, colleges and universities, the scientific institutions, the press, the publishing houses, and the film industry. The middle class was the principal force that shaped the policy of planned industrial development in the heyday of Congress rule. It was careful not to upset the big businessmen too much, even though several industries were nationalised. After all, the Congress depended on the financial support of businessmen at the time of elections. On the other hand, the Congress also promised to reform the pattern of landed property created under colonial rule, abolish the hereditary claims of zamindars who extracted rents from their tenants but did nothing to improve cultivation, and give ownership rights to peasants. This called for a careful balancing act. Political leaders, bureaucrats, and publicists spoke of balanced growth that would strike a compromise between the demands of different sections of society. For this, it was necessary to have a central planning organisation of experts. Political leaders in government were told to use the powers of the state to develop the economy by following the advice of experts.

This gave rise in the field of politics to the art of speaking in two voices. One voice proclaimed loudly that the new nation-state was rapidly moving along the path of development, progress, and even socialism. These were big words. But they were not empty words, except they were vague and could mean many things. That is exactly what was needed in order to appeal to the variety of social groups whose support the ruling Congress party had to secure. But the actual laws and policies of the government had to be more specific. Any concrete step designed to benefit one group could displease another. Thus, attempts to carry out land reforms might generate enthusiastic support among millions of small farmers but made the locally powerful landlords very unhappy. The latter were the ones who controlled the rural vote. So while Congress leaders and their public spokesmen continued to shout about land reforms, government officials and lawyers at the local level quietly exploited loopholes in the law to enable landlords to retain control of their properties. On all subjects and at every level, there emerged a gap between policy and its implementation. Policies were clothed in high-sounding but vague slogans while implementation was slipshod. This was not because of inefficiency or incompetence. It was a necessary part of the politics of balancing the interests of various powerful groups. If there was corruption in the failure to strictly implement the laws, it was part of the system by which the country was ruled.

Because of the zeal to industrialise quickly and thus create a modern and dynamic economy, and the failure to implement land reforms, agriculture could not keep pace with the growth of the urban population. By the middle of the 1960s, there was a massive food crisis in the country. Shiploads of wheat had to be imported as aid from the United States to supply the ration shops in India's cities. Once the immediate crisis was managed, it became necessary to change the direction of development policy. The strategy of green revolution was adopted to subsidise big farmers and encourage them to increase the production of food crops. This led, in the 1970s, to the growing political power of big farmers, especially in northern India. The Congress went into decline there and various regional groups and leaders emerged. The latter first joined forces under Jaya Prakash Narayan to oppose Indira Gandhi and, after her defeat in 1977, assumed power as the short-lived Janata Party. Even though the Congress came back to power in 1980, the support base for the regional parties was already formed among the relatively prosperous farmers of northern India as well as in Tamil Nadu and Andhra Pradesh.

The size and character of the middle class also began to change. In the first three decades after independence, the Indian middle class was intimately tied to government service and the public sector. The best institutions of higher education, including engineering and medical colleges, were funded by government. Student fees were nominal. The best students sought jobs in government or the public sector. But as secondary education expanded rapidly from the 1970s, there emerged a bifurcation in the cities between English-medium and vernacular-medium schools. The effects were felt in higher education after the disturbances in 1989 over the implementation of the Mandal commission recommendations on reservations for Other Backward Classes (OBC) and the liberalisation of the economy in 1991. The elite section of the middle class increasingly dissociated itself from the public education system, preferring to send its children to expensive English-medium schools and private colleges and universities in order to prepare them for lucrative jobs in the private sector. Secondary education became split into two distinct streams. City schools affiliated to the central boards catered to the English-speaking elite section, while schools in district towns and villages which were under state boards taught in the regional languages and laid the ground for a rapid growth of the regional middle classes.

It also produced a new dynamic of social aspirations. Young men and women in small towns and villages who had received some education became strongly motivated to leave their traditional occupations and move to the city in order to seek a better life. Their education opened them to the attractions of the glittering lifestyle of the elite depicted in cinema, television and advertising. Life in the city was a hard struggle for most of them. But they were sufficiently disenchanted with the circumstances into which they were born and sufficiently seduced by the prospect of a lucky break for them to continue to crowd into congested city suburbs. As I will soon explain to you, this division of the middle class into an all-India elite section and the regional sections constitutes a very important factor in contemporary Indian politics.

### Changes in Political Power

The fundamental change of economic policy ushered in by the liberalisation decisions of the Congress finance minister Manmohan Singh in 1991 led, over the next few years, to a major change in the balance of power between big business and big farmers. The green revolution strategy adopted in the late 1960s had made the big farmers a powerful force not only in the states but even in national politics. You may have heard of Charan Singh, the Jat leader from western UP, who was a major figure in the Janata Party, played a key role in bringing down Morarji Desai's government and briefly became prime minister in 1979.[1] Charan Singh was a very articulate spokesman for the big farmer interest in national politics. He bitterly criticised

---

[1] Chaudhary Charan Singh (1902–1987) was Prime Minister of India from July 1979 to January 1980. He then founded the Lok Dal which in 1996 became the Rashtriya Lok Dal under his son Ajit Singh.

Nehru's industrial policy for promoting the interests of urban elites to the detriment of India's villages. He argued for more government support for the larger farmers who could rapidly increase agricultural production, create jobs in the countryside, and reduce the population pressure on cities. He managed to organise farmers as a distinct and visible group. By the 1980s, other leaders such as Mahendra Singh Tikait and Sharad Joshi followed his lead to demand greater support for farmers and access to export markets for farm products.[2]

But this spell of prominence of big farmers in national politics did not last long. Reforms introduced after the liberalisation decision saw the withdrawal of government from many sectors of the economy. Corporate business houses began to flourish. Foreign investments started flowing in just as Indian companies opened manufacturing units abroad. The economy grew at rates unheard of before. India was no longer an underdeveloped country but an emerging economy. The elite middle class began to send its children to foreign universities and take vacations abroad. The boom in exports was steered by middle-class scientists and engineers who became stars of the Indian pharmaceutical and information technology (IT) industries. The urban middle class was now sold on the magic of the free market, globalisation, and the brilliance of Indian entrepreneurs. The farmers were reduced to a declining pressure group in state politics.

These changes in the relative power of different social groups had their effects on the political scene. Indira Gandhi had thrown aside the old Congress model of an election machine

---

[2] Mahendra Singh Tikait (1935–2011) is famous for organising in 1988 a march of about five lakh farmers in the heart of New Delhi, forcing the Rajiv Gandhi government to concede his demands for a rise in sugarcane prices and free water and electricity for farmers. Sharad Joshi (1935–2015) was the founder of the Shetkari Sangathana, a major farmers' organisation in western India.

based on strong state-level leaders and built a party that was completely centralised, held together by total loyalty to a single leader. The degree to which the Congress had become defined by what was effectively a monarchical form of leadership was revealed after Indira Gandhi's assassination in 1984 when, without following any formal procedure either in the party or in parliament, President Zail Singh, always a loyal Congressman, swore in Rajiv Gandhi as the next prime minister. The tradition was followed after Rajiv Gandhi's death when Sonia Gandhi was acclaimed as the undisputed leader of the party, even though she had no political experience at all. Even when P.V. Narasimha Rao or Manmohan Singh was prime minister, it was clearly understood that all power must flow from Sonia Gandhi as head of the party. Whether at the central level or in the states, all major policy decisions, all appointments, or the choice of ministers or candidates for elections were decided by a so-called high command which answered only to her. When, from the time of the parliamentary elections of 2014, Rahul Gandhi began to be projected as the natural successor to the leadership, the Congress was, for obvious reasons, dubbed a dynastic party.[3] It was clear that the framework of the party had solidified into a centralised power structure headed by what was effectively a royal family and nothing could change it.

You must know that after Rajiv Gandhi, whose government came to an end in 1989, no prime minister has been able to run a ministry in New Delhi without the support of other parties. Even the BJP which had an absolute majority in parliament in 2014 and 2019 included allied parties in its ministry. This is significant. It means that political power in India is now distributed in such a way that no single party can command authority all over the country. The regional parties are firmly

---

[3] Rahul Gandhi was elected vice president of the Congress Party in 2013 and led the campaign for the parliamentary elections of 2014.

in place in many states. The BJP's majority is localised in western and northern India; hence, it has to secure the support of regional allies in order to form a ministry that is reasonably representative of all regions.

## All-India Power Groups

There are two major social groups in India that have a strong interest in centralising the power of government. One of them consists of the big corporate business houses. They have factories and offices in various parts of the country and do business in every state. In the era of planning, they were dependent on licences from the central government to set up manufacturing units. After liberalisation, that is no longer necessary. But matters like corporate taxes, monetary policy, banking, interest rates, stock market regulation, labour laws, and environmental policy are still in the hands of the central government. Everything related to foreign exchange and international trade and investment is also controlled by the central authorities. Not surprisingly, the leaders of corporate houses try hard to influence central policies in their favour. They do so through their trade associations as well as by seeking to influence public opinion through the media. They also use more invisible methods such as financing the election campaigns of national parties and developing close personal relations with important political leaders.

In the years following liberalisation, when the private sector was expanding and economic growth was rapid, big business encouraged state governments to compete with one another to offer special terms such as land allotments or tax concessions to large corporate houses to come and invest in their states. A big industrialist invited to set up an automobile factory in West Bengal would say to the chief minister, "But the Haryana government is offering us much better terms. I must be able to show something more to convince my board that we should come to

West Bengal." It was a great time for corporate leaders because both central and state governments were keen to please them.

But the honeymoon did not last after the global financial crisis of 2008. As growth rates began to slow down, businessmen became wary of making big investments. It was no longer a situation in which competition in a free and expanding market would give everyone the chance to invest and make profits. Rather, corporate houses began to look for special treatment. Some of this happened in legitimate and transparent ways such as, for instance, when they appealed to the government for tax breaks for particular sectors, or relaxation of labour laws to facilitate the outsourcing of labour, or of environmental regulations to open new mines. Other methods were covert and sometimes illegal, such as defaulting on large bank loans without being penalised or arranging for preferential treatment in securing government contracts. In the era of planning and licences, when doing business was a matter of finding your way through a maze of regulations, industrialists had little choice but to seek favours from politicians and bureaucrats. With liberalisation, that era had supposedly come to an end. But from 2010 onwards, a new phase of crony capitalism began in India. The last years of the Congress-led UPA government were rife with accusations of high corruption involving ministers and business houses.

You may have heard of Anna Hazare, the Gandhian activist, who went on a fast in Delhi in 2011 demanding stricter laws against corruption in government.[4] The Anna movement attracted a lot of support among the urban middle class and contributed to the defeat of the Congress in the 2014 elections. It also produced a new urban political party – the Aam Aadmi Party.

---

[4] Anna Hazare went on a fast in April 2011 at Jantar Mantar in New Delhi demanding a law to set up an independent institution of Lokpal with powers to prosecute ministers and bureaucrats on charges of corruption.

The emotional charge generated by the anti-corruption sentiment among the urban middle class is interesting because it shows the gradual convergence of this sentiment with the demand for a strong centralised state that would strictly implement the law and reform the economy in favour of a free market. Everyone was agreed that corruption was bad and should be stamped out. Yet no one could deny having participated in small, and perhaps even large, acts of corruption. If you are in a hurry to find a reserved seat on a train or get something done in a government office or obtain a document from a court, you will have to find the right person who will do it for an extra payment. Sometimes, the extra payment could be quite substantial, such as when getting admitted to a good college or securing a schoolteacher's job. And, of course, anything to do with a police station means that palms must be greased. The usual justification for this is: "That's the only way things can be done. It's the system." People would blame the plethora of regulations which set up hurdles at every step and thus create the opportunity for unscrupulous employees and their touts to extract a bribe. In fact, most people seem to make a distinction between corruption as a necessary part of life and corruption as greed. In the first case, one regards oneself as the innocent victim of a system. In the other case, dishonest people try to get rich through corruption: such people must be identified, condemned, and punished. Curiously, even big businessmen will admit to systematic corruption and claim that if one did not participate in it, one would never get any business done in India.

By the time of the 2014 general elections, business circles as well as the urban middle class voiced a strong preference for a corruption-free and market-friendly government that would have fewer and more transparent regulations, do away with land or labour laws that restrict the expansion of private industry and reward merit and enterprise. Narendra Modi, chief minister of Gujarat, was projected as the leader who had demonstrated his ability to lead the nation to this golden future. There may have been a blot on his career left by the horrific killings of Muslims in Gujarat in 2002. But he had managed to put the episode behind him and build an image of himself as the maker of a new Gujarat – rich, confident, brimming with high-technology industries. Even though the prosperity and dazzle were confined to urban areas and the condition of Dalits, tribals, and Muslims had declined significantly, it was just the right kind of image, expertly projected through news reports and advertisements financed by corporate houses, to appeal to the urban middle class elsewhere in India.

In the days leading up to the 2014 general elections, pressure grew within the BJP to declare Modi as the party's prospective prime minister. He came from a backward-caste family and had struggled with poverty to enter a life of dedicated service in the RSS. But he did not represent the Gandhian model of renunciation. Rather, he would project the young and dynamic face of a party committed to a prosperous future, leaving behind its history of social conservatism and communal discord. Modi promised to end unnecessary subsidies and doles and radically reform taxation and labour laws to make Indian industry globally competitive. In his election speeches, he made no mention of Hindutva or the Ram temple at Ayodhya.

I have closely watched every general election in India since independence. Of the leading business houses in the 1950s and 1960s, some, such as the Birlas, had strong ties with the Congress leadership. Others, such as the Tatas, kept their distance from politics. Most responded to calls from political leaders to contribute to their campaign funds but rarely expressed open support for any political party. In the period after the 1980s, when there was no single dominant party any more, business houses seemed to hedge their bets by making contributions to rival parties; 2014 was the first election I have seen where the entire business community of India openly and collectively voiced its support for Narendra Modi. The English-language media which echoed the views of the upper middle class enthusiastically cheered him on.

## Regional Power Groups

But these all-India groups constitute a small, even if highly influential, part of the Indian people. Most other power groups have interests that are more regional. Their impact is on state and local politics. Among them are businessmen who own companies that may not be listed among the 500 most important firms in India but are nevertheless engaged in manufacturing, commerce, or services that employ, as sectors of the economy, hundreds of thousands of people. Medium- and small-size factories and workshops, construction firms, wholesale and retail outlets, agricultural processing, road transport, hotels and restaurants, etc. are sectors that are mainly organised regionally or locally. Needless to say, most of agriculture in most states is carried out by medium and small farmers. All of these groups have to deal mainly with state and local governments. Consequently, they involve themselves in state politics to further their interests.

As you know, the economies of Indian states vary greatly. Some, like Maharashtra or West Bengal, have industrial histories going back to the time of British rule. Others, such as Gujarat or Karnataka, have become highly industrialised in recent decades. The location of big industries, as I have already explained, earlier depended very much on central policies. But the prospects of regional industry, agriculture, commerce, and services have always had close links with the policies of state governments.

There are many variants here. Tamil Nadu is an interesting example where a regional political movement based on solidarity among non-Brahman castes has produced an entire class of small and medium entrepreneurs from among prosperous farming families. The two Dravida parties in the state were vehicles for the rise of these new business groups. They used their caste networks to raise capital, enforce contracts, and recruit labour. They also used their influence over local political leaders to evade tax liabilities, labour laws, and pollution regulations. This is how the district town of Tiruppur has emerged as the knitwear capital of India, with tens of thousands of garment factories employing lakhs of workers. Similarly, Sivakasi has become famous for firecrackers, matchboxes, and colour printing. Most of these enterprises are small, but their combination in a particular location and the social solidarity among their owners and workers have made them powerful in regional politics.

There are other examples where state government policies produced new entrepreneurs at the regional level. In coastal Andhra, a fertile agricultural region, prosperous farmers belonging to the Reddy and Kamma castes used their political influence to take advantage of the facilities offered by a big city like Hyderabad, capital of Andhra Pradesh, to start new industries and financial operations. This in turn created resentment among the people of Telangana who felt Hyderabad was being used by outsiders to enrich themselves while the Telangana districts remained backward. Haryana is another example where the state government promoted the new industrial and financial city of Gurgaon, making use of its proximity to the national capital. It offered generous compensations to farmers who had to give up their land; many of them used the money to set up transport and other businesses. Goa and Kerala have become showpiece examples of the state government's efforts to promote tourism, creating thousands of small enterprises employing lakhs of men and women. Similarly, Himachal Pradesh is an example of a state government's success in promoting fruit orchards and agro-processing industries. One can give many other examples.

Such dynamism in envisioning an economic future for a state requires leadership by the regional middle class. Leaders of political parties come out of this class; so do those who lead in the field of culture and shape public opinion. As a rule, entrepreneurial energies are released when there is a social churning that breaks down older hierarchies of property and caste in a regional culture. Most of the states of southern and western India have seen such a churning in the decades after independence. On the other hand, in a state such as West Bengal, the traditional Hindu upper castes consolidated their social and cultural dominance even as they embraced a leftist political ideology. As a result, even with significant land reforms, there has been no regeneration of regional business enterprise in West Bengal. Variations in the social formation of the regional cultures are an important indicator of economic disparities between regions in India.

I have described to you these economic and social disparities the way I understand them. You may have heard other descriptions, such as those preferred by your Marxist friends. I have tried many times to fathom what they say about classes and class struggle in Indian society, but must confess that I don't understand their language. So if you want to find out if my description agrees with the Marxist analysis or not, you should probably ask one of your professors. You may have also heard the ruling groups in India described as a Brahman-Bania combine. I understand why this may seem like a good description but it is too simplistic. There are undoubtedly many big businessmen in India who come from Bania families, just as a large section of the upper middle class is Brahman. But most Brahmans and most Banias are actually among what I have called the regional middle classes. So the label "Brahman-Bania combine" does not capture the division between the all-India and the regional power groups which I think is quite crucial in understanding the underlying conflicts in Indian society today.

## Relations Between the All-India and Regional Levels

Let me focus on the more recent period. Although Narendra Modi's government came to power in 2014 with the strong backing of the all-India business houses and the upper middle class, it was unable to deliver what they expected because of the pressures it faced from the regional formations, including state governments run by the BJP. The slowing down of growth after 2009 meant that state governments were collecting less revenue while expenditures to keep up programmes of subsidising influential groups such as farmers or small entrepreneurs and maintaining the subsistence levels of the poor were rising. Whenever a regional or local election loomed on the horizon, state governments had to announce new projects of social expenditure to prevent voters from shifting their support to the opposition. The Modi government did not dare bring in drastic changes to land or labour laws as desired by the corporate houses. The only significant reform it was able to carry out was to replace various state taxes with a uniform Goods and Services Tax (GST) for the whole country. This had been under negotiation from the time of the Manmohan Singh government, but the final form it took following much wheeling and dealing with the states was a hugely cumbersome tax structure. Nevertheless, it did shift the balance of decision-making in favour of the centre.

An act of daring displayed by Modi in his first term was his surprise decision in November 2017 to demonetise high-value currency notes. It made no economic sense and caused enormous difficulties for ordinary people. Modi claimed his decision would uncover huge quantities of black money. He said he was punishing the corrupt rich who hoarded money. Many people believed him even though the end result was a massive dislocation of small business, agriculture, and the informal sector.

Even though this gamble worked for the BJP in the UP elections of 2017, the party soon faced major agitations in Maharashtra, Madhya Pradesh, and Rajasthan by farmers who demanded that their loans be waived. Farmer suicides began to mount. There were movements among peasant castes such as Jats, Gujjars, and Patidars claiming job reservations. In 2018, the

BJP suffered a series of election defeats in Rajasthan, Madhya Pradesh, and Chhattisgarh, while its ally – the Akali Dal – was ousted from power in Punjab. This was also the time when the scandals broke of businessmen Vijay Mallya and Nirav Modi having fled the country after looting the banks of crores of rupees. And allegations began to be made for the first time that the two business houses of Ambani and Adani had been specially favoured in the granting of several major government contracts. All this meant that the time was not propitious for Modi to introduce pro-business reforms.

The turn towards Hindutva as the central slogan of BJP politics was signalled in Uttar Pradesh where the saffron-clad chief minister Yogi Adityanath launched a vigorous campaign of cow protection. It prompted vigilante groups in UP and elsewhere to pounce on defenceless Muslims on allegations of cow slaughter or trading in beef. The issue of building a Ram temple on the vacant site of the destroyed Babri mosque in Ayodhya was also raked up. In Karnataka, the journalist Gauri Lankesh was murdered for writing articles that allegedly criticised Hindu social practices.

But much more telling was the way in which Hindutva sentiments were merged into the question of national unity. Any criticism of the security clampdown and massive deployment of forces in Kashmir was painted as an endorsement of militancy. Student activism on university campuses was targeted as a threat to national security. In fact, any criticism of the Modi government, even by the most respectable and law-abiding parties and leaders, was alleged to be a tacit support for those who were out to destroy the unity of the country. The effect of this campaign was to tighten the focus of all of the government's activities to a single objective – the defence of the nation against its enemies – and to project Modi as the singular and supreme leader who must be supported by all in this hour of crisis.

You must remember the terror attack in Pulwama in February 2019 and the air strikes in Pakistan soon after. They completely changed the tone of the political debate leading up to the general elections. Superseding all of the mounting grievances of numerous groups all over the country, one question dominated the election campaign: "Modi vs. who?" Forgotten was the fact that India was a multi-party parliamentary system of government as well as a federation of twenty-nine states and six union territories (before the status of Jammu and Kashmir was changed in August 2019). Modi's image as the single leader of national authority successfully converted the general election into a presidential contest. The multi-party opposition scattered over different states could not throw up a rival leader to match him. In the process, the BJP also managed to centralise the principal issues of government.

## Centralisation of Power

The combination of Hindutva sentiments with a call for national unity was channelled into a series of moves by the Modi government in its second term. In July 2019, soon after it came to office, it passed a law banning the practice of divorce by "triple talaq" common among Indian Muslims and providing for the imprisonment of the guilty husband. This was hailed as a move against the oppression of Muslim women. In August, the government made inoperative Article 370 of the constitution by which Jammu and Kashmir had been given special status as a state within the federation. Not only that, it was demoted to the rank of a union territory under direct control of the central government. Ladakh district, which has a Buddhist majority, was separated and made another union territory. In November, following the Supreme Court judgment on the Babri Masjid dispute, the central government announced its decision to facilitate the building of the Ram temple. A dhoti-clad prime minister was the chief devotee at the foundation ceremony in

Ayodhya. It was the first time a place of religious worship was to be sponsored by the state after Somnath was rebuilt. In December, the Citizenship Amendment Act was passed and the home minister announced in parliament that the exercise for a National Register of Citizens would be carried out in every state of India. When protests against the CAA continued in cities across the country, the government attributed them to foreign sponsors across the border, the liberal media, and so-called urban Naxals. Once again, student activists on university campuses became the target of attacks by BJP supporters and the police. But, despite a high-pitched election campaign in which it mobilised every big gun in its arsenal, the BJP was resoundingly defeated by the Aam Aadmi Party in the Delhi assembly elections in February 2020. Soon after, large-scale communal violence broke out in Delhi in which more than fifty people were killed over several days while the police merely stood by and watched.

The alarm was first raised about the Covid pandemic in early March 2020. The prime minister went on television on 23 March to announce a national lockdown. The focus was on cities, since that is where the virus was entering through travellers from abroad. The lockdown tried mainly to protect the urban middle class which usually had safe jobs and could often manage to work from home. Since supply chains were broken because shops were closed and transport disrupted, those making their living from small business and agriculture were badly hit. But the worst sufferers were informal sector workers who were mostly self-employed, had no savings and often lived far away from their village homes. You will surely remember those harrowing scenes on television and social media of thousands of migrant workers walking hundreds of miles to return to their villages. It seemed the bureaucrats in Delhi who were daily announcing detailed guidelines to the whole country on what to do to fight the epidemic had completely forgotten about the existence of these lakhs and lakhs of migrant workers in our cities. It finally fell on the state governments to do something to facilitate their return and provide them with some subsistence at home.

The efforts to use the legislative power of the central government to further extend business-friendly reforms were expedited during the pandemic period while normal politics remained suspended. In July 2020, the government announced a new education policy for the whole country without consultation with the states, even though education is a concurrent subject on which both centre and states can make laws. Its purpose, as I have told you before, was to lay the foundation for the education of managers and workers skilled in the latest industrial and communication technologies. In September, the Industrial Relations Code bill was introduced making it harder for workers to strike and easier for employers to retrench their employees. A few days later, three laws were passed to facilitate the entry of corporate business into the market for agricultural commodities, thus threatening the continuation of *mandis* in states like Punjab and Haryana where farmers usually sell their crops at the minimum support price announced by government. These laws were rushed through parliament without proper scrutiny by experts or committees, even though agriculture is a state subject in the constitution. As the prime minister often remarks, a crisis is also an opportunity. Clearly, the government is not averse to using the emergency conditions of the pandemic to push through the pro-business reforms it had failed to execute under normal conditions. The thrust towards the centralisation of powers continues with a decisiveness that indicates firm ideological resolve.

## The Problem with Centralised Power

"But what is the harm in centralising power?" you may ask. "Will not a decisive leader at the centre with full powers of supervision and policymaking for the whole country make for a strong nation?" If that is what you think, I must say you are terribly wrong. Here is why.

First, the more power is concentrated at the centre, the greater the relative power of the all-India groups, i.e. corporate business houses and the English-speaking upper middle class. As I have already explained to you, their concerns are addressed mainly by the central government. They would much prefer to deal with a single powerful authority at the centre than to have to influence dozens of state and local authorities who may not at all be sympathetic towards them. But greater power to the all-India groups necessarily means greater inequality – both between regions and between different sections of the people. Let me explain.

During the period of rapid growth from the late 1990s, new investments in industry came to be concentrated largely in the southern and western states. There were economic reasons for this, having to do with the advantages of geographical location. There were also social and political reasons related to the cultural background of the entrepreneurs and the facilities offered to them by particular state governments. But once the concentration of growth industries increased the prosperity of those regions, average wage rates began to rise and local labour became more and more expensive. What happened then is interesting. Instead of the business houses looking to invest in states where labour was cheap, they took advantage of the fact that, unlike travelling across international borders, labour was free to move all over India. Hence, they employed labour contractors to mobilise migrant workers from poorer states like Uttar Pradesh, Bihar, and West Bengal to come and work in western and southern India on short-term contracts. Thus, the effects of industrial growth not only remained unequally distributed across regions, the disparities between the developed and less developed regions grew wider. This has now become a permanent feature of the pattern of development chosen by the Modi government.

Within the growth region itself, the inequality between the big investors, highly paid managers and professionals, and those who receive rents and dividends, on the one hand, and the rest of the population, on the other, increased rapidly. Even if average incomes rose, the inequality between the top and the bottom rose faster. Not only that, the expansion of industries meant the acquisition of land to build factories, townships, airports, roads, bridges, and other infrastructure. Farmers lost their land, and even if they were compensated, they were rarely able to start a new life as successful entrepreneurs, as the official propaganda suggested. Most of those who moved out of agriculture joined the vast informal sector in towns and cities. This, again, is an inevitable part of the growth pattern chosen by the Modi government. It seems to believe in the theory propagated by American economists in the 1970s that rapid growth of private capital would create enough wealth in the top layers of society that would gradually trickle down to the bottom layers and make everyone better off. I am told that most economists no longer believe in this fairy tale and that inequalities in the United States and Britain have become much worse in the last few decades. India seems to be headed in the same direction.

There is yet another dimension to the inequality between the all-India and the regional middle classes that is not usually recognised. The urban upper middle class has a far greater proportion of upper castes than the regional middle classes. As it is, the higher rungs of the private sector have almost no representation from the scheduled castes or tribes. The entry that was allowed to these groups through reservations in the central government services has recently shrunk because recruitment has been greatly reduced. Not only that, lateral entry into these services at middle and higher levels has increased, and the reservations rule does not apply to lateral recruitment which takes place without going through the entry-level competitive examinations. Besides, a new 10 per cent reservation has been introduced for economically backward sections. That is a category defined in such a way that most upper-caste applicants become eligible for the quota. As a result, the recent centralisation of powers has seriously undermined the effects of the changes that began after the Mandal commission recommendations were implemented and has pushed the pendulum back in the direction of upper-caste dominance.

The second problem with centralised power is that it becomes arbitrary and unaccountable. If decision-making is concentrated in a single authority, which in fact ends up being a single person – the supreme leader – then all the whims and fancies of that leader which are part of the personal mystique of almost magical qualities that are attributed to him or her are inextricably mixed with the exercise of authority. Decisions that are opaque or difficult to explain are assigned to reasons best known to the all-knowing leader. Supporters and fans will claim that their leader has powers of intuition that ordinary people lack and so it is best not to try to analyse their decisions too much. This is, of course, a licence for arbitrary power. But those who justify centralised power will claim that the supreme leader must not be hemmed in by rules and procedures. Since the leader's commitment to the defence of the nation and the cause of justice is beyond question, one must trust him or her with the exercise of unlimited power to do good for the people.

One can find many instances of such arbitrary and whimsical exercise of power by leaders who have been raised to the position of supreme authority in state politics. The phenomenon of the absolute leader is, therefore, not confined only to the centre. Think of M.G. Ramachandran or Jayalalithaa in Tamil Nadu, N.T. Rama Rao in Andhra Pradesh, Mayawati in Uttar Pradesh, or Mamata Banerjee in West Bengal. With Narendra Modi, too, were you able to explain why he wanted everyone to light lamps and blow conch shells at nine o'clock at night for exactly nine minutes to drive away the Covid pandemic? His devotees (*bhakt*) said, "He knows best. It must be for our good. We must follow his instructions." Even in the case of more serious decisions such as demonetisation, the reasoning was quite unclear, but even then his supporters were happy to leave the thinking to him. When there are allegations of favouritism towards particular business houses, the response is that the leader knows who will do the job best. This is, of course, abandoning entirely the people's role in a democracy and reducing the people themselves to a passive and obedient mass.

The third problem with centralised authority follows, paradoxically, from what is considered its great strength. Concentration of power in the person of a single leader reduces the focus of all opposition to that person. All of his or her words, actions, character traits, and weaknesses become central to criticisms of the performance of the government itself, just as every misdeed or failure of the government can be attributed to the leader. The propaganda machinery will try its best to keep the leader apart from party or government functionaries, but the logic of central power identified with the person of a leader will necessarily implicate the latter in the former, offering a single target to all critics. As a result, opposition politics too will converge on the leader's person. The regime's enemies will indeed become the leader's enemies.

The fourth problem with centralised personal authority is that of succession. Absolute and arbitrary personal authority inevitably means that impersonal rules of decision-making are undermined and institutional systems degenerate. The fundamental principle of bureaucracy that the office is distinct from the person is forgotten. The ultimate source of authority is attributed to the supreme leader who attains the status of an absolute monarch. Institutions in such a centralised system become so dependent on the authority of the leader that they fall apart in his or her absence. It is not surprising at all that when the monarch-like leader departs, his or her followers take recourse to the traditional practice of anointing the offspring as successor. We see this not only in the case of the Congress Party but also in the National Conference and the People's Democratic Party in Jammu and Kashmir (the Abdullahs and the Muftis), the Shiromani Akali Dal (the Badals), the Samajwadi Party (the Yadavs), the Shiv Sena (the Thackerays), the Rashtriya Janata Dal (the Yadavs), the Dravida Munnetra Kazhagam (the Karunanidhis), and the YSR Congress Party (the Reddys). What happens when the line of succession is not clear was shown by the vicious disputes that broke out within the AIADMK after Jayalalithaa's death. Interestingly, while the BJP is relentless in its criticism of such dynastic politics, it is silent on the monarchical style of leadership itself. But can one have the one without the other? The BJP will be put to this test in the future.

## More Power to the States

The most pernicious effect of concentrating power in a centralised authority is increasing inequality among the people. The euphoria of a political victory achieved under the flag of the supreme leader does not last long. Sooner or later, the resentment and suffering caused by the dominance of some groups over others will come to the fore. Agitations will break out, conflicts will emerge. Opponents will attack the ruling leader as the source of all their miseries, while followers will flock around to defend him or her. The arena of democracy will begin to look like the battlefield of civil war.

If one has to push back against the centralisation of powers that is now taking place, one must begin by rejecting the idea that a single strong leader makes for a strong collective, whether that collective is a party or state or nation. The reduction of political initiative to a single leader nullifies the idea of popular sovereignty and is, therefore, fundamentally anti-democratic. It is no argument to claim that the monarch-like leader is chosen by the people. That would be to suggest that the people must choose to hand over their democratic rights and powers to their favourite leader and agree to be ruled by him or her. In other words, they must surrender their sacred role as the source of sovereignty in a republic. How can that be democratic? It is, in fact, an invitation to authoritarianism (*tānāśāhī*).

I have explained to you at length why I think a shift in the federal balance towards more powers for the states is a necessary condition not only for halting the slide towards greater centralisation but also for creating room for the reduction of inequalities among the people. The most immediate consequence of the shift will be that a party which secures a majority in parliament by virtue of a lopsided support base in a few regions will no longer exercise the huge powers it does today because of the centralisation that has taken place. Even if the party happens to project a monarch-like leader, that leader would not have the scope to claim dominance over the whole country by virtue of being in power at the centre. Central political leadership will be effectively tempered by regional leaders, thus reducing the danger of authoritarianism. The resentment caused in many states by the dominance of some will be dissipated.

Second, greater power for the states would mean greater flexibility in development strategy according to regional and local conditions. I have mentioned before how social and political movements in particular states have encouraged the rise of new entrepreneurs who have, in each case but in a different way, transformed their economies. The examples of Kerala, Tamil Nadu, and Goa show that, with the necessary initiative from state governments, excellent results can be achieved in human development indicators such as livelihood, health, and education.

I should also bring to your attention the example of Bangladesh. At the time of partition in 1947, the eastern districts of Bengal were almost entirely agrarian since most industries were located in and around Calcutta. During the period when the region was in Pakistan, and especially under military rule, the people of East Pakistan complained of being treated like a colony of Punjab. When it became independent in 1971, Bangladesh was one of the poorest countries in the world, worse than almost every state in India. I was recently shown a report by a United Nations agency which calculates that the human development index for Bangladesh has now almost caught up with the Indian average and that its performance is better than every state in the central and eastern region of India, including Assam, Bihar, Chhattisgarh, Jharkhand, Madhya Pradesh, Odisha, Rajasthan, Uttar Pradesh, and West Bengal.[5] Specifically, Bangladesh does better than most Indian states on indicators such as life expectancy, schooling, and gender equality.[6] This has become possible largely because Bangladesh, instead of trying to introduce high-technology industries that create little employment, has encouraged the spread of innumerable small- and medium-sized workshops, mainly producing garments for export, which employ millions of workers, mostly women. This has resulted in the absorption into the organised labour force of migrants from rural areas, greater economic security of women, and better health and education of women and children. Of course, Bangladesh being a sovereign nation-state has a different political status from Indian states, but the comparison shows what could be achieved if the poorer Indian states had greater and more flexible decision-making powers to suit their particular conditions.

There is one more reason why greater economic resources to states will benefit especially the poorer sections of the people. The national growth strategy followed in India recently has

---

[5] According to the UNDP Human Development Report 2020, the human development index for Bangladesh was 0.632 and for India 0.647. The indexes for the relevant Indian states were: Bihar 0.576, Uttar Pradesh 0.596, Jharkhand 0.599, Madhya Pradesh 0.606, Odisha 0.606, Chhattisgarh 0.613, Assam 0.614, Rajasthan 0.629, West Bengal 0.641.

[6] Life expectancy at birth is 72.6 years, expected years of schooling is 11.6 years, gender development index is 0.904. These are better numbers than most Indian states.

meant the inevitable decline of small farmers and the swelling of the ranks of informal workers. State and local politicians have to bear the brunt of helping these people find a livelihood and sustain themselves and their families. The regional parties in particular, especially the AIADMK in Tamil Nadu and Telugu Desam in Andhra Pradesh, took the lead in devising government schemes to provide subsidised food, clothes, housing, healthcare, and other amenities to the poor. Such schemes have now been adopted by every state government in India. Needless to say, a part of the revenues earned by the states have to be spent in this way. Business lobbies and the upper middle class criticise such spending as populist waste that does not build any productive assets. But come election time in a state, the party in power at the centre, whether it is the Congress or the BJP, joins in the chorus in announcing special schemes for the poor to help the party's prospects in the state. Since the centre has far more resources, the states in turn have to look to the centre to transfer some funds to help them meet their mounting expenditure for the poor. This creates a condition where the central government prefers to have large discretionary funds which it can use to gain political leverage rather than hand over the statutory financial power to the states. You must have heard central ministers come to a state and announce: "Vote for us in the state elections and the centre will give you more assistance. In fact, the prime minister will deliver a special package for the state." If this logic were to prevail, the people of every state would have to elect the same party to the state government as at the centre. That would obviously mean the end of federalism. Since the need for anti-poverty spending is now recognised by all, it is far better to give greater financial powers to the states which have to deal directly with the poor than to encourage this kind of partisan arbitrariness.

A related, but even more pernicious, political consequence of the lopsided power of the central authorities in relation to the states is the ability of the party in power at the centre to topple state governments. The indiscriminate use of Article 356 which gives the governor the power to dismiss a state government may have been curtailed somewhat because of the intervention of the Supreme Court, but that has not stopped the use of threats as well as inducements to get members of a state assembly to change sides to bring down the government. You have seen how the BJP, after having been defeated in elections in Karnataka and Madhya Pradesh, nonetheless managed to engineer defections in the Congress and the Janata Dal (Secular) in order to come to power. Central investigative agencies and tax authorities are deployed to intimidate legislators, and astronomical sums of money are offered in addition to the promise of political office. Not only is this a betrayal of the people's mandate as expressed in an election, but it also distorts the federal principle by forcibly manipulating a political convergence of the states with the centre.

Third, I have already discussed at length the question of language in relation to the coming together of people into the Indian nation. The crucial issue here is that of education. The constitution had originally declared education a state subject, based on the perfectly good reasoning that education is intimately tied with the language of instruction which varies from state to state. But education was transferred to the concurrent list during the Emergency in 1976 and has remained there ever since. Every party in power at the centre has used laws and administrative regulations to influence the institutions of education all over the country. Initially, the emphasis was mainly on higher education which, it was argued, required a degree of standardisation throughout India. Central bodies such as the University Grants Commission (UGC) not only introduced national standards for the qualifications and pay scales of teachers but also enforced uniform models for degrees, curricula, examinations, scholarships, national eligibility tests, etc. From the 1990s, the central government increasingly began to suggest national policies for secondary education. Bodies such as the Central Board of Secondary Education (CBSE) became the most influential examination board in the country and the National Council of Educational Research and Training (NCERT) produced textbooks for use everywhere in India. The culmination of this trend came with the announcement of the National Education Policy in 2020, which lays down a single framework of education all over the country from the primary to the doctoral level.

There is little doubt that centralised power to regulate education has resulted in giving priority to the all-India groups at the expense of the varied needs of the regions and their cultural aspirations. The central government periodically announces its plan to create world-class universities and invite the best universities of the United States and Britain to open campuses in India. At the same time, the push for privatisation of higher education and the channelling of government support to science, technology, engineering, and mathematics has meant that even though there is massive demand for college education among broad sections of the people, state universities are increasingly deprived of funds. As a result, even as there are more college graduates in every state, the quality of education keeps falling. The gap between the elite all-India stream and the regional stream has reached all the way down to the primary level – one stream training the next generation of the elite and the other merely expanding the vast pool of poorly educated members of the regional middle classes, unhappy with their traditional occupations but ill-equipped for the jobs to which they aspire.

If the people of India are to reclaim control over the education of the young, it is vitally important that this gap be obliterated. To do this, what is needed is the universalisation of quality bilingual education – in English and an Indian language. I am saying this after having watched the education scene, especially at the school level, for many years. In the days before independence, there were few schools and access to education was largely restricted to the upper castes and propertied sections. But all students, even those living in cities, went to the nearest school in the neighbourhood. Those from less privileged backgrounds who managed to get into a school received the same education that students from the richest families got. There was no distinction. Every school taught English. As a result, many hard-working and gifted students from relatively poor families were able to distinguish themselves in university examinations and become successful professionals. The recent divide between the elite and the regional streams has meant a sharp difference in the quality of education available to the two groups.

Many intellectuals decry the sprouting of private English-medium schools everywhere, even in rural areas. They must try to understand why so many people feel that their children must learn English to succeed in life. If there is a sense of cultural inferiority here, it is born out of a genuine sense of deprivation and injustice. To make fun of this aspiration is to justify the cultural pretensions of the elite. The ability to read and speak English gives to young men and women from less privileged families a feeling of self-confidence and the belief that they can achieve what was denied to their parents.

I have no doubt at all that English should be accepted as the official or link language of communication across the different regions of India. Its biggest advantage is that, as a language, its use is not concentrated in any particular region of the country. Hence, unlike Hindi, it does not give to the people of a region an additional instrument of domination. English is regionally neutral. To say that it smacks of colonial rule is a silly argument because, as I have shown you, almost every institution and practice of government that we use today is carried over from the days of British rule. Of course, one could still say that English bears the mark of an elite language used by the privileged class. But that is exactly why I am arguing that English should be made available in every school in the country. That would, over time, erase the stamp of elitism which attaches to that language now.

I have also watched with great interest the career of Hindi after independence. There are two distinct tendencies here. One is marked by official efforts to produce a Sanskritised Hindi by getting rid of the numerous Arabic-Persian words in the commonly spoken Hindustani and spreading this new language through official media. I remember a time in the 1950s when many people in north India used to complain that they did not understand the Hindi news broadcast on All India Radio. This effort has now achieved considerable success as the next generations have learnt the new Hindi in schools and colleges. By contrast, the other tendency represented by the Hindi entertainment and advertising industry, sensitive to the actual speech of different sections of the people, continued with the spoken Hindustani for a much longer time. In productions that claimed some literary distinction, especially in the lyrics of songs in Hindi movies, the prestige of Urdu literary styles carried a lot of weight. In recent years, the language of the commercial and social media has reflected the popular hybrid language that has emerged, unashamedly mixing Hindi with English. This is even seen in the commercial and social media in the regional languages where there is uninhibited borrowing from both English and Hindi.

The effort to use the powers of government to thrust official Hindi on those who do not understand it causes much resentment. When ministers or bureaucrats decide that they will answer letters from Tamil Nadu or West Bengal or Meghalaya in official Hindi, or if those who speak in English in official meetings are frowned upon and sometimes even reprimanded, people from those regions naturally see it as an attempt by Hindi speakers to dominate over others. The recent trend of labelling those who do not speak Hindi as guilty of a lack of patriotism is particularly galling. It reveals the prejudice that those from the Hindi heartland, speaking the official Sanskritised Hindi, are the only genuine Indians by birth and that others must emulate them to qualify as patriotic Indians. Instead of unifying the nation, it actually creates festering divisions.

On the other hand, Hindi has actually spread much more smoothly through the non-official channels of cinema, television, advertising, and, more recently, social media. The fact that this Hindi does not conform to the officially sanctioned form is actually its strength. Every living language has two forms – the standard form officially enforced through schools, the bureaucracy, and the print media, and the popular colloquial form which flows without strict regulation, freely borrowing from other languages and adopting new words, idioms, and even grammatical rules as more and more people accept the innovations. In the case of Hindi in India, the first form has been administered in a heavy-handed manner by official agencies following politically influenced policies. The second form has actually encouraged many more people from other regions to willingly learn and use the Hindi language. A reduction in the powers of the central government to dictate language policy might actually help the popular acceptance of Hindi without causing political antagonism.

Finally, there is one question I want to raise and answer. When I have discussed the issue of Indian federalism with others, some have asked me, "But aren't there autocratic leaders in the states too? And what happens if there is a particularly nasty state government? How will it help the people if such a government has even greater power to do harm?" In recent times, the example of Uttar Pradesh has been mentioned as a state with an extremely repressive government which explicitly targets Muslims as undeserving of any benefits and slams sedition charges against anyone daring to criticise it. More powers to such a government? Some of my friends are horrified by the idea.

But you have to consider the question more carefully. The rules of democracy cannot always preclude the election of oppressive governments. There are many reasons why a majority of voters may choose a government which later turns out to be bad. That is exactly why they are offered a chance to throw out the government at the next election. Sometimes there is a temptation to use the powers of the central government to dismiss a state government on the ground that it has failed to govern. We have seen the terrible misuse of this constitutional provision in the past, which is why the Supreme Court has laid down strict conditions on its application. In any case, this supposed remedy to bad government in the state usually comes up when a different party is in power at the centre. That possibility does not even arise in a situation like Uttar Pradesh today. So let us face the plain fact. Democracy places the responsibility of electing state governments on the people of the state. They must also accept the responsibility of removing a government they do not like. After all, who can remove a central government with enormous powers if it becomes tyrannical? If the people's sovereignty is to have any meaning, the people must accept its responsibility as the source of all powers.

## A National People's Federation

I have earlier explained to you why it is wrong to think of the Indian republic as it is now constituted as having a long history going back into the ancient past. To do this is inevitably to impose the history of a part of the Indian people on the whole. The Tamil people have a long history; so do the Marathi or the Kashmiri or the Manipuri or indeed the Santali people. What is referred to in history as Bharatavarsha or Aryavarta or Hindustan can also be given long chronologies. But none of these entities coincide with the present territorial boundaries of India. Indeed, the Indian republic did not exist before 1950. To give this republic a proper foundation among the Indian people as a nation rather than in the legal history of the state, we must recognise the specific and different ways in which the people of the various regions of India came together to form the new democratic and federal nation-state.

I have also defined the three principles with which the truth of this democratic federation (*lokătāntrik sangh*) can be properly expressed. First, the people of each language region must be recognised as different and respected as such. The claim that all Indian languages are derived from Sanskrit and that all that genuinely belongs to Indian culture (*bhārătīya saṃskṛti*) must conform to the norms of upper-caste North Indian society is patently unacceptable. Second, the people of each state must be recognised as equal. The people of Kerala, Meghalaya, Kashmir, and the Andaman and Nicobar Islands must be treated as different from but equal to the people of Uttar Pradesh or Maharashtra. Third, the needs and preferences of the people must have priority over the claims of the government machinery. National security must mean above all the life and freedom of the people. In other words, people cannot be asked to give up their freedoms for the sake of the health of the state. In fact, they should not even be asked to pay additional taxes to enable the government to buy fancy warplanes. That is because the people (*lok*) have given birth to the state (*rājya*) and not the state to the people.

This, I say, represents the truth of our nationalism. The Indian republic is a national people's federation (*rāṣṭrīya lokăsangh*) This description correctly expresses the truth that the different components of the people, each with its own history and culture, agreed to come together in 1950 to form a federal republic on the basis of equality and mutual respect for their distinct identities. Equality is the essential principle of democracy.

This truth of Indian nationalism is hidden under the cover of many falsehoods. I have told you how the British conquered territory in this part of the world, and which portions were included in the British Indian empire and which left out. There was no cultural logic to this process of imperial conquest. The provinces of British India were distributed between the new states of India and Pakistan in 1947 supposedly on the basis of religion. But the actual process by which this division took place varied: in many cases, the decision was made by the provincial legislature, but in some, plebiscites were held among the people. The division left large religious minorities in both countries. It is false to claim that Pakistan was a country of Muslims and India of Hindus; both had to find an acceptable place for minorities in their new constitutions. The princely states were brought within India mostly by negotiation with their rulers, but the terms were often quite different. In a few cases, the integration happened through armed action, and sometimes the annexation was ratified by a popular vote. The French colonial territories were brought into India by diplomatic negotiation, but the Portuguese territories were annexed by military force. The constitution acknowledged these variations in the terms of inclusion into the Indian republic by allowing for special conditions under Articles 370 and 371. Consequently, it is false to claim that the relation of every part of India to the whole is the same. Even when the parts are equal (*barābar*) in status (*sammān*), they are not the same (*ek*) in quality (*guṇ*).

I have also argued that India is in truth neither a Hindu Rashtra nor a pluralist democracy. The attempt to foist a Hindu identity on the Indian nation, and hence define citizenship by religion, provides a justification for blatant oppression against minorities. To claim that this is only to complete the unfinished business of partition is to betray all of those millions who chose to stay in this country and live in solidarity with all other Indians within the same constitutional republic. The proponents of

Hindutva seek to falsify and uproot the constitutional principles agreed upon in 1950 and erect a sectarian (*sāmpradāyik*) republic in its place. I sometimes think the present chief minister of Uttar Pradesh is showing the way towards a future in which Hindu dominance (*parākramāvād*) will try to spread over the entire country.[7]

The claims of pluralist democracy are also false. This may be a little more difficult to see because the attractive slogan "unity in diversity" effectively conceals the many inequalities inherent in pluralism. The supposed harmony infused into Indian civilisation by Advaita metaphysics hides the deeply embedded hierarchies of caste, gender, and region. Even if the existence of different cultural practices is recognised, they do not come together as the sum of equal parts. No adherent of pluralism will admit that the religious rites of the Bhil or the Naga are as important for describing Indian civilisation as the verses of the Sāmaveda or the poetry of Tulsidas. The "unity" that pluralist diversity is supposed to have produced is that of a single Indian civilisation evolving from ancient Vedic times by bringing within its fold other peoples and cultures. But this "unity" always ensures that the moral superiority of the Brahmanical high culture is retained. The core principles of this high culture can never be reconciled with the principle of equality which is fundamental to democracy. Powerful social movements, such as Buddhism and the sects established by Sufi and Bhakti saints, which tried to spread the message of equality were successfully tamed by giving them a place, but always an inferior place, within Indian civilisation. The greater degree of equality in tribal cultures is slighted as the characteristic of uncivilised people. I am convinced that no attempt to present

---

[7] This appears to be a reference to M.S. Golwalkar's claim that true national integration can only be achieved by assimilation of others into Hindu culture through *parākramāvād*. This is discussed in Chapter 4 of the book.

*varṇāśram* as only a form of division of labour with no inherent hierarchy, or Hinduism as inclusive of Dalit and Adivasi populations, will ever achieve a truly democratic union of the people of India. The unity of plural but unequal components is not a democratic unity.

I have described to you in some detail the many inequalities of wealth, income, caste, gender, and region that plague Indian society today. I have also argued that what we need above all is to change the federal balance of power in the direction of the states. Not for once am I claiming that giving more power to the states will remove all of those inequalities. That would be an absurd claim to make. What I am saying is that by making the regional cultural formation the primary field of struggle for greater equality, we would provide a new beginning for the democratic struggle for social justice which was halted and in many ways reversed by the rise of Hindutva politics.

This is not a call for a radical or revolutionary onslaught on the present system of government. Quite the contrary. It is a realistic proposal to infuse a more democratic content into the constitutional structure that we already have. What needs to be established, on every issue and at every point, is the priority of the people over the politician, the bureaucrat, or the judge. Yes, laws will be made, administered and adjudicated, but not merely to satisfy an influential or even a considerable section of the population. If democracy comes to mean the permanent rule of a regional, linguistic, or religious majority, it turns into a tyranny. Ambedkar sounded this warning a number of times in the Constituent Assembly. He was acutely aware that even though the constitution was offering an excellent legal structure for democracy to be practised, Indian society remained deeply undemocratic. The effort must be renewed to push forward the practice of democracy in the economic, social, and cultural fields.

The task is not impossible. You are well aware of the effort that has been made in Europe to build something like a common economic, cultural, and political structure under the European Union. The task was not easy there because the nations and states of Europe have a long history of bitter warfare among themselves. Yet they have been able to achieve a considerable degree of federal co-operation, even though each member state retains its sovereign status (and Britain has recently exercised that sovereignty to leave the Union). By comparison, India has achieved the constitutional task of federal union far more easily. What it needs to do now is achieve greater economic and social justice by deepening the practice of democracy in every part of the country.

### What You Can Do

The protests in 2019–20 against the Citizenship Amendment Act showed that it is possible for groups of active citizens to organise peaceful and democratic protests without being led by political parties. In many cases, parties are unwilling to associate themselves with such protests because they would not help their electoral chances. In any case, they suspect movements they do not themselves control. But once such a movement achieves a degree of visibility, political parties and leaders express their support and take up the issue. When the CAA law was rushed through parliament in December 2019, the opposition leaders were unsure of how to react and put up almost no resistance. Many were afraid that if they opposed the law, they would be accused of defending Muslim infiltrators. But as they watched the protests spread from city to city, spontaneously drawing large crowds of young and apolitical people, one opposition party after another began to declare its rejection of the CAA. That is how the existing political system can be infused with greater popular and democratic content.

You also saw the crucial role that young people played in that movement. There is a particular reason for this at the present moment. The young are more educated than the older generation of Indians. They are also much more familiar with the new technologies of communication through the mobile phone, internet, and social media. As a result, they are in a far better position to bridge the gap between the elite and the regional cultural worlds. Even when they are educated in a vernacular medium, they are much more aware of what is going on in the rest of India and indeed the rest of the world. As a result, they are in a crucial position to bring change to the provincialism of regional and local cultures. I know of a young Santal woman from Jharkhand who used to work in a hospital in Delhi. When she went back to her village to visit her sick mother, the village elders saw her wearing city clothes, using cosmetics, and speaking on the phone to strangers in Delhi. They were alarmed that one of their daughters might be seduced by a man from the city. They locked her up and refused to let her return to her job in Delhi. She finally managed to escape, but sadly was unable to go back home for a few years. Today, I am sure there are more and more women in Jharkhand villages who are going out to study or work in cities. They are the ones who will bring change to their local cultures. Along with greater income and knowledge, they will instil the desire for greater justice in their communities.

You must support them, but not by condemning the backwardness of tribal culture. This is where you must be careful not to repeat the mistake that the liberal elite often makes. I am reminded of my own experience many years ago. I used to live then in a village near Patna on the bank of the Ganga. One day, I saw a Brahman I used to know standing waist-deep in the river, cupping his palms full of water, raising it towards the sky and letting the water fall back. I asked him what he was doing. He was annoyed and said gruffly, "Can't you see I am offering *tarpan* to my ancestors in heaven." I quietly turned around and started throwing water on to the river bank. This time the Brahman asked me what I was doing. I said, "I am watering my kitchen garden." He looked puzzled and said, "But you live in the next village. That's at least a mile from here!" I said, "If the water you are throwing up in the sky can reach your ancestors in heaven, then why shouldn't the water I am throwing on the bank reach my kitchen garden?" The Brahman went away muttering a few insults about how low-caste people have no knowledge of religion.

Thinking about this incident later, I realised that I had not done the right thing. Even though my rational mind was repelled by what I thought was a senseless Brahmanical ritual, I had forgotten that people live not only in the real world of material things but also in a world of their imagination (*kalpanā*). Indeed, they give meaning to the real world by attaching imagined ideas to things. The Brahman obviously did not believe that the water of the Ganga would actually reach his forefathers in heaven. Rather, by making this symbolic offering, the ritual helped him remember his debt to his ancestors. This is important for Brahmans who are so conscious and proud of their ancestry (*vaṃś*). One can, therefore, definitely criticise the Brahmanical claim of superior status by birth and the thoroughly unjust social inequality that claim has perpetuated. But when one ridicules the ritual of *tarpaṇ*, one forgets that the social life of every community is filled with innumerable imaginary meanings. Even the solidarity of the nation is an imagined idea. But when millions of people believe in it, it becomes a reality.

I used to have long arguments about this with E.V. Ramasamy in Madras. He was convinced that the irrational claims of religion had to be blown away by ridicule and satire. I thought he was not sufficiently sensitive to the emotional needs of the people. While ruling groups and religious authorities did try to secure the backing of the wealthy and keep the labouring poor under control by appealing to religion, the rich too needed religion to cope with the unpredictability of economic and political conditions, just as the poor held on to their own religious beliefs to soften the harshness of their lives. If one wants to change the conditions which make religion a tool of oppression, one must also be mindful of how religion makes life more meaningful. Periyar did not agree with me. But I think his method of shock and scorn ultimately did not yield much result.

So you must remember to respect the sentiments of people even as you try to change their values and practices. It may seem difficult but it can be done. I have seen how the beliefs and lifestyles of the people of this country have changed since the time of independence, not just in cities but even in the villages. The spread of transport, schools and colleges, cinema, television, and now the mobile phone has carried new objects, images and ideas to the remotest parts of the country. People do not wish to live in the old way. They aspire to something more satisfactory and just. But the changes have come haphazardly, brought by many forces along many channels. There is no coherent sense of direction to the way people are deciding to change their ways of living.

In fact, many such changes in occupation and lifestyle, and the impact that such changes often have on local power relations between groups, create new hostilities. To give you just one example, the Pallar was once a Dalit caste of bonded farm labourers in Tamil Nadu who now call themselves Devendra Kula Vellala and claim identity with the Pallava kings who ruled the region a thousand years ago. This group is now locked in a ferocious, and often violent, conflict with the Thevar caste of dominant farmers who cannot accept the public assertion of cultural identity by a group that it continues to regard as socially inferior. There are many examples I could give from other states of such conflicts among non-elite groups that have experienced the shock of democratic change. One of the most tragic examples I know is from the Vidarbha region where Kunbi cotton cultivators, who have a long experience of dealing with

Marwari moneylenders and the uncertainties of the market, have responded to indebtedness with a string of suicides. I found out that the Marwaris had recently withdrawn from rural moneylending and their place had been taken by Mahars who had returned to the village after years in government service or small trade and were investing their savings in the business of moneylending. Kunbi farmers, who earlier were quite used to borrowing from Marwari outsiders, now found it unbearable to be indebted to Dalits from their own village. Suicide is the final response to their imagined humiliation.

It is in this fluid and confusing social situation that the forces of Hindutva have been able to advance their moral vision of the Hindu Rashtra. As I have explained to you, that vision is not restricted only to winning elections. The army of Hindutva has spread into the entire country. Its dedicated soldiers have spent years working with schools, health centres, and religious institutions in remote districts, Dalit mohallas, and Adivasi villages. By inviting marginal people to be good Hindus, they have offered a sense of inclusion and worth to those who had been excluded from the larger national society. But the latter have by no means been recognised as equal to the upper castes. Mere inclusion is not equality. In fact, this inclusion has been accompanied by an aggressive cultural effort to project a bellicose version of the Hindu religion which shuns the tenderness and piety of the Bhakti sects and instead projects Ramchandra as a muscular warrior-king with bow and arrow. This new militarist Hinduism with its war cry of "Jai Shri Ram", which solidified in northern India with the Ayodhya temple movement, is now making inroads into the rest of the country, pushing out regional Hindu rituals and festivals. Needless to say, it singles out for exclusion and often violent suppression the Muslim, and sometimes the Christian, minority.

I am asking you to speak against this attempt to impose on the whole country a single, thoroughly politicised, Hindu religion as *the* national culture. It is not that this aggressive cultural politics of Hindu-Hindi nationalism is not being resisted. But the resistance is often taking the form of a retreat into a conservative and insular provincial culture. Older generations are trying desperately to hold on to their familiar values and are annoyed because the young want something new. They do not see that the Hindutva campaign under Modi has managed to respond to some of the aspirations of the youth all over the country. What the BJP has done is channel those aspirations towards the cause of a militant and intolerant Hindu Rashtra. To resist that effort, you cannot fall back on an old way of provincial life that no longer satisfies the desire for greater equality, freedom, and opportunity.

That is why I am urging young people like you to bridge the cultural divide between the elite and the masses. This must be done in the field of education by making the English language universally available to all. But it must also be done by spreading in the regional languages the knowledge and ideas that are now restricted to the few who have facility in English. I am urging you and your friends to speak, write, perform, debate, and organise in the regional language with which you are most familiar. You must come out of your English-speaking bubble to converse with those who don't read English. It will be hard work. But I promise you that if you make the effort, you will learn far more about India than you will ever do from your websites.

So I am not asking you to call your friends to come out on the street and throw stones at the police. In fact, the fight against the politics of Hindu nationalism can and must be fought not only in the arena of politics but also outside it. Remember, the emotional power that people feel when they think of their attachment to the nation is generated in the imagination. And that imagination is ignited by stories and poetry and songs and drama. It is through language that those emotions are conveyed. That is why I am urging you and your friends to immerse yourself in the language of solidarity. It is through the solidarity of people that a political agenda can emerge for a more democratic and just federation.

Let me remind you once more of the era of the freedom movement in India. Not only political leaders, but poets, novelists, journalists, dramatists, actors, singers, and painters played a major role in mobilising the people in the cause of nationalism. In fact, if you ask me, I will say that they played an even more crucial role than political activists in spreading the message of the struggle. How else do you think people across India were so emotionally affected by Gandhi's fasts or Bhagat Singh's execution? I believe writers and artists working in the various regional languages prepared the ground on which politicians and lawyers constructed the Indian republic.

I am calling on your generation to begin a new cultural movement for a more just and equal people's federation. Leaders and parties will follow. This moment is crucial. The regime has shown its fangs. Opposition parties are confused because they cannot think beyond their immediate and narrow electoral calculations. The organised media is either too scared or has been bought over. Charvak has seen moments like this before. The enthusiasm in political circles in Punjab, Bengal, and Maharashtra created by the actions of armed revolutionaries and political leaders like Lajpat Rai, Tilak, and Aurobindo Ghose in the early-twentieth century was crushed by severe police repression. But writers and artists stuck to their task and kept the people's imagination alive so that when Gandhi arrived with a new political message, the people were ready to act in a way never seen before.

Charvak is counting on you.

# Index

Aam Aadmi Party 284, 293
Abbas, Ghulam 95
Abdullah, Sheikh Mohammad 69, 94; family of 299
Adani (business house) 291
Aden 55
Adigal, Maraimalai 201, 201n
Ādisūra 193, 193n
Adityanath, Yogi 291
Adivasi 24, 38, 72, 116, 117, 126, 165, 166, 167, 174, 206, 221, 246, 250, 286, 312, 317. *See also* Scheduled Tribe; tribe
Advani, Lal Krishna 251
Afghan army 51, 108
Afghanistan 13, 22, 49, 50–1; Amir of 50, 51
Africa 7, 21, 62
Afridi (tribe) 85
Afridi, Sher Ali 58
Ahir 151
Ahmadi 169
Ahmed, Sultan 84n
Ahmedabad 116, 122
Ahmednagar Fort 142
Ahom (rulers of Assam) 38, 39, 195, 206, 257
Aitchison's *Treaties* 29
Aiyangar, Aramavudh 83
Aiyar, C.P. Ramaswami 72
Aizawl 214

Ajivika 235
Ajmer 116, 183
Akali Dal. *See* Shiromani Akali Dal
Akbar 6, 143, 146
Akhand Bharat 127
Aksai Chin 30, 32, 33
Alamgir. *See* Aurangzeb
Alexander 11n
Ali, Fazl 184n
Ali, Laik 86, 87, 88
Ali, Mir Osman (Nizam of Hyderabad) 81–91, 95, 98, 221
Ali, Mohammad 151–2
Ali, Shaukat 152
Aligarh 149; Anglo-Oriental College at 149, 152
All Assam Students Union (AASU) 261–2
All India Anna Dravida Munnetra Kazhagam (AIADMK) 204, 287–8, 299, 302
All India Muslim League 41–50, 68, 75, 95, 96, 137, 153, 209n, 222
All India Muslim Personal Law Board 169, 176
All India Radio 204, 306
All India Shia Personal Law Board 169
Allahabad 150
Alwar 75

321

Amanullah (king of Afghanistan) 51
Ambedkar, Bhimrao Ramji 118, 136–7, 156–7, 156n, 158, 158n, 168, 197–8, 199, 248, 264, 312; on principles of Indian federation 218–23
America 57: North 6, 7; South 7
American (people) 22
Ambani (business house) 291
Amritsar 43, 51, 205n; Treaty of 93
*Ānandamaṭh* 187
*anārya* 16, 105, 106, 114
Andaman and Nicobar Islands 22, 23, 55–61, 66, 101, 102, 183, 309
Andamanese (people) 56–8
Andhra Pradesh 62, 78, 81, 84, 91, 183, 184, 204, 221–2, 248, 279, 288, 297, 302
Aney, Madhav Srihari 119n, 126
Anglo-Afghan War 50
Anglo-Burmese War 38, 56
Anglo-Gorkha War 36
Anglo-Sikh War: First 93; Second 31
Angola 63
Annadurai, C.N. 202, 203
Anushilan Samiti 119
Ao, Shilu 213
Arab (people) 11, 11n, 21
Arabia 112
Arabian Sea 54, 55
Arabic 150, 306
Archaeological Survey of India 12
Ardagh, John 32
Armed Forces Special Powers Act 226, 226n
*arthaśāstra* 2, 239

Arunachal Pradesh 27, 30, 33, 166, 208n. *See also* North East Frontier Agency
*ārya* 13, 17, 18, 20, 25. *See also* Aryan
Arya Samaj 113
Aryan 12, 13, 14, 22, 24, 104–6, 110, 114, 143, 200, 201, 202, 216
Aryavarta 193, 199, 308
Asafjahi 89
Asia 7, 21, 28, 62: Central 11, 13, 14, 15, 24, 50, 104, 144, 157; East 21; South 22, 116, 176; Southeast 21, 22, 61, 143
Asoka 6, 7–8, 106, 143, 146
Asom Gana Parishad (AGP) 262
Assam 28, 30, 38, 39, 48, 49, 76, 78, 116, 181, 205, 210, 222, 228, 247, 257–66, 301; hill districts of 205–11; population growth in 259n; western 257. *See also* Brahmaputra valley
Assam Rifles 209, 212
Assamese: (language) 19, 195, 206, 215, 258–9, 264–5; (people) 222, 258–60, 262–5
*asur* 16–17
Asur (tribe) 17
Atatürk, Kemal 157, 163
atheism 202, 204, 248
Athens 9–10, 25
Auchinleck, Claude 97, 98
Aurangabad 195n
Aurangzeb 41, 144, 245
Aurobindo, Sri. *See* Ghose, Aurobindo
Australia 21, 56
Australian 166
Austroasiatic languages 19, 22, 61

Autonomous Hill Council 76
Avesta 12, 14
Awadh 34, 149, 220
Axom Jatiyo Mohaxobha 259n
Axom Xongrokhwini Xobha 259n
Ayodhya 35, 105n, 106, 114, 177, 178, 244, 251, 286, 291, 317
Ayyanar 174. *See also* Ayyappan
Ayyappan 174–6
Azad, Abul Kalam 191
Azad, Prithvi Singh 59
Azad Gomantak Dal 63–4
Azad Kashmir 99

Babel, Tower of 208
Babri Masjid 173, 251, 291; legal dispute over 177–8, 292
Badal, Parkash Singh: family of 299
Bahadur Shah Zafar 102, 242
Bahawalpur 79
Bahujan Samaj Party 253
Bajrang Dal 166
Bakarganj 47
Bal, Loknath 59
Balochistan 12, 14, 22. *See also* Baluchistan
Baltistan 96, 99
Baluchistan States Union 79
Banaras. *See* Varanasi
*Bande Mataram* 187
Banerjee, Mamata 297
Banerjee, Upendra Nath 59
Banerji, Rakhaldas 12
Bangladesh 52, 53, 127, 128, 129, 141, 169, 176, 192, 193, 194, 261, 300–1. *See also* Bengal; Pakistan, East
Bania 171, 253, 289
Baramulla 96

Bardoloi, Gopinath 209, 209n, 210, 210n
Baroda 152
Basavanna 117
Bauti 222
Bay of Bengal 55
Beijing 32
Bengal 38, 39, 41, 45–9, 50, 54, 59, 60, 61, 111, 116, 138, 148, 149, 153, 182, 187–92, 194, 204, 224, 258–9, 264, 271, 319; East 48, 49, 122, 218; north 190; population 188n; south 246; south-west 47, 48. *See also* Bangladesh; Pakistan, East; West Bengal
Bengali (language) 19, 49, 181, 187, 189, 190, 192, 194, 200, 201, 257, 258, 259; (people) 189, 192–4, 204, 258–64
Bentinck, William 54
Berar 84
Bhagavad Gita 139, 195n
Bhagirathi (river) 46, 48
Bhakna, Sohan Singh 59
Bhakti movement 144, 247, 311, 317
Bharat Itihas Sanshodhak Mandal 195n
Bharat Mata 179, 189, 190, 193
Bharatavarsha 17, 308. *See also* India
Bharathi, Subramania 190, 200
Bharatiya 109, 110
Bharatiya Jana Sangh 118, 155, 156, 184
Bharatiya Janata Party (BJP) 125, 126, 170, 173, 174, 176–7, 187, 199, 227, 250, 251–6, 262,

263, 265, 266, 274, 282–3, 286,
   289–93, 299, 303, 318
Bharatiya Vidya Bhavan 86n
Bharatpur 75
*Bhaviṣyapurāṇa* 105
Bhil 18, 19, 311
Bhima (river) 198
Bhima Koregaon 198
Bhojpur 151, 220
Bhojpuri (language) 220
Bhopal 69, 75, 94
Bhumihar 151
Bhutan 28, 34, 36, 41
Bhutto, Shah Nawaz 80
Bhutto, Zulfikar Ali 80
Bibhishana 106n
Bidar 89
Bihar 48, 151, 220, 221, 227,
   252, 253, 274, 296, 301;
   government of 251
Biharsharif 172
Bijapur 144, 146, 196n
Bikaner 44
Birla (business house) 286
Bodo 222
Bodoland 222
Bohra 113
Bolivian 21
Bombay: city of (*see* Mumbai);
   province of 55, 80, 86n, 91,
   149, 153, 181; state of 162,
   182, 184, 219, 220
Bombay Parsi Panchayat 169
borders of India 20, 26–7, 65–6;
   with Bangladesh 51–3; with
   Bhutan 27; with Burma 38;
   with China 27–33, 65; with
   Nepal 27; with Pakistan 41–50
Bose, Subhas Chandra 60, 70, 191
Brahma Sutra 139

Brahman 1, 2, 13, 24, 92, 108,
   122, 148, 150, 154, 176,
   193, 194, 196–8, 200–2, 226,
   240, 246, 247, 289, 314–15;
   anti- 198; Chitpavan 154;
   Deshastha 148, 196; Konkanas-
   tha 148; *kulīn* 271; Marathi
   199; Namboodiri 122; non-
   201, 202–3, 234, 287 (*see also*
   Non-Brahman movement);
   Rarhi 148; *smārta* 163;
   Varendra 148
Brāhmaṇa (literature) 16
Brahmanical religion 19, 20, 39,
   92, 116, 143, 144, 167, 174,
   196, 199, 201–2, 236, 247, 248,
   253, 257–8, 311, 315
Brahmaputra (river) 29, 108;
   valley 257, 258
Brahmi 8
Brahmo (religion) 161n; Samaj
   140, 161, 161n, 162, 192
Brahui 14
Bṛhaspati 1–2
Britain. *See* United Kingdom
British 56, 97, 103, 152, 153
British Commonwealth 82
British Empire 7; in India 11n,
   40, 62, 102, 104, 109, 119,
   121, 124, 134, 144, 145, 146,
   152, 163–4, 167, 181, 190, 198,
   200, 209, 226, 228, 237, 241–2,
   257, 260, 277, 287, 305, 310;
   policies of 27, 32, 34, 36,
   37–8, 41, 50–1, 53–63, 67–70,
   136, 149, 164, 180, 182, 192,
   205–6, 208, 209–10, 212,
   258
Bucher, General 87
Buddha, Gautama 8, 106, 107

Buddhism 7–9, 11, 20, 50, 92, 106–7, 106n, 117, 141, 143, 199, 235, 247, 311; Navayāna 248
Buddhist 200; (people) 1, 8, 39, 48, 94, 110, 111, 112, 139, 161, 169, 171, 234, 248, 292; Neo– 248; vihara 8, 135, 234, 235
Burdwan 47
Burma 20, 40–1, 60, 210, 211, 213, 263. See also Myanmar
Burmese 56, 58; army 38; rulers 38, 206, 257

Cachar 259, 260; hills 38
Calcutta (see Kolkata): University of 23, 23n
Caroe, Olaf 29, 49–50
caste 13, 19, 25, 108, 110, 115, 116, 117–18, 120, 122, 125, 134, 136–7, 142, 148, 154, 156, 161, 167, 168, 171, 196, 197–8, 201, 206, 244–57: agricultural 151, 246–7, 248; artisan 246–7; landowning 248, 249, 267–8, 272, 316; lower 151, 193, 246, 251–4, 266–7, 272, 315; middle 246; untouchable (see Dalit); upper 116, 149, 151, 193, 199, 227, 246, 249, 250, 251–4, 256, 267–8, 271, 289, 296, 305, 309, 317. See also jāti; Other Backward Classes; Scheduled Caste; and names of individual castes
Catholic. See Christianity: Roman Catholic
Catholic Bishops Conference 169

Cauvery (river) 180
Ceded Districts 84
Cellular Jail 58–60, 103
Census: 1881 188n; 1931 250, 256; 1951 208n; 2011 256, 256n, 259n; 2021 256
Central Board of Secondary Education (CBSE) 304
Central Provinces 77, 84
centralisation of power 145, 146; in federal system 125, 243–4, 283–7, 292–300
Ceylon. See Sri Lanka
Chakma 39
Chakravarty, Trailokya 59
Chaliha, Bimala Prasad 210
Chamar 151
Chamber of Princes 68, 69, 70
Champa 19
Chandannagar 61, 62
Chandernagore. See Chandannagar
Charvak 1–3, 319. See also Charvaka
Charvaka (school of philosophy) 1–2. See also Charvak
Chatham Island 56
Chattopadhyay, Bankimchandra 187–90, 187n, 192
Chau, John Allen 22
Chaudhuri, Jayanto Nath 90
Chauri Chaura 152
Chetti 247
Chhatari, Nawab of 83, 84
Chhattisgarh 166, 220, 221, 291, 301; Union 76
Chhattisgarhi (language) 220
chhit mahal. See enclave
Chicago 139, 166

China 5, 11, 20, 22, 27–33, 34, 35, 37, 38, 49, 50; People's Republic of 30, 212, 214, 236; Republican 28. *See also* Qing Empire; Tibet
Chinese (language) 215
Chiplunkar, Vishnushastri Krishnashastri 194, 194n
Chitral 79, 96
Chittagong Hill Tracts 39, 46–7, 48
Chogyal 36–7
Chokhamela, Sant 117, 117n
Christian: (people) 25, 76, 110, 112–17, 121, 126, 139, 148, 161n, 171, 200, 208, 209, 214, 327; missionaries 61, 165, 166, 208, 212, 215–16, 258
Christianity 22, 61, 110, 126, 142, 148, 163, 216; American Baptist 258; Anglican 212; Orthodox 157, 169; Protestant 169, 216; Roman Catholic 116, 169, 170
Chushul, treaty of 31
cinema 115
citizenship in India 124, 228–9
Citizenship Act 1955 228; Amendment 2003 228, 229; Amendment 2019 128, 229, 263, 293, 313: protests against 130–1, 243, 263, 293, 313
Civil Disobedience movement 119
class: big farmer 279, 280–1, 287, 288, 294; business 255, 274, 275, 277, 283–5, 287–8, 289, 290, 291, 294, 302; inequality of 290, 295–7, 301–2; landlord 274, 275, 277, 278; medium and small farmer 287, 290, 294, 296, 302; middle 149, 208, 211, 214, 215, 216, 254, 255, 266–7, 269–73, 276–7, 281, 284–6, 288, 296, 304; poor 290, 302, 305, 315–16; upper 149, 150, 151, 182, 315–16; upper middle 146, 163, 289, 290, 295–7, 302, 304; worker 288, 293–4, 296, 301, 302
Cochin 69, 70, 164
Colebrook–Cameron reforms 54
Colombo 54
communal riots 118, 119, 151, 153–4, 293
communism 122, 126
Communist Party of India (CPI) 265; in Kerala 73; in Telangana 81–2, 88, 89, 91
Communist Party of India (Marxist) (CPI(M)) 265
Congress. *See* Indian National Congress
Congress Socialist Party 63, 70
Constituent Assembly of India 68, 156, 165, 167–8, 209n, 210, 210n, 312
Constitution of India 73n, 97, 125, 161, 180, 181, 186, 203, 204, 215, 240, 242, 248; religious freedom in 157–9, 161–3, 165–7, 211; secularism in 156–7; Articles 5–11 228; Article 25 158n; Article 26 158n; Article 28 159n; Article 30 159n; Article 51A (Fundamental Duties) 236–7, 243; Article 356 303, 307; Article 370 77–8, 99, 100,

155, 292, 310; Article 371
77–9, 213, 310; Directive
Principles 168, 237; Part A
states 78, 97, 182, 184; Part B
states 78, 97, 182, 184; Part C
states 183, 184; Preamble 131,
156; Sixth Schedule 76, 210–
11; Union Territory 183
Cooch Behar 35, 39, 51–2
Coorg 183
corporate business 255, 280–1,
283–4, 290, 291, 294, 295–6.
*See also* class: business
Covid pandemic 131, 179–80,
254, 293, 298
cow protection 151, 196. *See also*
Gaurakshini Sabha
crown colony 41, 55
Cunha, Tristao de Braganza 62–3
Cutchi Memon 167

Dacca. *See* Dhaka
Dadra 63, 64
Dalai Lama 28, 30
Dalit 116, 117, 126, 148, 165,
167, 174, 197–8, 199, 219, 222,
247, 248, 249, 253, 256, 266–8,
272, 286, 312, 316, 317. *See
also* Harijan; Scheduled
Caste
Daman 61, 63, 65
daṇḍanīti 238–43, 267
Dani, Ahmad Hasan 11n
*Danial Latifi v. Union of
India* 173n
Danish East India Company 61
Dar, S.K. 183n
Darjeeling 34, 36, 47, 48, 222
Das, Chitta Ranjan 138
Das, Pulin 59

DNA 20–1; mitochondrial 20,
23; whole genome sequence
20–1, 23, 24; Y chromosome
20, 23
Dawoodi Bohra 162
Dehradun 87
Delhi 102, 116, 149, 154, 155,
180, 225, 237, 250, 266–7, 284,
293, 314; Government of 180;
Sultanate 6, 11n, 145, 196n. *See
also* New Delhi
democracy 121, 126, 127, 146,
147, 185, 219, 222–3, 225–6,
252–4, 277–9, 281–3, 286–7,
290–2, 307–9, 311–13
Denisovan 21
Depressed Classes. *See* Scheduled
Caste
Desai, Morarji 280
Deshpande, Dattatreya 63
Dev, Narendra 191
devadasi 162
Devagiri 195n
Devaswom 75–6, 164–5
development: agricultural 277,
279; human 301, 301n;
industrial 276, 278, 283–4,
287, 295–6, 300, 301
Devendra Kula Vellala 316
Dhaka 47
dharma 107, 196, 241–2
*dharmaśāstra* 2, 110, 133, 160,
163, 240
Dinajpur 47, 48
Disaster Management Act 253
*Discovery of India, The* 142–4
Diu 61, 65
*Dnyāneśwarī* 195, 195n
Dogra 31, 51, 93, 96
Dost Muhammad 50

Dravida Munnetra Kazhagam (DMK) 203–4, 220, 249, 287–8
Dravida Mahajana Sabha 247n
Dravida Nadu 203, 204
Dravidar Kazhagam 201n
Dravidian: (people) 12, 13, 14, 200–4, 217; (languages) 14, 16, 17, 19, 24, 123; movement 201–4
Duars 35
Durand line 51
Durga 190
Duryodhan 26
Dutch Empire 53–4
Dutt, Batukeshwar 59
Dyer, Reginald 51

East Godavari 62
East India Company 34, 36, 38, 50, 53, 54, 84, 93, 163, 198
East Pakistan Renaissance Society 48
Eastern States Union 76
education 149, 233–44, 246, 252, 279–80, 303–7. *See also* National Education Policy 2020
Egypt 5, 9–10, 64
Emergency, state of 37, 156, 236, 237, 243, 249, 303
empire 6, 18, 127
enclave 51–3
England 123
English: (language) 5, 102, 103, 109n, 118, 119, 141, 142n, 149, 153, 157, 163, 181, 182, 185, 187, 189, 190, 194, 203, 208, 215, 216, 217, 227, 231, 247, 249, 258, 276, 286, 294, 304,

305; education in 149, 279, 305–6, 318; (people) 113
Eritrea 21
Europe 7, 13, 15, 18, 24, 61, 113, 114, 115, 120, 121, 141, 157, 212, 225, 312–13: Eastern 7; Central 7; Western 6, 24, 25
European 56, 57, 123, 144; (people) 24; nationalists 25, 115
European Union 313
Ezhava 246

Farakka 46
Faridpur 47
fatherland 109, 110, 112, 114, 194. *See also pitribhu*
federation: balance of power in 299–303, 312; Indian 125, 180, 182–5, 217, 218, 222, 223–6, 229–30, 244, 250, 254–7, 292; of peoples 186, 229, 259, 309, 319. *See also* linguistic states
Ferozepur 42, 44
First Indians (people) 21–2, 23, 24
France 7, 61–3, 67, 102, 103, 123, 157
French (people) 113

Gaekwad, Fatehsingh Rao (Maharaja of Baroda) 76
Gaekwad, Pratap Singh (Maharaja of Baroda) 76
Gaidinliu, Rani 208–9, 209n
Gandhara 11n. *See also* Qandahar
Gāndhārī 50
Gandhi, Indira 37, 156, 172, 205n, 236, 237–8, 243, 244, 248, 279, 281, 282

Gandhi, Mohandas Karamchand 41, 49, 70, 73, 75, 103, 107, 109, 118, 127, 132–8, 147, 151–2, 154–5, 181, 211, 276, 319
Gandhi, Rahul 282, 282n
Gandhi, Rajiv 172, 262, 281n, 282
Gandhi, Samaldas 80
Gandhi, Sonia 282
Gandhian 49, 106n, 108, 114, 138, 284, 286
Ganga: (river) 314, 315; plains of 146
Gangtok 37
Garhwal 34
Garo: hills 38, 39; (people) 38, 208
Gauhati University 259
Gaunda 247
Gaurakshini Sabha 151
Gautama 120
German (people) 113
Germany 23, 115, 120
genetic science 20–5
Ghadar movement 59
Ghaggar (river) 15
Ghaznavi, Mahmud 41, 81
Ghaznavid 11n
Ghazni, Mahmud of. *See* Ghaznavi, Mahmud
Ghose, Aurobindo 187, 189, 190, 319
Ghosh, Atulya 47
Ghosh, Barin 59
Ghosh, Ganesh 59
Gilgit 96, 98, 99
Giza 9
Goa 61–5, 66, 78, 84, 116, 169–70, 196n, 204, 215, 222, 224, 288, 300

Godse, Nathuram 154–5, 154n
Golconda 144
Golwalkar, Madhavrao Sadashivrao 119–26, 142, 155, 185, 186, 238, 242, 311n
Gond 14
Goods and Services Tax (GST) 254, 254n, 290
Gorakhpur 152
Gorkha 34, 36, 51
Gorkhaland 222
Government of India 29, 32, 35, 36, 40, 41, 63–4, 69–100, 154, 161, 213, 214, 225, 228, 231, 250, 256, 261–4, 289–94
Gracey, Douglas 98
Greece 5, 9–10, 14, 25
Greek: (people) 25, 104; (rulers) 240
Guha Thakurta, Manoranjan 59
Gujarat 12, 63, 69, 73, 78, 86, 134, 161, 165, 166, 167, 184, 220, 227, 248, 251, 285–6, 287
Gujarat University 122
Gujarati: (language) 86n, 115, 181, 219; (people) 73
Gujjar 290
Gulbarga 89
Gupta, Atul 45, 46
Gupta Empire 6, 107, 108, 143, 145
Gurdaspur 43, 44, 95
Gurgaon 288
Gurkha. *See* Gorkha
Guru Granth Sahib 117
Gwalior (state) 74

Hafiz 111
Haj pilgrimage 165
Hanafi law 176

Hanuman 106n
Harappa 12; civilisation 10–16, 22, 105, 143; people of 24
Hardinge, Lord Charles 93
Harijan 136–7, 250. *See also* Dalit; Scheduled Caste
Harsha 125
Haryana 12, 13, 18, 75, 185, 270, 283, 288, 294
Hathras case 266–8, 272
Havelock Island 61
Hazare, Anna 284–5, 284n
Hedgewar, Keshav Baliram 119
Heraka religion 208
High Court 163; of Bombay 162, 162n; of Calcutta 161n
Hill Tipperah 39. *See also* Tripura
Himachal Pradesh 183, 288
Himalayan Frontier Tracts. *See* North East Frontier Agency
Himalayas 6, 17, 21, 27, 29, 32, 34, 105, 105n, 120
Hindi: (language) 5, 8, 18, 19, 123, 126, 150, 185, 199, 200, 201–3, 220, 227, 253, 305, 306–7, 318; anti- 202–3, 204, 220, 231; (people) 110, 110n
Hindu: (civilisation) 110–11, 115–16, 140–2, 216, 318; (people) 16, 42–50, 58, 73, 75, 79, 81–91, 94, 102, 104–31, 133–8, 139, 148–53, 156, 158, 160–3, 166–72; 173–8, 184, 191, 192, 193, 197, 199, 225, 226, 227, 249, 251, 252–3, 256, 260, 263–5, 271, 289, 310, 317; majority 126, 142, 151, 159, 171, 176, 177; non- 219, 247; temples 135, 160–3, 164–5, 174–6, 177–8; undivided family 171
Hindu Mahasabha 45, 46, 48, 112, 118, 126, 147, 153, 154, 155, 156
Hindu Rashtra 106–31, 142, 166, 186, 193, 199, 227, 238, 243, 310–11, 317
Hinduism 111–13, 117, 118, 139, 140, 141, 144, 146, 154, 158, 161–3, 168, 196, 199, 201–2, 204, 248, 291, 311, 317
Hindustan 104, 308
Hindustani: (language) 150, 306; dharma 197
Hindusthan 102, 104, 108, 109, 112, 113, 114, 122
Hindutva 112–17, 119, 142, 176, 227, 244, 253, 257, 286, 291, 292, 311, 312, 317–18
*Hindutva* 31n, 104–18; *Essentials of* 103
Hitler, Adolf 115
Hirakud dam 72
Holkar, Yeshwant Rao (Maharaja of Indore) 74
Holland 157
*Homo erectus* 21
Hooghly. *See* Hugli
Huang Ta-chen 31
Hugli 47, 62
Huna 11n, 106
Hunza 79, 96
Hyderabad: (city) 222, 288; (state) 68, 69, 81–91, 94, 95, 96, 98, 100, 127, 149, 182, 184; army 88, 89

India: borders of (*see* borders of India); British 39, 49, 50, 52,

58, 60, 73n, 93, 163, 224, 228, 310; central 14, 19, 20, 116, 206, 301; as civilisation 143–5, 199, 309, 311; constitution of (*see* Constitution of India); eastern 22, 301; French territories in 61–2, 180, 310; Government of (*see* Government of India); island territories of 53–61; north 14, 17, 22, 50, 74, 89, 97, 111, 114, 122, 126, 143, 146, 147, 148, 149–53, 172, 199, 202, 203, 220, 225, 226–7, 233, 251, 252, 253, 279, 283, 309, 317; north–east 27, 38–40, 75, 122, 126, 148, 166, 195, 205–18, 225, 226, 249, 257, 265; north-west 240; Portuguese territories in 61–5, 180, 310; princely states of (*see* princely states); republic of 131, 132, 309; south 62, 81, 143, 200, 203, 220, 289, 295; Union of 37, 40, 164, 210, 215, 224; western 74, 126, 206, 226, 227, 251, 252, 253, 283, 289, 295
Indian (people) 6, 10–11, 14, 18, 20, 199, 225, 228
Indian Air Force 89, 97
Indian Army 64, 86, 89–91, 97, 98, 100, 213, 214
Indian Christian Marriage Act 169
Indian Civil Service 40, 71
Indian Mutiny (*see* Revolt of 1857)
Indian National Army 60
Indian National Congress 6, 42–50, 55, 68, 69, 70, 71, 75, 78, 86, 86n, 90, 95, 97, 102, 112, 114, 124, 127, 132, 137, 146, 147, 152–3, 154–6, 170, 172–3, 174, 181–2, 183, 187, 190–3, 191n, 200, 209, 227, 237, 241, 248–50, 251, 252, 256, 257, 265, 274–82, 284, 286, 297, 299, 302, 303; All India Committee (AICC) 69; Andhra Provincial Committee 181; in Assam 209, 210, 259; Bengal Provincial Committee 181; Faizpur session of 209n; Goa Committee 62; Gujarat Provincial Committee 181; in Hyderabad 81, 88, 91; Kathiawar Committee 80; Kerala Provincial Committee 181; Madras ministry of 202, 203; Swarajist wing of 138; Sylhet District Committee 181
Indian Navy 61, 64, 97
Indian Ocean 55
Indian Penal Code 167
Indo-European languages 13, 14, 15, 19, 22, 24, 123
Indo-Greek rulers 50
Indo-Nepal treaty 34
Indonesia 20, 55, 127
Indore (state) 74
Indra 16
Indus (river) 15, 104, 105, 108, 114. *See also* Sindhu
Indus-Saraswati civilisation 15, 18
Indus Valley civilisation. *See* Harappa civilisation
Industrial Relations Code 294
informal sector 290, 293–4, 296, 301–2
Inner Line 39
International Mother Language Day 193

Iran 15, 50, 127, 144
Iranian (people) 22
Islam 110, 122, 126, 128, 142, 143, 157, 163, 165, 172. *See also* Muslim
Ismail, Mirza 83
Italian (people) 25, 113
Iyothee Thass 247–8, 247n

Jadonang 208, 209
Jaipur 83
Jain (people) 1, 110, 111, 161, 169, 171
Jainism 20, 92, 117, 142, 161, 235
Jaintia 39; hills 38
Jalandhari, Hafeez 93–4
Jallianwala Bagh 51
Jalpaiguri 47, 48
Jammu 94, 95, 99. *See also* Jammu and Kashmir
Jammu and Kashmir 31, 44, 65, 69, 77, 78, 79, 83, 85, 88, 92–100, 153, 176, 182, 204, 222, 224, 225, 226, 291, 292, 299, 309; army 98; constituent assembly of 78, 97; constitution of 99. *See also* Azad Kashmir; Jammu; Kashmir
Jana Sangh. *See* Bharatiya Jana Sangh
*janatā* 18
Janata Dal (Secular) 303
Janata Party 249, 252, 279, 280
*Jānatā rājā* 198, 198n
Japan 29, 60, 211, 236
Japanese (people) 21, 60
Jarawa 56, 57
Jat 248, 249, 280, 291
Jatav 253

*jāti*: (caste) 12, 17, 19, 23, 25, 107n, 110, 120–1, 148, 167, 207, 245–6, 249, 271; (nation) 19, 259. *See also* caste; nation
Jayalalithaa, Jayaram 165, 204, 297, 299
Jayanta, Bhatta 92, 92n
Jessore 46, 47
Jew (people) 55, 113, 113n, 120, 139
Jharkhand 17, 166, 221, 301, 314
Jinnah, Muhammad Ali 69, 73, 75, 82, 83, 85, 86, 88, 89, 96, 98, 114, 138
Johnson, William 31
Johnson-Ardagh line 32
Joshi, Sharad 281, 281n
Julaha 148, 151
Junagadh 79–81, 85, 85n, 91, 100, 155, 224
Justice Party 200, 202, 247

Kaaba 116
Kabul 50
Kachari 39, 206
Kafur, Malik 196n
Kaibarta 246
Kailash, Mount 127
Kalapani 35
Kalat 79
Kaliachak 46
*Kāmasūtra* 235
Kamba Ramayana 111
Kamma 249, 288
Kamrup 257
Kanauj 193
Kandy 54
Kannada (language) 19, 91
Kanpur 153

Kanungo, Hem Chandra 59
Kanyakumari 26, 66
Karachi 80, 89
Karaikal 61, 62
Karaikudi 200
Karakoram mountains 31, 32
Karimganj 49, 260
Karnataka 81, 89, 161, 180, 184, 204, 287, 291, 303
Karunanidhi, Muthuvel 203; family of 299
Kashgar 31
Kashmir 26, 32, 44, 66, 67, 91, 92, 94, 98, 110, 111, 127–8, 146, 148. *See also* Azad Kashmir; Jammu and Kashmir
Kashmiri 116, 215, 225, 308
Kathiawar 72, 73, 79
Kathmandu 34
Kaurava 50, 200
Kautilya 239–41, 244
Kayastha 150, 193; Chandraseniya Prabhu 199
Kazakhstan 22
Kerala 53, 62, 72, 116, 122, 146, 148, 174–5, 184, 204, 208n, 246, 288, 300, 309; Government of 164–5, 174
Khalistan movement 205n
Khalji, Alauddin 195, 195n
KHAM coalition 250
Khan, Bacha. *See* Khan, Khan Abdul Ghaffar
Khan, Hamidullah (Nawab of Bhopal) 69, 75
Khan, Khan Abdul Ghaffar 49–50, 99
Khan, Liaquat Ali 75, 80
Khan, Mahabat (Nawab of Junagadh) 79–80
Khan Sahib 49
Khan, Syed Ahmad 148
Kharan 79
Khasi 20, 38, 207, 208, 210n; hills 39; Siems 76, 207; states 76
Khasi-Garo-Jaintia Hills 208, 258
Khilafat movement 41, 103, 152
Khmer 61
Khoja 113
Khudai Khidmatgar 49, 50
Khulna 46, 47, 48
Khyber-Pakhtunkhwa 13, 50. *See also* North West Frontier Province
Khyber Pass 51
Koch 35, 39
Kohima 211
Kol 18, 19
Koli 250
Kolkata 34, 46, 47, 48, 119, 151, 187, 190, 258, 300
Konar, Harekrishna 59
Konkan 196n, 220
Koregaon 198
Kripalani, Jivatram Bhagwandas 155
Krishna 111
*Kṣa-kiraṇe* 118
Kshatriya 13, 39, 246, 250, 272
Kuki 208, 214
Kumaon 33, 34
Kumbh Mela 111, 117, 165
Kun Lun mountains 32
Kunbi 316 17
Kunzru, Hriday Nath 184n
Kurmi 253
Kurukh 14
Kurukshetra 26, 200
Kushana 11n
Kushtia 48

Kushwaha 252
Kutch 183

Laccadive, Amindivi and Minicoy Islands. *See* Lakshadweep
Ladakh 31, 33, 34, 49, 94, 100, 222, 292
Ladakhi (language) 222
Lahore 43, 44, 85, 93, 98, 222
Lakshadweep 53, 66, 208n
Lakshmi 190
Lal Beg 253
Lal, Jagat Narain 183
Laldenga 215
Lall, Panna 183
language(s): and federalism 181–5, 219–20, 257, 264, 303–7; of India 111, 115–16, 123, 185–7, 232, 279, 304–5, 309, 314, 318
Lankesh, Gauri 291
Las Bela 79
Latin 18
Latur 82, 91
Lawande, Vishwanath 63
Left Democratic Front 174
Left parties 252
liberalism 126, 136, 147, 157, 163, 166, 242, 314
Lightfoot, Captain 29
Lingayat: (caste) 161; (religion) 161
Linguistic Provinces Commission 183n
linguistic states 125, 181–5, 219–21, 225. *See also* language(s): and federalism
Linlithgow, Victor Hope, Lord 71
literacy rates 208, 208n
Lohia, Ram Manohar 63
*lok* 6, 18, 19. *See also* people

London 42, 55, 83, 88, 102, 161n, 212
Lucknow 137
Lushai Hills 207, 208, 212, 214, 216, 258. *See also* Mizoram
Lushei: (language) 216; (people) 208, 214, 216. *See also* Kuki; Mizo

Macartney, George 31
Macartney-McDonald line 32
Macaulay, Thomas Babington 54
MacDonald, Ramsay 136
Macmahon, Henry 28
Macmahon line 27, 28–30
Madhesia 35
Madhya Bharat, Union of 74, 75, 76, 183
Madhya Pradesh 166, 182, 220, 221, 227, 290, 291, 301, 303
Madras: (province) 53, 149, 162, 181, 202, 247, 248; (state) 182, 203, 219, 220, 315
Madrasi 108
Madurai 200
Mahabharata 26, 50, 52, 111
Mahar 117, 117n, 198, 248, 317
Maharashtra 6, 59, 78, 81, 111, 148, 154, 184, 190, 194–9, 204, 218, 220, 224, 248, 253, 287, 290, 309, 319; Dharma 194–7, 226–7
Maharashtrian 204
Mahé 61, 62
Mahishya 246
Majlis-e-Ittehad-e-Muslimeen 82, 83, 86
Makran 79
Malabar 53, 153, 167, 181
Malaya 60. *See also* Malaysia

INDEX 335

Malayalam 19, 181
Malayali 53, 116
Malaysia 127
Malda 46, 47, 48
Maldives 53–4
Mallya, Vijay 291
Manasarovar 127
Manchu Empire 31
Mandal, Bindheshwari Prasad 250; report of commission 250–2, 279, 297
Manipur 78, 146, 180, 208n, 209, 217, 218, 226, 226n
Manipuri 38, 206, 308
Manonmaniyam Sundaranar 200, 200n
Manto, Saadat Hasan 45
Manu 239
Manusmriti 202
Maoist: ideology 214; insurgency in Nepal 35
Mapillah 167
Maratha 74, 108, 144, 154, 196, 248, 252; Empire 6, 102, 108, 145, 193, 194–5, 196, 198, 226
Marathi: (language) 91, 102, 107, 108, 117, 118, 184, 194–6, 197, 198, 200, 201, 219; (people) 198, 308
Marathwada 88, 220
Marseilles 103
Marshall, John 12
Marwari 151, 317
Marxist 289
Maurya Empire 6, 11n, 114, 143, 145, 146, 237
Mayawati 253, 297
Mayo, Richard Bourke, Lord 58
McDonald, Charles 32
Meenakshipuram 165

Medina 116
Meghalaya 208, 208n, 218, 306, 309
Mehrgarh 22
Meitei 20, 39
Menezes, Julião 63
Menon, V.P. 71, 71n, 72–5, 83, 95–6, 97
Midnapore 47
migration: from Bangladesh 129; to Britain 129; to the United States 129
Mīmāṃsā 234, 235n
minorities 251, 310; rights of 122, 124, 136–7, 158–9, 161–2, 219, 248, 257
Mirpur 96
Mishra, Pratap Narayan 150n
Mithila 220
Mizo: (language) 216; (people) 20, 215–18
Mizo National Front (MNF) 214–15
Mizo Union 214
Mizoram 78, 208, 208n, 214–18, 224. *See also* Lushai Hills
*mleccha* 108
Modi, Narendra 60, 176, 253, 285–6, 289–94, 296–8, 318
Modi, Nirav 291
Mohammed 113
Mohenjo-daro 10, 12, 105
Moitra, Mohit 59
Mookerjee, Syama Prasad 155
Monckton, Walter 83, 84, 87, 88
Mongolian 16
Moradabad 172
motherland 190, 194, 200
Mountbatten, Lord Louis 42, 43, 50, 69, 71, 72, 73, 79, 82–9, 97

Mozambique 63
Mufti Mohammad Sayeed: family of 299
Mughal Empire 6, 11n, 31, 52, 143, 145, 146, 149, 181, 197, 237, 257
Muivah, T. 214
Multan 11n
Mumbai 55, 63
Munda 18, 19
Mundari (language) 14, 17, 61, 115
Munshi, Kanhaiyalal Maneklal 86, 86n, 87, 88, 89–90, 155
Murshidabad 46, 47, 48
Muslim: elite 81, 149–50, 249; (people) 41, 42–50, 53, 54, 58, 75, 78, 81–91, 94, 102, 103, 108, 109, 110, 112–17, 119, 121, 124, 126–30, 133–8, 148–53, 161, 167–73, 174, 177–8, 191, 192, 200, 219, 225, 228, 250, 251, 253, 256, 260, 261–5, 271, 286, 291, 292, 307, 317; rulers 122, 135, 143, 227, 252
Muslim Conference 94, 95, 96
Muslim League. *See* All India Muslim League
Muzaffarabad 96
Muzaffarpur 172
Myanmar 41, 55. *See also* Burma
Mymensingh 38, 260
Mysore 70, 74, 77, 78, 79, 83, 91, 213, 247

Nadia 47, 48
Naga 20, 38, 180, 207–8, 209, 211–13, 311: Angami 38, 207; Chang 213; Kabui 208; Sema 213
Naga Hills 38, 40, 211–14, 258
Naga National Council (NNC) 211–13
Naga National Organisation (NNO) 213
Nagaland 41, 66, 78, 208n, 209, 211–18, 224, 225; independence declaration of 211; People's Sovereign Republic of Free 213
Nagalim 180, 214
Nagamese 215
Nagar Haveli 63, 64
Nagari 150
Nagpur 119, 151, 199
Naik, Narayan 63
Nalanda 232, 234
Namgyal: (rulers of Bhutan) 35; (rulers of Ladakh) 31
Nanak, Guru 144
Nanded 88
Napoleonic wars 55
Narayan, Jaya Prakash 279
Narayana Guru 246
Nasik 103
Nasser, Gamal Abdel 64
*nāstik* 1
nation 18, 19, 123, 185; democratic logic of 184, 185, 244, 303, 318–19; Indian 6, 17, 41, 142–3, 179, 185–7, 193–4, 203, 204, 218, 222, 224, 226–30, 259; modernity of 5–7; –state 5–7, 113, 176, 185, 210, 244, 276, 277, 309. *See also jāti; rāṣṭra*

National Conference 69, 78, 94–5, 100, 299

National Council of Churches in India 169
National Council of Educational Research and Training (NCERT) 243, 243n, 304
National Education Policy 2020 231–8, 243, 293, 304
National Register of Citizens 228, 262–3, 293
National Socialist Council of Nagaland (NSCN) 214, 216
nationalism 4, 41, 140–1, 178: Hindu 112, 114, 118, 126–31, 147, 170, 171, 172, 173, 185, 187, 193, 199, 226, 233, 234, 251, 253, 265, 310–11, 318; Indian 58, 60, 153, 187, 192, 197, 199, 203, 204, 205, 208–9, 215, 216, 226–9, 233, 276–7, 309–10; Assamese 259; Marathi 199; Mizo 216; Naga 216; Tamil 203, 204
Nationalist Congress Party (NCP) 274
Nazi 115
Neanderthal 21
Nehru, Jawaharlal 29, 30, 32, 33, 42, 43, 64–5, 67, 69, 75, 78, 80, 86, 87, 89, 97, 99, 100, 132, 142–7, 155–6, 167–8, 183, 183n, 184, 186, 191, 191n, 209, 210, 212, 244, 281
Nehru, Motilal 55
Neil Island 60
Nellie 261
Nepal v14, 34–5, 36, 37, 41, 116
Nepali (language) 222, 263
New Delhi 41, 55, 83, 84, 87, 99, 211, 261, 281, 282. *See also* Delhi

Nichols-Roy, J.J.M. 210n
Nicobar Islands 61. *See also* Andaman and Nicobar Islands
Nicobarese (people) 61
Nigerian 21
Nilambara 92
Nirbhaya case 266–7
Nivedita, Sister 114
Nizam of Hyderabad. *See* Ali, Mir Osman
Nizamuddin 116
Non-Brahman movement 200–2, 204, 247
Non-Cooperation movement 119, 134, 136, 152
Noorani, A.G. 90n
North-Western Provinces 150. *See also* Uttar Pradesh
North Cachar Hills 209
North East Frontier Agency (NEFA) 28, 29, 33. *See also* Arunachal Pradesh
North Sentinel Island 22
North West Frontier Province (NWFP) 13, 49–50, 85, 96, 99, 167. *See also* Khyber–Pakhtunkhwa
Northern Circars 84
Norwegian (people) 25
Nyāya 92n, 121, 234, 235n
*Nyāyasūtra* 120

Oceania 20
Ochterlony, David 34; Monument of 34
Odisha 166, 204, 247, 301. *See also* Orissa
Odiya 19
Oli, K.P. Sharma 35
Onge 23, 57–8

Oraon 14, 19
Orientalist 14
Orissa 69, 72, 76, 77. *See also* Odisha
*Oru Paisa Tamizhan* 248
*Orunodoi* 258
Osmanabad 88
Osmania University 81
Other Backward Classes (OBC) 250, 252–4, 255, 256, 279
Oxford University 140, 149, 152

Pakistan 10, 21, 22, 32, 41–50, 51, 67–100, 127, 128, 153–4, 156, 169, 176, 182, 193, 212, 225, 292, 300–1, 310; East 48, 52–53, 67–73, 193, 199, 212, 259, 260, 301. *See also* Bengal: East
Pakrashi, Satish 59
Pali 8
Pallar 316
Pallava 316
Panchama 108
Pandava 200
Pandharpur 117, 196
Panipat 108
Panikkar, K.M. 184n
Pāṇini 195
Panja, Jadabendra 47
paramountcy 28, 67, 68, 69, 76
Paraiyar 247, 248
Paris 62, 103
parliament: British 41; Indian 159, 160, 168, 172, 176. *See also* Rajya Sabha
Parmanand, Bhai 59
Parsi 55, 113, 113n, 119, 139, 161n, 169. *See also* Bombay Parsi Panchayat
Parthenon 9
partition of India 41–50, 118, 127, 153, 154, 180, 252
Patel, Vallabhbhai 67, 70–6, 71n, 78, 80–81, 82, 83, 85–90, 128, 153, 155–6, 183, 186
Pathankot 95
Patiala (state) 75
Patiala and East Punjab States Union (PEPSU) 75, 76, 183
Patidar 248, 249, 291
Patnav 314
people, the 6, 18, 19, 222, 224, 225–6, 229–30, 237, 242, 244, 275, 277, 303, 309, 312; alliances among 265, 318–19; sovereignty of 6–7, 299–300. *See also lok*
People's Democratic Party (PDP) 299
Periyar. *See* Ramasamy, E.V.
Persian: (language) 30, 94, 111, 149, 150, 195, 306; (people) 104
Persian Gulf 229
personal law: Christian 111, 167; Hindu 111, 156, 159, 160–2, 163–4, 167–8; Muslim 111, 160, 163–4, 167–8. *See also* uniform civil code
Peshwa 108, 144, 198
Phizo, Angami Zapu 211–14, 211n
Phule, Jyotirao 197, 197n
Phule, Savitribai 197, 197n
Pillai, Manonmaniyam Sundaram. *See* Manonmaniyam Sundaranar
*pitribhu* 109, 109n, 112, 117, 194

# INDEX 339

plebiscite 310; in Bhopal 75; in Goa 65; in Gwalior and Indore 74; in Hyderabad 85, 86, 87, 98; in Jammu and Kashmir 37, 65, 85, 97, 98, 99; in Junagadh 80, 81, 224; in NWFP 49–50, 85, 224; in Sikkim 37; in Sylhet 49, 224
pluralism: philosophy of 139–42; in societyv132–8; in the state 132, 142–7, 193, 227, 232, 237, 265, 310, 311–12
Pondicherry. *See* Puducherry
Poona. *See* Pune
Poonch 96
Port Blair 56, 58, 60, 103
Portugal 61–5, 67, 84, 170
Portuguese Empire 54, 62, 169–70, 195, 196n
Prabhas Patan 81
Praja Mandal 69, 72; in Bhopal 75; in Junagadh 80
Prakrit 8–9, 17, 105
Prasad, Rajendra 70, 153
Prayag 165
princely states 28, 37, 40, 67–100, 164–5, 180, 224, 310; in Gujarat 69, 73, 165; in Orissa 69, 76; in Pakistan 79; in Rajasthan 165; in the Khasi hills 207; Unions of 72–77. *See also individual princely states*
Prithviraj 111
Privy Council 161
Puducherry 61, 62
Pulwama 292
Punakha, treaty of 36
Pune 103, 136, 154, 195n, 198n, 274

Punjab 11, 12, 13, 15, 31, 41–5, 47, 49, 50, 59, 60, 75, 79, 93, 95, 111, 153, 155, 182, 185, 204–5, 291, 294, 319; (in Pakistan) 301
Punjabi (language) 115, 184
*punyabhu* 112
Puranas 19, 112, 118, 247
Purandare, Babasaheb 198n
Puri 165
Purkhi 222

Qandahar 50. *See also* Gandhara
Qaumi Taranah 94
Qasim, Muhammad bin 41
Qing Empire 28, 31, 32, 34, 36
Quit India movement 119, 142

Rabadi 250
race 12, 13, 17, 23, 106, 107n, 110, 115, 120–1, 136; Hindu 114, 123, 127
Radcliffe, Cyril 42–50
Radha 111
Radhakrishnan, Sarvepalli 140, 140n, 141
radio 30, 115
Rai, Lala Lajpat 319
Raichoudhury, Ambikagiri 259
Rajagopalachari, Chakravarti 89, 202
Rajasthan 12, 161, 165, 290, 291, 301; Union 74, 76, 183
Rajkot 80
Rajput 73, 74, 108, 143, 194, 197, 227, 250, 252
Rajput, Ganesh Rai 245
Rajpramukh 73, 91
Rajshahi 46

# 340 INDEX

Rajwade, Vishwanath Kashinath 154, 194–7, 194n
*rājya* 5, 18, 110, 238–40
Rajya Sabha 176
Ram Janmabhoomi movement 173
Ramachandran, M.G. 204, 297
Ramakrishna Mission 161, 161n, 162
Ramanuja 140
Ramasamy, E.V. 201–3, 201n, 248, 315–16
Ramayana 111, 117
Ramchandra 35, 105, 106, 114, 227; temple of 177–8, 244, 251, 286, 291, 292–3, 317
Ramdas, Sant 196, 196n, 198
Ramdas Swami. *See* Ramdas, Sant
Rangpur 38, 46, 51–2
Rao, N.T. Rama 297
Rao, Peshwa Baji II 198
Rao, P.V. Narasimha 282
*rāṣṭra* 5, 7, 18, 19. *See also* nation
Rashtriya Janata Dal (RJD) 252, 274, 299
Rashtriya Lok Dal (RLD) 280n
Rashtriya Swayamsevak Sangh (RSS) 118, 119, 125, 154, 155, 185, 187, 199, 209, 242–3, 286
Ratnagiri 103
Rathayatra 111, 117, 165
Rau, Benegal Narsing 77, 210n
Razakar 82, 88–9, 90, 91
Razvi, Kasem 82–6, 88
Red Fort 89
Red Sea 21
Reddy 248, 288
Reddy, Y.S. Rajasekhara: family of 299
referendum. *See* plebiscite

religious: conversion 139, 165–7; denomination (*see* sect)
reservations 137, 219, 245, 247, 250, 252, 255, 268, 296–7
Revolt of 1857 56, 57, 102, 109, 121, 242
Rohilkhand 220
Roman (script) 215
Roman Empire 130
Rome 25, 112, 116
Ross Island 60
Roy, Indubhushan 59
Roy, Khoka 59
Roy, Narayan 59
Roy, Rammohan 140
Roy, Subodh 59
Russia 27–8, 29, 32, 50, 51

Saadulla, Syed Muhammed 209, 209n
Sabarimala 174–6, 177
Saha, Gopimohan 59
Sahni, Daya Ram 12
Śakuni 50
Sakya Buddhist Society 248
Salazar, Antonio 62, 64, 65, 84
Samajwadi Party 252, 299
Saṃhitā 16
Sāṃkhya 235n
*sāmrājya* 18. *See also* empire
Sanatan Dharma 108, 112, 113, 118, 121
Sangam literature 18, 200
*Saṅgīt sannyāsta khaḍga* 107
*Saṅgīt uhśāp* 117
Sankara, Adi 140
Sankardev, Srimanta 258n
Sannyasi rebellion 190
Sanskrit 8, 13–19, 27, 104, 104n, 105, 111, 115, 123, 133, 139,

143, 150, 187–90, 194, 195, 200, 201, 208, 226, 232–6, 306, 307, 309
Santal 19, 24, 308, 314: Hembrom 19; Kisku 19; Murmu 19; Tudu 19
Santal Parganas 19
Santali (language) 115
Santiniketan 192
Sanyal, Sachin 59
Saraswati: (river) 15; (goddess) 190
Sarkar, Benoy Kumar 23–4, 23n
Sarnath 7–10
Satnami 108
Saurashtra Union 76, 77, 183; constituent assembly of 78
Savarkar, Ganesh Damodar 59, 102
Savarkar, Vinayak Damodar 31n, 59, 60, 101–18, 119, 121, 123, 124, 125, 126, 194
Scandinavia 157
Scandinavian (people) 21
Scheduled Caste 45, 136–7, 171, 219, 250, 255, 256, 296. *See also* Dalit
Scheduled Tribe 256, 296. *See also* Adivasi; tribe
Scindia, Jivaji Rao (Maharaja of Gwalior) 74, 74n
Scott, Michael 212
Scottish 25, 27, 30
Scythian–Parthian kingdoms 11n
sect 113, 115, 116, 121, 133, 135, 158, 161–3, 246, 247, 311. *See also individual sects and denominations*
secularism 126, 134, 146, 147, 152, 232; legal disputes over 160–78; Nehruvian 143, 147, 153, 156–9, 237, 238
Self-Respect movement 201–2, 201n, 204
Sen, Niranjan 59
Sentinelese (people) 23
Shah, K.T. 156n
Shah Bano Begum 172; case of 172–3
Shah, Yusuf Adil 96n
Shaiva 92, 134; neo- 201
Shaka 106, 107
Shakespeare, William 111
Shakta 116
Shankaravarman 92
Sharia 167
Shariat Act 167
Sharmila, Irom Chanu 226, 226n
Shetkari Sangathana 281n
Shia 134, 169
Shillong 209, 260
Shimla 28, 33; Agreement 28–30
Shinde, Jivaji Rao. *See* Scindia, Jivaji Rao
Shinde, Vithala Ramji 197, 197n
Shiromani Akali Dal 47, 75, 184, 291, 299
Shiv Sena 198–9, 274, 299
Shivaji 108, 144, 154, 196, 197, 198, 199, 226
Sialkot 44
Siddha medicine 247
Sikh: (people) 41–4, 47, 75, 96, 108, 110, 111, 112, 144, 156, 161n, 169, 171, 184; kingdom 31, 93
Sikhism 117, 142
Sikkim 34, 36–7, 41, 65, 78, 224
Sikkimese (people) 20, 215
Simhala. *See* Sri Lanka

Simla. *See* Shimla
Sinari, Prabhakar 63
Sind. *See* Sindh
Sindh 10, 11, 11n, 12, 41, 80, 111
Sindhu: (people) 104, 106, 107; (river). *See* Indus
Sindhusthan 104–5, 108
Singh, Ajit 280n
Singh, Ananta 59
Singh, Bhagat 319
Singh, Chaudhary Charan 280–1, 280n
Singh, Duleep 93
Singh, Gulab 31, 93
Singh, Guru Gobind 14
Singh, Hanwant (Maharaja of Jodhpur) 73
Singh, Hari (Maharaja of Jammu and Kashmir) 44, 69, 85, 94–8
Singh, Kartar 59
Singh, Manmohan 280, 282, 290
Singh, Ranjit 31
Singh, Swaran 237
Singh, Tara 42
Singh, Vishwanath Pratap 250, 251
Singh, Zail 282
Singh, Zorawar 31
Sinhalese 54
Siva 246
Sivakasi 288
sixty-four *kalā* 232, 234–5
Smriti 112
Solanki, Madhav Singh 250
Somnath temple 81, 155, 251, 293
South Africa 137
South Korea 218
Soviet Union. *See* Union of Soviet Socialist Republics

Spanish Empire 7
Sphinx 9
Special Marriage Act 169
Sri Lanka 54, 105, 105n, 110, 114, 130, 248
Srinagar 96, 97
Staines, Graham 166
Stalin, J.V. 236
state, the 5, 185, 225–6; authoritarian 237–8, 244, 255; centralised 145, 227, 243–4, 254–7, 285; imperial structure of 181, 185, 210, 224, 237; Indian 212, 217, 218, 226, 228. *See also* statelessness; *rājya*
statelessness 206–7
States People movement 69, 71, 89, 95, 224. *See also* Praja Mandal
States Reorganisation Commission 184, 184n
Steppe pastoralists 24
Sudra 13, 246, 247
Suez Canal 64
Sufi 133, 144, 246, 253, 311
Sugandha 92
Sugauli, treaty of 34,
Sugriva 106n
Sultanate. *See* Delhi Sultanate
Sunderlal, Pandit 90
Sunni 134, 153, 176
Supreme Court of India 161, 161n, 172, 173, 174–5, 177–8, 292, 303, 307
Survey of India 29
suzerainty 28
Swadeshi movement 187, 190
Swaminarayan Sampraday 161, 161n
Swat 79

INDEX                                343

Swatantra Party 86n
Sylhet 49, 224, 259, 260

Tagore, Rabindranath 111, 140–1, 187, 191–2, 191n
Tai 38; -Ahom 195
Tajikistan 22
Takshashila. *See* Taxila
Tamil: (language) 18, 19, 111, 115, 190, 200–4, 217, 219, 247; (people) 18, 130, 203, 217, 308; (region) 146, 247
Tamil Nadu 62, 165, 180, 199, 202, 203–4, 224, 249, 279, 297, 300, 302, 306, 316
Tamil Thai 200, 203, 218
Tandon, Purushottam Das 156
Tanti 148
Tata (business house) 286
Tawang 28, 29
Taxila 11, 232, 234
Telangana 69, 81, 82, 88, 184, 221–2, 288
television 115
Teli 252
Telugu (language) 19, 91, 115, 182, 183, 184, 219, 221
Telugu Desam Party 19, 302
Terai 34
Thackeray, Bal: family of 299
Thailand 20
Thakur 151, 245, 267
Thevar 316
*Thirukkural* 18, 200
Thiruvalluvar 200
Tibet 20, 27–32, 36, 37, 49, 127; South 30; Western 32
Tibetan (script) 222
Tibeto-Burman languages 207
Tikait, Mahendra Singh 281

Tilak, Bal Gangadhar 154, 190, 197, 319
Tipu Sultan 53
Tiruppur 288
Travancore 68, 69, 70, 72, 74, 94, 164, 213
Travancore-Cochin Union 75, 76, 77, 78, 79
tribe 207, 208, 210–11, 314
Trinamool Congress 193
triple talaq 176–7
Tripura 48–9, 217
Tripuri 39
Tuensang 213
Tulsidas 311
Turkey 152, 157, 163; Sultan of 114, 152
Turkmenistan 22
Twenty-four (24) Parganas 47

Udaipur 73
Ukepenofu 207–8
ulema 241
uniform civil code 167–72
Union of Soviet Socialist Republics (USSR) 49, 63, 64, 121, 157, 163, 236
Union Territory 53, 62, 65, 292
United Arab Republic. *See* Egypt
United Kingdom 63, 64, 102, 129, 157, 210, 228, 296, 304, 313
United Liberation Front of Assam (ULFA) 205, 205n, 263
United Nations 42, 63, 64, 65, 80, 85, 86, 98, 100; Development Programme (UNDP) 301
United Progressive Alliance (UPA) 284

United Provinces 111, 150, 151, 152, 153. *See also* Uttar Pradesh
United States of America 63, 64, 123, 129, 136, 157, 225, 228, 231, 233, 236, 278, 296, 304
University Grants Commission (UGC) 303
untouchability 133, 134, 136–7, 154, 156. *See also* caste; Dalit
Upanishad 139, 140
Urdu 111, 149, 150, 193, 227, 306
Uri 96
Uttar Pradesh 86n, 182, 220, 221, 227, 243, 245, 248, 252, 253, 266, 290, 292, 296, 297, 301, 307, 309, 311; government of 266; western 220, 280
Uttarakhand 221
Uzbekistan 22

Vaidik. *See* Vedic
Vaiśeṣika 235n
Vaishnav 92, 116, 134, 247, 258, 258n
Vaisya 13
Vajpayee, Atal Bihari 228
Vallabhi 232
Valmiki 253, 267
*Vande mātaram* 187–93
Varanasi 116, 117, 150
Varkari 117, 117n, 195n, 196
varna. *See varṇāśram*
*varṇāśram* 13, 92, 108, 110, 121–2, 143, 196, 239, 240, 242–3, 244–5, 249, 312
Vatican 169
Vātsyāyana 235
Veda(s) 1, 6, 11, 16, 18, 20, 110, 111, 235: Rig 12, 13, 18; Sama 311; Yajur 16
Vedanta 235n: Advaita 121, 139–40, 142, 146, 163, 238, 311; Neo- 161n; *viśiṣṭadvaita* 140
Vedic: civilisation 25, 226; people 1, 13–18, 20, 25, 50; religion 92, 107, 108, 112, 121, 143
Veerashaiva 161
Vellala 201, 247
viceroy 58
Vidarbha 184, 220, 248, 316–17
Vietnamese (language) 61
Vijayanagara Empire 6, 145
Vikramaditya 107
Vikramshila 232, 234
Vindhya Pradesh Union 76, 183
Vishnu 118
Viswa Hindu Parishad 251
Vithala 196
Vivekananda, Swami 114, 139, 166
Vokkaliga 249
Vrindavan 117

Wahabi 58
Wangchuk (rulers of Bhutan) 35
Wavell, Lord Archibald 68, 71
*We or Our Nationhood Defined* 119–21, 125–6
West Bengal 35, 46, 47, 48, 62, 193, 283–4, 287, 289, 296, 297, 301, 306
Wheeler, Mortimer 12
women 16, 109n, 117, 118, 128–9, 131, 133, 166–7, 170–1, 173, 176–7, 266–273, 292, 301
World War I 51, 153
World War II 41, 54, 60, 211, 236

Xavier, St Francis  116
Xinjiang  31, 32
Xuanzang  8

Yadav  249, 252
Yadav, Lalu Prasad  251; family of  299
Yadav, Mulayam Singh  299
Yanam  61, 62
Yemen  21, 55: South  55
Yerawada Jail  103, 136

Yoga  235n
Younghusband, Francis  27, 29
YouTube  129
Yudhiṣṭhir  52
Yunnan  38
Yuvajana Sramika Rythu (YSR) Congress Party  299

Zainul Abedin  92, 93n
Zhou Enlai  32, 33
Zoroastrian. *See* Parsi

www.ingramcontent.com/pod-product-compliance
Lightning Source LLC
Chambersburg PA
CBHW031431230426
43668CB00007B/497